TO
IN   R

D1101899

WULFRUN
COLLEGE

PAGE ROAD, WOLVERHAMPTON WV6 0DU
Tel: Wolverhampton (01902) 317700

EDUCATION,
ASSESS
...st date below.

SOCIET

76 9108491 1

ASSESSING ASSESSMENT

Series Editor:
Harry Torrance, University of Sussex

The aim of this series is to take a longer term view of current developments in assessment and to interrogate them in terms of research evidence deriving from both theoretical and empirical work. The intention is to provide a basis for testing the rhetoric of current policy and for the development of well-founded practice.

Current titles

Patricia M. Broadfoot: *Education, Assessment and Society: A Sociological Analysis*
Sue Butterfield: *Educational Objectives and National Assessment*
Caroline Gipps *et al.*: *Intuition or Evidence? Teachers and National Assessment of Seven-year-olds*
Caroline Gipps and Patricia Murphy: *A Fair Test? Assessment, Achievement and Equity*
John Gray and Brian Wilcox: *'Good School, Bad School': Evaluating Performance and Encouraging Improvement*
Christopher Pole: *Assessing and Recording Achievement*
Malcolm Ross *et al.*: *Assessing Achievement in the Arts*
Harry Torrance (ed.): *Evaluating Authentic Assessment*
Alison Wolf: *Competence-based Assessment*

ASSESSING
ASSESSMENT

EDUCATION, ASSESSMENT AND SOCIETY

A SOCIOLOGICAL ANALYSIS

Patricia M. Broadfoot

Open University Press
Buckingham · Philadelphia

Open University Press
Celtic Court
22 Ballmoor
Buckingham
MK18 1XW

and
1900 Frost Road, Suite 101
Bristol, PA 19007, USA

First Published 1996

A catalogue record of this book is available from the British Library

ISBN   0 335 19601 2 (pb)   0 335 19602 0 (hb)

Library of Congress Cataloging-in-Publication Data
Broadfoot Patricia.
     Education, assessment, and society: a sociological analysis/by Patricia
M. Broadfoot.
        p.   cm. – (Assessing assessment)
     Includes bibliographical references and index.
     ISBN 0–335–19602–0. – ISBN 0–335–19601–2 (pbk.)
     1. Educational tests and measurements – Social aspects – Great
Britain.   2. Educational tests and measurements – Social aspects –
France.   3. Educational sociology – Great Britain.   4. Educational
sociology – France.   I. Title.   II. Series.
LB3056.G7B76   1996
371.2′6′0941–dc20   95–25352
                                                                                                    CIP

Typeset by Type Study, Scarborough
Printed in Great Britain by St Edmundsbury Press Ltd, Bury St Edmunds,
Suffolk

*For my children
James, Laurence and Elanwy
who have taught me so much.*

CONTENTS

SERIES EDITOR'S INTRODUCTION

Changing theories and methods of assessment have been the focus of significant attention for some years now, not only in the United Kingdom, but also in many other western industrial countries and many developing countries. Curriculum developers have realized that real change will not take place in schools if traditional paper and pencil tests, be they essay or multiple choice, remain unchanged to exert a constraining influence on how teachers and pupils approach new curricula. Similarly, examiners have been concerned to develop more valid and authentic ways of assessing the changes which have been introduced into school syllabuses over recent years – more practical work, oral work, problem solving and so forth. In turn psychologists and sociologists have become more concerned with the impact of assessment on learning and motivation, and how that impact can be developed more positively. This has led to a myriad of developments in the field of assessment, often involving an increasing role for the teacher in school-based assessment, as more relevant and challenging tasks are devised by examination agencies for administration by teachers in schools, and as the role and status of more routine teacher assessment of coursework, practical work, group work and so forth has become enhanced.

However educationists have not been the only ones to focus much more closely on the interrelation of curriculum, pedagogy and assessment. Governments around the world, but particularly in the United Kingdom, have also begun to take a close interest in the ways in which assessment can influence and even control teaching, and in the changes in curriculum and teaching which could be brought about by changes in assessment. This interest has not been wholly coherent. Government intervention in the UK has sometimes initiated, sometimes reinforced the move towards a more practical and vocationally oriented curriculum and thus the move towards more practical, school-based assessment. But government has also been concerned with issues of accountability and with what it sees as the maintenance of traditional academic standards through the use of externally set tests. The overall effect has been that as certain sorts of responsibility for assessment have been devolved to school level, the parameters within which such responsibility can be exercised have been more tightly drawn.

It is precisely because of this complexity and confusion that the present series of books on assessment has been developed. Many claims are being made with respect to the efficacy of new approaches to assessment which require careful review and investigation. Likewise many changes are being required by government intervention which may lead to hurried and poorly understood developments being implemented in schools. The aim of this series is to take a longer term view of the changes which are occurring, to move beyond the immediate problems of implementation and to interrogate the claims and the changes in terms of broader research evidence which derives from both theoretical and empirical work. In reviewing the field in this way the intention of the series is thus to highlight relevant research evidence, identify key factors and principles which should underpin the developments taking place, and provide teachers and administrators with a basis for informed decision-making which takes the educational issues seriously and goes beyond simply accommodating the latest policy imperative.

Patricia Broadfoot's book represents a particularly timely and important contribution to this agenda since it provides an extensive overview of work on assessment in different, usually discrete and sometimes even hostile, disciplines, pursuing an explanation of not only what is happening in the field of assessment, but why it is happening. Thus Broadfoot reviews the development of assessment as a crucially important mechanism within emerging education systems and investigates both the social context and the social consequences of this development. She argues that most work on assessment has been and remains concerned with the technical – the techniques of measurement – rather than with the purposes and effects of such a dominant and all-pervasive social practice. She explicitly brings together varying perspectives and traditions in order to 'address the separate dynamics of the classroom, the school, the local and the national context as these mediate idiosyncratically the general imperatives of industrial and post-industrial society'.

Thus she investigates the purposes and consequences of assessment within schools with respect to teaching and learning, within education systems with respect to accountability, and within economies with respect to the division of labour and the articulation of the school system with the labour market. She argues that changes in assessment reflect changes in the priorities and preoccupations of society as a whole, especially with regard to the increasing complexity of the division of labour and the increasing regulation of so many aspects of social life. Thus assessment arose in the context of increasing social competition for roles within emerging industrial societies, developing both to regulate and legitimate the process and outcomes of the competition. Latterly, assessment has been sustained and developed still further because of the insistent pursuit of rationality and the increasing use of technicist procedures to obscure fundamental, and some would argue, irreconcilable value differences in increasingly differentiated postmodern societies.

These are broad and at times abstract arguments, and Broadfoot herself acknowledges the possibility of superficial generalization and over-deterministic explanation. She avoids such pitfalls by the depth of her theoretical understanding and the wealth of empirical evidence which she brings to bear on the argument. This is particularly exemplified in her comparison of developments in England and France, very similar in phase of industrial development and complexity of social system, yet very different in key particulars with regard to assessment, particularly with respect to the issues of central/local control of the school system and its attendant procedures of examination and evaluation.

Thus Broadfoot reminds us that our sometimes parochial concerns (parochial in terms of both national systems and subject disciplines) should be situated within broader accounts of the growth of assessment and can be analysed as manifestations of much longer term and more fundamental trends in the development of schools systems, and indeed in the regulation of social behaviour. This is an ambitious book which admirably succeeds in meeting the aims it sets for itself.

Harry Torrance

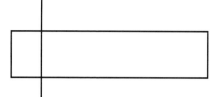

ACKNOWLEDGEMENTS

During the years it takes to research and write a thesis, one receives help from many different quarters. Some of this help is quite gratuitous, where the source is a timely article or a chance remark. Nevertheless, it is the insights and stimulus provided by the work of the invisible college of colleagues in the academic community that make any particular project possible. Thus my primary debt is to the many scholars in this field on whose work I have drawn even though, as is the way of these things, they are for the most part unaware of this debt.

To many other people I owe more explicit thanks. I am truly grateful to the many French and English teachers, academics and administrators who have helped me with my crucial role in getting me started on this research and to Nigel Grant for convincing me of the importance of comparative studies. Roger Dale and Stewart Ranson played an important role in the development of some of the theoretical ideas in this book.

To my colleagues at Bristol University I am indebted for support and encouragement over many years, especially to Marilyn Osborn and Peter Robinson who share my fascination with France and the lessons to be learned from its profoundly different educational traditions.

For many years I have been a member of the Nuffield Assessment Seminar. The meetings of this group have provided me with invaluable opportunities for scholarly debate in the field of assessment and have played a vital role in the development of my thinking.

I am grateful to The Economic and Social Research Council who have funded a succession of comparative French–English projects: Constants and Contexts in Educational Accountability: a comparative study 1979–1981; Teachers Conceptions of Their Professional Responsibility in England and France 1984–1987; Primary Teachers and Policy Change 1993–1994; and The Quality of Primary Education: Children's Experiences of Schooling in England and France 1995–1997. Each of these projects has in its own way helped to develop the thinking on which this book is based.

I also wish to express my sincere thanks to Mrs Sheila Taylor who has battled with various drafts of this manuscript with great skill and unfailing cheerfulness.

Above all, my thanks are due to my long-suffering family: to my husband David for his unfailing understanding and support, and to my children who have cheerfully tolerated the impact on family life that writing a book inevitably makes.

PART I

RATIONALE

1

THE SOCIAL ROLE OF ASSESSMENT

Assessment is a central feature of social life. Passing judgement on people, on things, on ideas, on values is part of the process of making sense of reality and where we stand in any given situation. Even very small children can make assessments. They can respond to a simple question such as 'Did you have a nice time?' with the appropriate response of 'Yes' or 'No'. This implies the activation of a set of mental processes involving a mental review of the event being referred to, and the application of certain more or less conscious criteria of what would constitute a 'nice' time. Although we are rarely called upon to make explicit what is typically an implicit process of making judgements, there are occasions when the process is more overt and formalized, the criteria are subject to greater scrutiny as to whether they are reasonable and just and the collection of evidence on which to base the judgement is carefully controlled. Thus while we would be surprised in any social setting to be asked to justify an evaluation that was part of a personal response, we would be equally surprised if this same process of evaluation did not involve the application of systematic criteria in any more public judgement, whether this is deciding which candidate to vote for in an election, which applicant to appoint to

a given job or who to make the treasurer of the local gardening club.

One of the most highly charged evaluative settings is that of education. The evaluation concerned may be that essentially informal, even intuitive, personal response characteristic of all social interaction, where each actor has to make judgements about other actors as the basis for predicting the impact of any particular action in a given social setting. When teachers decide whether and how to intervene in a breach of discipline they are doing just this. The evaluation may on the other hand be more deliberate, involving the collection of evidence concerning a pupil's learning through tests or observation in order to know how best to help and encourage him or her.

Teachers need, too, to evaluate their own teaching in order to judge the value of particular teaching strategies and to discover to what extent the class as a whole has mastered a particular unit of work and thus can usefully be moved on to the next topic. Teachers have many techniques available to enable them to make such judgements. Research shows (for example, Flanders 1970; Boydell 1974; Stubbs 1976; Brown and McIntyre 1977) that on average teachers may spend almost half their time on oral questioning, partly of course as a teaching tool to move the lesson on, but mainly to assess the understanding of individual pupils and, in aggregate, the class as a whole. In addition, marking written work, chatting to pupils and even facial expressions will reveal relevant diagnostic information.

To the extent that the teacher is relating to the needs and interests of the individual pupil, this purpose of assessment would seem to approximate perhaps most closely to a child-centred interpretation of education. As Rousseau so well demonstrated in *Emile*, the concept of an organized sequence of learning experiences depends upon the teacher's ability to judge the pupil's understanding and needs at any particular time. Certainly studies of English primary school teachers' approach to assessment confirm that this intuitive, individualized, constant monitoring by the teacher has been their typical view of the role of classroom assessment (Broadfoot, 1996).

Appearances are deceptive, however, for during the ongoing interaction between teacher and pupil, and even between the pupils themselves, over the weeks and months pupils themselves are also engaged in self-assessment. Pupils come to an often unconscious assessment of their performance in relation to each other as they strive to achieve the socially defined goals which underlie the teacher's activities. Although the teacher may seek to respond to the variety of pupil needs and interests, pupils often have to be categorized by the teacher as a result of both implicit and explicit assessment so that they can be given 'appropriate' teaching. This is often in relation to various pre-existing stereotypes (Becker 1952), such as 'lazy', 'dull' or 'bright'. Gradually, pupils too come to recognize that only particular kinds of achievement are valued and they learn to assess themselves and adjust their expectations accordingly (Pollard *et al.* 1994).

At the extreme, evaluation may take the familiar and highly visible form of a formal examination hedged around with rules of procedure to ensure that all those being judged have a strictly comparable stimulus and context in which to produce the evidence on which the evaluation will be made. For whereas the 'formative evaluation' which is part of the process of teaching and learning is inherent in all educational activity worthy of the name, mass schooling systems have also evolved a quite different sort of more formal evaluative activity – which may be termed 'summative evaluation'. This 'more or less formalised procedure usually separated from the classroom situation' (Ottobre 1978: 12) comes at the end of a particular stage of school activity and has a quite different role from that of 'formative evaluation'. Its purpose is the externalization of information about the process of education so that those not personally involved in it can still be provided with reliable information about the learning that has taken place (Harlen *et al.* 1992). On the basis of such information, the characteristics, and hence quality, of pupils, teachers, institutions and even the education system as a whole can be judged. For 'insiders' such formalized judgements provide useful standards against which to measure their own progress, be they pupils, teachers or administrators. The internalization by pupils of such assessments results in time in the very clear differences of behaviour and motivation characterizing those labelled 'bright' and marked out for success and those 'less able' pupils destined for failure. While it may be deplored educationally, this 'cooling out' process (Goffman 1952; Clark 1962, 1982) is highly effective in limiting the frustration that would be endemic in those education systems in which there are a large number of pupils aspiring to a limited number of opportunities. For 'outsiders', the information generated by 'summative evaluation' can provide an apparently rational basis for discriminating between individuals when there is a need to select. Such information is also the basis of accountability in the sense that it provides for judgements to be made on the quality of the education being offered.

This kind of explicit educational evaluation is usefully distinguished by the term 'assessment', which may be taken to mean the deliberate and overt measurement of educational performance in order to provide information for purposes beyond the immediate interactive learning situation.

Some writers (e.g. Satterley 1981) distinguish between 'assessment' as the actual process of measurement and 'evaluation' as the subsequent interpretation of such measurements against particular norms of performance. In formative evaluation these two stages are often synchronous. As teachers scan pupils for signs of non-attention or difficulty, they are also simultaneously interpreting what they see in terms of the criteria identified by their previous experience. In more formal assessments, however, there may be a more explicit distinction between the production of scores, often including a measure of standardization, and the subsequent interpretation and use of those scores for various purposes such as reporting and pupil selection. Generally, however, assessment may be taken to refer both to those deliberate and planned procedures of measurement and to the uses to which the information so generated is put, as these have evolved as part of mass educational provision, while evaluation refers to the more general process of judgement and feedback outlined above.

The repertoire of assessment techniques might include teacher-marked essays, exercises and class tests; standardized tests, periodic school examinations and public examinations; standard assessment tasks; school records, reports to parents, testimonials and references, profiles and portfolios; and more rarely formal evaluations by outside agents such as school psychologists.

This already lengthy list of assessment techniques would be further added to, particularly in those education systems where schools enjoy a measure of autonomy, by the senior management of the school in their concern for the way in which the consumers outside the school, such as the parents of actual and prospective pupils, the local community in general, employers and further and higher education establishments, would judge the products of the school and, hence, its activities. Equally, senior managers at least will be concerned with their own assessment of school effectiveness as expressed in those indicators upon which the management hierarchy outside the school – the local education authority inspectors, advisers and officials, and local political representatives – come to form their judgements about the quality of education provided in that particular school.

There is also, in every country, a third level of concern which preoccupies those charged with *national* responsibility for educational provision and standards, such as a ministry of education, a national inspectorate and, ultimately, the elected government. Indeed, educational assessment in various forms has been of central importance in the creation of educational systems *per se* through the rationalization of educational provision and the control of educational practice.

Thus educational assessment is not just about judging *individual* potential and performance. It has always been just as much about judging *institutional* quality. Some of the earliest manifestations of formal educational assessment were the 'quality assurance' exercises of the medieval craft guilds, which were designed to ensure a common standard to be achieved by all craftsmen who aspired to join (Frey 1992). Similarly, inspection of all kinds is an assessment concept which has an equally long history and, in the English context at least, its emphasis on the evaluation of *institutional* quality through school inspection by Her Majesty's Inspectors (HMI) predates the use of assessment for more individual purposes.

Recently, however, the crucial role played by assessment within the education system *as a whole* has become increasingly evident. Governments around the world, beset by problems of rising unemployment, public spending requirements increasing exponentially and a pressing need to be internationally competitive, have sought the resolution of these problems in the creation of education systems which are both more responsive to imposed national priorities and more effective in achieving these. The use of formal assessment arrangements to effect control through the language of accountability has become a typical and prominent feature of education policy-making. Such accountability arrangements can take many different forms. In some countries, the emphasis will be on quality *assurance* procedures which involve, for example, requirements that teachers should be provided with regular appraisal opportunities in order that they can be encouraged continually to improve their professional skills. Or such quality *assurance* might take the form of a national requirement for school self-evaluation to be undertaken, so that each institution is involved in continually seeking to remedy the weaknesses that the members of that institution themselves identify. In other countries, the emphasis may be more on quality *control* procedures, including, for example, the inspection of individual teachers and the publication of results against a range of performance indicators, most typically school examination results.

However it is done, the use of formalized assessment procedures for this purpose is an extremely powerful policy mechanism for exerting control over the education system. Whoever has the power to determine the criteria against which such assessments are made has the power to influence the priorities pursued by teachers, parents and pupils throughout the land. The current international preoccupation which measuring quality – whether this is in state services or industrial production – has brought into sharp focus this aspect of the social role of assessment. The British government's concern during the 1990s to generate user 'charters' for a whole range of state and other services is a classic model of the way in which assessment is involved in any 'quality' exercise. The criteria for assessment are the principles of the charter and the process of evaluating the evidence against these principles – whether by a private individual or as a more formal part of the state bureaucracy – is an exact mirror of the assessment process as it is applied to individuals within the education system.

So integral to the mass provision of education has the ideology and the associated practice of formal assessment become that the two would now appear to be inseparable. Any attempt to release education from the constrictions of assessment procedures, whether at individual, institutional or systemic levels, would be likely to result in the collapse of the system itself. From the most informal micro interaction of the classroom, through class tests and certificate examinations right up to the macro levels of national and international monitoring of standards, it is possible to trace a single underlying rationale, an ideology which embodies the contradictory purposes of mass education and powerfully controls the nature of its goals and rewards.

The scope of this book comprehends the whole range of such organized evaluative activity within the education system, from the judgements pupils themselves and their teachers form in the classroom about learning through to the way in which various, more formal means of recording and reporting pupils' progress in the school as a whole provide for the accountability of the individual teacher, the school, the local authority and, ultimately, national educational provision as a whole. The book's particular focus is on the choice of approaches to formal assessment which characterize a particular time and place as these are determined by policy-makers' attempts to balance the different purposes that educational assessment serves – priorities which, in turn, are likely to reflect continuity and change in the social context. These different purposes are explored briefly in the next section.

Selection, certification and control

This brief description of the pervasive and characteristic role of formal evaluative techniques in contemporary education systems explains why a sociological analysis of assessment policy is necessary. It will be argued that assessment techniques provide one of the principal mechanisms by which the changing bases for social control within the broader society which gave birth to mass schooling in the first place are translated into the educational process. More specifically, it will be suggested that the proliferating division of labour that the process of industrialization increasingly required posed quite novel problems of social control concerning how the allocation of such new roles and indeed the management of the state as a whole might be regulated and legitimated, and that it was formal assessment techniques within the educational process that provided the solution to this problem. Inherent in such an approach is the assumption that in developed societies with mass educational provision – as opposed to traditional societies categorized by non-formal educational provision – there is something generically different and characteristic about the way in which educational assessment operates. These 'developed' societies may be variously described as 'mass' or 'modern', 'industrial' or 'capitalist'. Capitalist societies are often further sub-divided into 'entrepreneurial', 'corporate', 'advanced', 'post-capitalist' and 'post-modern' manifestations. Nevertheless, all such societies share common features which differentiate them from pre-industrial societies. For the purposes of the present analysis these common characteristics are taken to be those identified by Aron (1980: 22):

> the simplest abstract definition of 'industrial society' involves three principal characteristics: where the vast majority of the labour force is concentrated in the secondary and tertiary sector; where there exists a constant impulsion, in contrast to the relatively stable character of traditional societies to expand productivity; and, consequently, where there is a rapid rate of technological innovation.

To the extent that these characteristics are present in any particular society, they are likely to give rise to a need for some rational – that is, apparently justifiable – basis to be found for the allocation of unequally desirable social roles. The most obvious rational justification is likely to be demonstrated *competence* to perform the role. Allied to the demonstration of competence, which is typically acknowledged through formal *certification*, is the idea of *competition* or selection, namely that individuals should be allowed to compete on an equal basis to demonstrate their claim to competence. The provision of a competition which is apparently open and fair suggests that those who are not successful in achieving their aspirations will accept the rational selection criteria being applied and, hence, their own failure. In so doing they acquiesce not only in their own defeat but in the legitimacy of the prevailing social order. To this extent the provision of an apparently fair competition controls the build-up of frustration and resentment among the least privileged.

The issue of *control* extends beyond that of the individual, however, to include control of the educational system as a whole. In some societies this systemic control will take the form of a powerful state bureaucracy whose activities regulate the process of education through the control of curriculum content, pedagogy and the institutional context. In other, more 'decentralized' societies where there is no such powerful state bureaucracy, control is likely to be exerted as much by the interaction of interest groups and various, less formal, normative pressures such as feelings of professional responsibility. Thus, as well as attesting competence, regulating competition and reducing the frustration of individuals, assessment procedures have a crucial role to play in providing for such systemic control. It is these themes of *competence*, *competition* and *control*, and the way they in turn influence the *content* of education, that arguably provide the analytical key to understanding the unique and characteristic role played by educational assessment procedures in industrial societies. Thus, the chapters that follow explore the way in which historical and contemporary developments in assessment policy and practice may be understood in terms of the interplay between these themes and the different priority accorded to each of them as social, economic and political factors dictate.

Yet, despite the fact that the panoply of marks and grades, tests and exams, reports and inspections, quality assurance and perform-ance indicators is one of the most characteristic features of contem-porary education provision, there has, as yet, been little attempt to explain *why* assessment procedures have come to have such a dominant role in contemporary educational provision. Although many educational administrators and most teachers would identify the periodic necessity of having to submit themselves and their pupils to some kind of formal evaluation as one of the most fundamental constraints on their professional practice, such constraints are rarely questioned. While there is no lack of research on most of the major aspects of assessment, such as its effects on pupils or the advantages and disadvantages of various different measurement techniques, more fundamental questions about the role of assessment in education, especially in relation to policy, have been left largely unexplored. Why is this?

One explanation for this omission is a relative lack of interest in educational assessment on the part of sociologists (Broadfoot 1991). Although assessment is an *implicit* issue in many major areas of sociological concern, such as the curriculum or social inequality, and more recently educational policy, in the past it has been compara-tively rare for sociological research to address educational assess-ment as an *explicit* topic and even more rare for such research to seek to explain the ubiquity of educational assessment. Certainly, the sheer scale of such a task and the theoretical complexities involved render it a daunting challenge. It is not surprising that fear of superficial generalizations and over-deterministic explanations have led most researchers to choose a more limited focus for studies in this area.

There is, for example, a substantial research tradition concerned with exploring the role of assessment as part of classroom inter-action. The powerful role that assessment can play in the social creation of identity through teacher and peer 'labelling' and, hence, in the shaping of pupil careers has been the subject of much research and some now classic studies such as those of Rosenthal and Jacobsen (1968), Good and Brophy (1970), Rist (1970) and Fleming and Anttonen (1971), as well as newer work (e.g. Pollard 1995).

Equally significant is the research tradition concerned with establishing aspects of the relationship between assessment and learning in which psychological concepts such as 'locus of control' and 'attribution', motivation, autonomy and learned helplessness have been very valuable in illuminating the interplay between affect and cognition in learning (Little 1987).

Crooks's (1988) literature review of research on the impact of classroom evaluation practices on students testifies to the significance of such practices either in encouraging or in inhibiting learning, depending on how they are used. But although such studies of the effects of assessment procedures in the process of schooling underline the latter's significance, they can in themselves throw but little light on why the extensive *formalization* of such procedures should have been a defining characteristic in the emergence of mass schooling systems

By far the greatest volume of assessment literature, however, is concerned with assessment *techniques*. While many studies are concerned with the development and refinement of different approaches to educational measurement, many more offer powerful critiques of assessment techniques and the effects and shortcomings of these same techniques in action. Typically these latter studies offer a more or less vitriolic condemnation of the harmful effects of particular kinds of summative assessment on pupil motivation and creativity, or they seek to expose the inevitable inaccuracies of any formal assessment process.

The development of reliable and manageable formal assessment procedures of individual capacity and achievement was clearly an important feature of evolving meritocratic policies for education. Their legacy, however, has been both to divert the focus of analysis away from the actual *effects* of the assessment procedures used and to concentrate attention on the measurement of student achievement for certification purposes. Although in Britain throughout the 1950s, for example, psychologists were assiduous in their attempts to uncover the inaccuracies of the 11-plus examination and hence the assumptions on which it was based (Simon 1953; Vernon 1978) there was little attempt to understand such procedures in terms of broader, social pressures. Today the same attention to the *development of procedures* rather than to *studies of their effects* is still evident. In the United States, for example, a recent review of research on assessment policy found that virtually all such studies were concerned with technical issues and that out of more than 500 studies reviewed, only 11 were concerned with the effects of such assessments (Elwein *et al.* 1988).

Thus the powerful and intense debates over rival *techniques* which have traditionally characterized research into educational assessment have helped to exclude discussion of more fundamental issues concerning the *purposes* and *effects* of such activity. Given that formalized assessment procedures are often involved with the determination of individual life chances, it is at first sight not surprising that in the intense concern for justice and public acceptability, relatively little thought has typically been spared for more profound questioning of the very principle of educational assessment and the organizational practices of contemporary education systems which are based on it. On the other hand, given the size and quality of the critical literature that now exists about the shortcomings of assessment procedures, the continued exclusion of any fundamental critique from the policy arena would seem hard to justify.

It is now widely accepted that any kind of educational measurement can be at best only a rough estimate of particular kinds of ability; that educational assessment is as much an art as it is a science; an instrument of power as much as a source of social liberation. Despite the statistical finesse which often characterizes the processing of results and the considerable quantity of research which has been directed towards improving the accuracy of assessment, the limitations of different techniques − whether concerned with student, institutional or systemic assessment − have been extensively documented in a large number of research studies since the seminal work of Hartog and Rhodes in 1935 (see Ingenkamp 1977; Raven 1991; Broadfoot 1995). At the individual level, the vagaries of pupil performance and especially of exam stress, of differences between markers and in the difficulty of questions, are only some of the more obvious causes of inaccuracy which would now seem to be largely unavoidable. Research has revealed, for example, that differences between examiners, such as speed of reading, fatigue and competence (see, for example, Lee-Smith 1990; Broadfoot 1992);

the order and speed of marking or even the examiner's personal social situation, may affect the marking process (Branthwaite *et al.* 1981) and cause considerable unreliability.[1]

Perhaps even more important, however, is that variations in contextual factors produce *real* differences in student performance which are not just measurement error (Wolf and Silver 1993; Filer 1995). Performances vary because assessment is fundamentally an interpersonal exercise which cannot be divorced from human subjectivity.

It may well be partly for this reason that examination results are typically a fairly weak guide to the likely quality of future job or higher education performance (Schools Council 1972; Oxtoby 1973). Indeed, Powell (1973) has documented a whole series of other influences on attainment in higher education, of which the most obvious are motivation and effort, but which also include the important affective dimensions which have traditionally been excluded from certification assessment, such as introversion and extroversion and confidence.

It is largely because the technical aspects of assessment are so readily amenable to systematic study that it is these very shortcomings of particular techniques which have dominated discussions about desirability. The debate – and there is currently a good deal of it – is conducted almost entirely in this arena, the arena of efficiency. The heated discussion which often accompanies proposals for relatively minor changes in assessment policy rarely touches on more fundamental issues. Rather, the focus of such discussion is overwhelmingly on reviewing current practice and on working out how it may be changed to become more efficient and thus, ostensibly, more just.

The same emphasis on short-term pragmatic issues has also been characteristic of research into educational assessment. This tendency to locate research problems essentially within the status quo is highly significant because of the legitimating influence of assessment procedures in reinforcing a particular understanding of the desirable nature of education. To put it another way, if only the *efficiency* of assessment practices is questioned – and not their purposes and effects – the debate, such as it is, will continue to centre on *means* rather than *ends*. Furthermore, since formal assessment procedures exert a strong influence at every level of the system, the criteria which inform them will continue to impose a particular interpretation of what the nature of education in contemporary society should be (Broadfoot 1986). To the extent that this is so, assessment procedures are likely to lead to inertia in the education system and its inability to respond to changing social needs.

Often the technical studies are themselves highly critical of the shortcomings of educational measurement whilst continuing to accept the need for such activity (e.g. Murphy 1982). Recently, however, there has been a strong international move towards a new assessment paradigm which emphasizes different criteria of assessment quality – most notably its impact on learning rather than the accuracy of measurement *per se*. There is a growing concern to find ways of collecting and interpreting evidence of student performance which are more appropriate for the contemporary educational emphasis on the inculcation of skills and personal qualities as well as knowledge (Resnick *et al.* 1995; Torrance 1995).

Parallel to the literature on various aspects of individual student assessment is a growing body of scholarship which explores the way in which assessment can contribute to the development of professional competence including that of teachers (Burke 1989; Jessup 1990; Gonczi 1994; Stones 1994). But, while the emergence of these new ways of thinking about assessment issues is of *fundamental* importance in shaping the character of the learning experiences that future students will encounter, it does nothing to reduce the significance of the relationship between education and assessment practice. If anything, the move towards a more 'evaluative state' which is explored in detail in Chapter 3 means that the familiar defining influence of assessment in determining the way in which we organize education is spreading to other state bureaucracies and industrial enterprises as the core management strategy. Given their growing pervasiveness, sociological analyses of the significance of such developments are urgently required.

However, to date there have been relatively few studies of educational assessment as a policy issue. Apart from some significant socio-historical studies – particularly of the emergence of the two most explicit manifestations of formal educational assessment, examinations and intelligence testing (e.g. Karier 1973; Montgomery 1978; Vernon 1978; Evans and Waites 1981; Sadler 1991; Noah and Eckstein, 1992) interest in assessment as a policy issue has been as recent as much of the interest in policy studies more generally. Historical studies of assessment have typically been nationally specific and thus not explicitly concerned with generalizing beyond the idiosyncratic concatenation of events they describe to the broader and common social currents underpinning them.

This is also true of much of the recent explosion of studies of assessment policy issues, which have been concerned to explain particular initiatives – such as the English National Assessment System – within their specific national and historical context. Important as such studies are (for example, Wilson 1975 in the United States; Sadler 1991 and Meadmore 1995 in Australia; Harlen *et al.* 1992 in the UK; Nisbet 1993 in Europe) in influencing the policy debate concerning choices of assessment strategy, they are not typically concerned with the more fundamental *common* pressures informing the initiatives in question; nor do they address the sources of the different patterns in policy response in different countries which may face very similar challenges.

Critics versus developers: the effects of disunity

Rarely have the various perspectives and traditions of research into educational assessment been brought together. The different professional communities represented and their different goals have encouraged at best a defensive neutrality, at worst an overt hostility. Even more rare have been the attempts to widen the focus of debate in order to situate such research traditions within a more general understanding of the relationship between education and society. Policy generators, policy implementors and policy critics remain isolated from each other, locked into their professional communities and idiosyncratic concerns. Sociologists in particular have been reluctant to address assessment issues and have been content not to intervene in the debate between politicians and psychologists, historians and pedagogues.

Why this should have been the case is a difficult question to answer. In part at least, the explanation is the same as that for the comparatively recent sociological interest in policy and in curriculum and classroom processes more generally, namely the long-standing preoccupation of sociologists with the structural factors of input and output within the educational system. Until the early seventies the domination of psychological perspectives concerned with the measurement of individual differences (see, for example, Ebel 1965, 1972; Pidgeon and Yates 1968; Thorndike and Hagen 1969; Bloom *et al.* 1971) and sociological perspectives concerned with the identification of educational disadvantage and the quest for equality (see, for example, Banks 1955; Floud and Halsey 1958; Halsey *et al.* 1961; Douglas 1964; Douglas *et al.* 1971) combined to support both the overwhelming dominance of positivist research techniques and the concentration of attention on the individual within the system. It was not until the early 1970s that British sociological perspectives underwent a radical change in focus with the advent of the 'new' sociology of education (Bernbaum 1977). But it was curriculum and, to a lesser extent, pedagogy which dominated the newer concern with tracing the operation of power and control through the content and processes of education (e.g. Young 1971; Whitty and Young 1976; Eggleston 1977). If Bernstein was atypical in his identification of *three* message systems in schooling – curriculum, pedagogy *and evaluation* – in his work on education codes (Bernstein 1977), even he gave evaluation far less attention than the other two message systems which were embodied in the key concepts of 'classification' and 'framing'. Evaluation appeared as a dependent, rather than as a defining, variable (see Chapter 4).

In the late 1970s, however, with the growth of interest in neo-Marxist political economy perspectives, sociologists of education began to take a more explicit interest in the origins and effects of formal assessment procedures (Mehan 1973; Hextall and Sarup 1977; Meighan 1977; Whitty 1978; Broadfoot 1979a, 1984; Hargreaves 1982a,b). Some of these studies (e.g. Scarth 1983; Turner 1984; Bates 1984) were directed at curricular messages as these are affected by assessment at school and classroom level. Others (e.g. Dore 1976; Collins 1979; Ranson 1984) were more macro-focused, concerned with the credentialling function of contemporary school systems.

During the 1980s the very substantial growth in visibility of assessment as a policy issue was reflected in a significant growth of scholarly interest in this field. Research topics have included the impact of changing policies regarding school examinations (e.g. Noah and Eckstein 1992); the organization and impact of national assessment (e.g. Troman 1988; Koretz 1991; Stake 1991); and more general discussions of the potential role of assessment in promoting quality in education (Horton 1990; Vedder 1992; Nisbet 1993). Important as these developments have been, however, they stop short of an attempt to bring the various currents of understanding concerning the social role of assessment together. Not only is the amount of work in this area still comparatively small, there remains a pressing need for more synoptic sociological studies of assessment policies and procedures which can provide some kind of bridge between these various traditions and perspectives and so foster a more general understanding of the origins and effects of formal assessment procedures in societies with mass education systems.

Only such comprehensive studies can explain this fundamental, and in some ways determining, aspect of educational provision and organization, and hence illuminate a major feature of social life. It is for this reason that in recent years the relative neglect of assessment activities as a focus for research by sociologists of education has begun to be rectified and it is in an attempt to contribute to this growing literature that this book has been written.

The scope of this book is broad – historical and comparative, structural and processual – and the danger of superficiality correspondingly great. Nevertheless, the importance of the issue is taken to justify the risks inherent in such a grand design. If it succeeds in its avowed purpose the book will provide a conceptual model which may be used to study the social role of educational assessment in all those societies which have formal educational provision. The understanding that such studies generate should in turn help those charged with designing and using assessment procedures to apply this powerful social tool in the full knowledge of its potential impact.

The book in outline

The subject of this book is thus, as its title suggests, an analysis of the part played by assessment procedures in the growth and development of the kind of mass educational provision which is typical of industrialized and industrializing societies. In order to bring what is potentially a vast project within the scope of a single study, most of the empirical analysis of this study is based on two case studies of assessment policy and practice in England and France. These two countries are taken to be sufficiently similar to each other in terms of their history and stage of development to be illustrative of the general theme of the role of assessment in industrial and post-industrial societies, yet sufficiently contrasting in certain key respects to illuminate important differences of emphasis in the use made of educational assessment. Only by means of constant attention both to commonalities across education systems and to contrasts between them can the kind of ethnocentric determinism which has character-ized so many macro-sociological studies of education be avoided.

The analyses that follow are constructed on the assumption that a truly comprehensive sociology of assessment must address the separate dynamics of the classroom, the school, the local and the national context as these mediate idiosyncratically the general imperatives of industrial and post-industrial society. As a contri-bution to the generation of such sociological understanding, this book is particularly concerned with exploring the social role of educational assessment as a policy device which can be used to direct and legitimate the social and political goals of educational systems.

The organization of the chapters that follow reflects this general goal and the book's particular comparative focus as a way of illuminating the tension between the general and the nationally specific. The first five, largely theoretical, chapters constitute Part I of the book and are primarily concerned with generating conceptual frameworks with which to structure an analysis of the range of assessment practices found in a contemporary education system. Part II of the book, which includes Chapters 6, 7 and 8, is much more empirical in focus, its aim being to elucidate and substantiate the analyses of Part I by means of detailed references to the two case study systems. Within this general framework, the chapters are divided as follows.

Chapter 2 provides a fairly general overview of the nature and significance of educational assessment. It has two major elements. The first element is concerned with establishing the pervasive presence and overwhelming importance of formal assessment pro-cedures in any form of mass education provision and, by so doing, to justify the importance of the topic as a whole. The second element is concerned with clarifying in fairly general historical terms the reasons which lie behind the steady growth in the number and significance of assessment procedures in formal education. Given the essentially sociological, rather than historical, focus of the study as a whole, Chapter 3 adopts a more contemporary focus. It provides a resumé of some of the more marked and generalizable trends currently identifiable in the assessment practices of industrialized countries. Thus Chapters 2 and 3 introduce the major theoretical arguments which are expanded in Chapters 4 and 5, at the same time setting a general empirical context for the more detailed case studies of Part II.

If the principal purpose of Chapters 2 and 3 is to establish the importance of educational assessment as a topic of study, the principal purpose of Chapter 4 is to explain *why* such evaluation procedures have become so integrally connected with mass education systems. This quest involves an examination of the generic characteristics of 'industrial' societies through the insights provided by sociological theory, notably that of Marx, Weber and Durkheim, and the more recent work of Bernstein, Foucault, Habermas and Marcuse. Whereas the focus of Chapter 4 justifies, and indeed requires, a very general and extended theoretical analysis about the common characteristics of such societies, it is equally important that these generalizations can be conceptually linked to the idiosyncratic characteristics of particular schooling systems.

Chapter 5 therefore extends a rather different level of theoretical analysis from that of Chapter 4. It is explicitly concerned with the provision and justification of an analytical framework for the empirical analyses of Part II. Thus, it is concerned with the way in which the common characteristics of mass education systems are mediated by the institutional archaeology and ideological traditions of a particular nation state. There has been a marked tendency in recent sociology of education for macro analyses to fail to distinguish between the common and the idiosyncratic features of different societies, particularly where such societies can be grouped under a generic term such as 'capitalist'. One of the principal themes of this book is that both general and contextually specific analyses are necessary for an adequate understanding of contemporary practice and that there are considerable dangers in extrapolating uncritically to all similar societies from analyses based on any one particular society.

Chapters 6, 7 and 8 serve the dual function of illustrating empirically these general arguments and, at the same time, demonstrating the importance of the national context in determining the precise manifestation of more general pressures and trends. The selection of two national education systems for detailed study, which differ radically in their ethos, organization and origins, reflects one of the major themes of the book, which is the relationship between educational assessment and social control. The growing currency of the concept of accountability and, subsequently, market forces in anglophone countries in the past decade has helped to focus attention on educational assessment as a vital element of *systemic* control alongside its already widely accepted significance as the chief instrument of individual selection and status legitimatization. The analyses of Chapters 6 and 7 address both these major dimensions in the role of educational assessment in an attempt to show how very different institutional manifestations of these key functions nevertheless provide for very similar outcomes in the way in which assessment procedures provide for certain critical functions to be performed by mass education systems.

Thus Chapter 6 offers an overview of the way in which assessment procedures have operated in the institution and development of mass schooling in France since the early nineteenth century. Such an analysis requires a more general account of the ideological and institutional traditions which have become characteristic of French education since the days of Napoleon Bonaparte. It is argued that the most notable of these traditions is that of strong central control. One of the major theoretical arguments of this study is that the way in which assessment procedures are used for control of the education system is a reflection of the degree of central control embodied in that system. This hypothesis is the principal reason for the choice of the case study material. Since the two systems under study – the French and the English – until recently differed radically in their degree of formal centralization, it was envisaged that they would highlight the very different ways assessment procedures have come to be used in individual social settings to fulfil the fundamental objective of system control.

To make the comparison between constants and contextually specific factors as clear as possible, Chapter 7 provides a very similar case study to that of Chapter 6, based this time on the development of educational assessment procedures since the early nineteenth century within the highly decentralized English context.

The eighth and final chapter of the book pulls together the various analytical strands of Parts I and II in a more speculative consideration of the implications of contemporary trends in educational assessment policy in the two countries under study. While the theme of Part I as a whole is the significance of the move from collective to individual social responsibility which was associated with the process of industrialization, Chapter 8 introduces what seems likely to be the next stage of this process, the move towards an increasingly technicist value-orientation to conceal the underlying power relations inherent in educational policy and practice. This latter development is taken to be a further stage in that pursuit of rationality which is a characteristic of industrial societies. A technicist value-orientation requires that those judgements which lie at the heart of any assessment procedure are transformed from being evaluations of an individual's qualities or achievements made against a more or less personal, value-laden set of chosen criteria into evaluations in which the criteria are apparently the absolute dictats of scientific efficiency. Against the relative values of personal choice, culture or belief and the whole realm of politics are pitted the impersonal, objective canons of scientific logic. The implications of the changes in assessment policy which can be identified in both France and England as a result of these contemporary trends provide a conclusion to the study as a whole since they underline the way in which assessment procedures reflect the broader social context. At the same time the current and almost unprecedented prominence of assessment policy in both England and France, as part of the move across Europe as a whole towards what Neave (1989) has termed 'The New Evaluative State', underlines the critical importance of further studies in this area. Radical new developments in the social role of educational assessment are beginning to be visible: on the one hand, a further strengthening of its technicist credentials and hence its power in the dissemination of ideas of 'quality assessment' into all aspects of life; on the other, the post-modern challenge which threatens the legitimacy of the whole edifice of educational assessment as it is addressed in this book.

Many of the empirical data for Part II of the book were collected in the course of four SSRC- and ESRC-funded studies directed individually or jointly by the author: 'Constants and contexts in educational accountability: a comparative study', which was undertaken between 1979 and 1981 (Broadfoot 1981c); 'Teachers' conceptions of their professional responsibility in England and France', which was undertaken between 1984 and 1988 (Broadfoot and Osborn 1988; Osborn and Broadfoot 1992); the Primary assessment, curriculum and experience study 1989–97 (Pollard *et al.* 1994); and the Systems, teachers and educational policy change study 1993–4 (Broadfoot *et al.* 1996a). Taken together these studies have spanned every level of each system from the minister's office to that of the classroom teacher. An equally important source of material was the rich fund of official and unofficial documentation generated in the course of the various projects. However, while much of the contemporary analysis draws on primary source material, the historical analyses are based largely on secondary sources.

Every effort has been made in the study to observe the canons of qualitative research, to use its concern with the meanings and perceptions of respondents to explore the reality as well as the rhetoric of educational practice. Analyses of the empirical data have been submitted to respondents at various stages to check the interpretations made and to generate further insights. In the same spirit, every effort has been made to avoid selective quotations which might deliberately perpetrate bias. The gradual sedimentation of ideas that has taken place over more than a decade of research in this area and the parts of it that have already been published offer some safeguards against any more or less deliberate bias. In the end, however, like all sociological accounts, this book can only be one, essentially personal, attempt to explain some aspect of social life. As such it is but a small part of an endless debate.

THE SOCIAL PURPOSES
OF ASSESSMENT

This chapter and the next are devoted to an elaboration of the central
argument on which this book is based, that historical and contemporary developments in assessment policy and practice may be
understood in terms of the interplay between the themes of
competence, competition and control and the different priority
accorded to each of them in the education system as social, economic
and political factors dictate. To justify the assertion that this
analytical framework is applicable to industrial societies in general,
it is necessary to review historical and contemporary trends in
assessment, evaluation and accountability procedures from a broad
empirical base. Such a review has a second equally important
function of providing a more general context within which the two
case studies which provide the bulk of the empirical evidence in the
book may be located.

   Although the so-called founding fathers of sociology – notably
Marx, Durkheim and Weber – stressed the importance of studying
social phenomena in their historical and international context, it is
perhaps only with the recent growth in prominence of international
issues generally that the importance of recognizing both national
cultural traditions and more general international currents in the

generation of educational policies has been recognized (Phillips 1989). Certainly, as far as assessment is concerned – whether of individuals, institutions or systems as a whole – a study of both historical and international contexts shows clearly the dilemmas inherent in its social role, for the issues that have dominated the debates on educational assessment appear to be common to most of the industrial and industrializing countries of the world (Ottobre 1978; Heyneman 1988). In any country with mass and extended education, the same dilemmas are apparent. In developing countries, which have typically modelled their education systems on those of the developed world, such dilemmas tend to be even more acute since selection and its legitimation are the crucial mechanisms for regulating the aspirations of the masses for the very few openings in the modern employment sector.

Assessment practices reflect and reinforce the often conflicting values embodied in education systems. Debates over the reform of assessment procedures frequently illustrate the tension that exists between, for example, educational goals defined by industry and those of teachers, or the conflicts between a market perspective and a more egalitarian one. It is clear that the degree of influence which various bodies associated with the education system are able to exert at any one time – itself a product of oscillations in the social, economic and political climate – is reflected in the kind of emphasis embodied in the assessment procedures adopted. To the extent that assessment practices are similar in different countries, they reinforce the importance of understanding education and, by definition, educational assessment procedures, in relation to the wider societal and indeed inter-societal forces acting upon it, and hence of not overestimating the internal autonomy and scope for change of any one educational system.

The pages that follow explore the sociological rationale for the emergence of assessment procedures as part of the development of formal educational provision. In attempting to map broad historical and contemporary trends in assessment policy and practice, this chapter and the next will emphasize the importance of seeking to understand the relationship between changes in the socio-economic context and the ways in which these are reflected in changing assessment practices as one of the main sources of leverage on the education system itself. Central to such an exploration, however, is a commitment to respecting the integrity of a given social context so that explanations reflect the mediation of common pressures and trends by the idiosyncratic culture and traditions of particular systems. The first part of the chapter addresses developments in assessment at the level of the individual, whereas the second part pursues its role in society more generally. This distinction is more arbitrary than real, however, for in practice the ebb and flow of different policies and the practices to which they lead is a complex compilation of a variety of tools and strategies in which, like the pieces on a chessboard, each has its scope and enforced limitations and must, therefore, be used in conjunction with other pieces with different powers and constraints to achieve the desired goal.

In Chapter 1 it was argued that as far as assessment is concerned, the enduring purposes are to promote and accredit competence, which in turn serves to influence the content of education; to manage the inevitable competition for limited rewards; and to control the priorities and operation of one of the principal state apparatuses. Building on the dynamic metaphor of the pieces on a chessboard, Chapter 2 explores each of these social imperatives in turn, showing how a varying pattern of checks and balances operating in different times and places nevertheless provides for the same result – the fulfilment of these three broad social imperatives through the manipulation of assessment policy.

The assessment of competence

Even in the most simple societies, children must be trained and subsequently demonstrate competence in the appropriate forms of behaviour and skills required by all members of that society. In some societies, competencies which are the result of such 'primary' socialization will be extended by means of 'secondary socialization' to include preparation for different roles in society. These are societies which are sufficiently complex to allow, and indeed require, their members to pursue a much greater variety of interests and to develop specific talents and skills. The inculcation of both general and specific competencies is increasingly provided for through the mechanism of formal schooling.

Whether education consists simply of the passing on of the unified body of skills necessary for survival, or is transmitted through the highly bureaucratized, elaborate and costly systems which complex industrialized societies have typically evolved to provide for the wide range of specialist skills they require, some kind of assessment of competence will be necessary, not least because the willingness of individuals to submit to such evaluation reflects and reinforces their commitment to joining that particular society. Many commentators have equated the public examinations of contemporary society with the 'rites of passage' of simple societies when a child is able and expected to take on the full obligations of an adult member of society. Such 'rites of passage' are essentially 'qualifying' tests; the time at which youngsters can demonstrate their mastery of the norms and skills necessary for effective participation in that society, thereby allowing the existing members of that society to judge their fitness to belong to it. Candidates cannot fail, however, since they are already destined for their future social roles from birth. Rather, the assessment constitutes a target for teachers and students alike to strive towards, in their efforts to ensure the possession of the necessary social competencies.

In such societies, the assessment procedures may well be undifferentiated, reflecting a society where there is little or no division of labour, except perhaps between boys and girls. All aspirant members will be adjudged at the same stage of their life, on the same relevant criteria of basic competence in necessary skills, in order to ensure the continued survival of the society. The emphasis of the test will be on validity; that is, that the skills assessed match as closely as possible the potential real life requirements. The emphasis is on competence; on qualifying, not on selection.

By contrast, the *rites de passage* (Firth 1969) of complex societies are typically highly differentiated, reflecting the range of competencies that are sought and the need to provide for successive stages of sorting and selection for different social roles.

The content of assessment

In simple societies, the content of assessment is largely determined by the competencies required. There is likely to be little discussion about the desirable content of 'education', and little need to discriminate between the members of a society in terms of their mastery of it. In more complex societies, these basic competencies may be comparatively insignificant compared to other criteria which define more specialized competencies. Still other criteria, as Bourdieu and Passeron (1977; Bourdieu *et al.* 1994) has pointed out, may be quite arbitrary, reflecting the cultural characteristics of dominant groups on which their power is based. Typically implicit rather than explicit, such criteria often constitute a considerable handicap to the success of children from other social groups in the educational system.

As the advent of capitalism began to break down the existing bases for social divisions and the expanding economy of subsequent industrialization created an unprecedented degree of social mobility in the early nineteenth century, the idea of competition for the more desirable social roles became an increasingly significant theme in assessment procedures. Clearly nepotism and wealth are incompatible as selection criteria with the more rationalist concerns embodied in the attestation of competence and open competition. Thus, as the creation of wealth is more and more associated with the recruitment and fostering of talent on a large scale, competition becomes ever more important. The basis of this competition, however – the form and content of assessment – has arguably been determined not so much by what the competition is *for* but rather by how such competition can best be *controlled*. That is to say, as the competitive element of assessment has increasingly come to predominate over its role in the attestation of competence, content has tended to be determined by its legitimatory power rather than its relevance to specific tasks. Or, in more psychometric terms, the preoccupation with the reliability of assessments has tended to eclipse concern with validity (Nuttall 1987).

Although such choices are never clear-cut in their origins, it will be argued that the predominance of formal written examinations and intelligence tests (including the other, later forms of standardized test modelled on them) in the recent history of education owes far more to the power of such devices to legitimate selection than it does to their content or predictive validity. Apart from the degree of irrationality this injects into the selection process, and hence into that of occupational allocation, the content of schooling is itself closely affected. It is a common assertion that the 'assessment tail tends to wag the curriculum dog' (Wilson 1975). Thus the content of assessment procedures is also very significant for the way in which it is likely to affect the entire teaching–learning process in both form and substance. Ironically, this relationship is now being explicitly capitalized upon in the measurement-driven instruction (MDI) movement, in which the 'washback effect' of assessment procedures is deliberately manipulated to encourage emphasis on particular learning outcomes. Public examinations are also used in the same way to effect changes in pedagogy (Airasian 1988; Kellaghan and Greaney 1992).

Following Foucault, Bernstein (1982, 1988) suggests that contemporary societies are characterized by a deep cultural 'fault'. This fault is the division between mental and manual labour, which is a product of an equivalent division between those who produce and those who reproduce forms of knowledge in society. One illustration of this 'fault' is the distinction between 'primary contextualizing' – that is, the creation of knowledge – the 'recontextualizing' of public examiners and curriculum planners in the form of school subjects, and the final stage of 'secondary contextualizing' carried out by teachers at various levels.

Those who control the process by which knowledge is 'recontextualized' into the particular versions of knowledge which become characterized in school subjects, curricula and textbooks are in a powerful position to determine what kinds of intellectual activity are the basis for high status. Thus the assessment procedures used may reflect and, in turn, reinforce not the knowledge and skills that the contemporary economy would appear to require, but rather an essentially arbitrary way of representing knowledge which happened to characterize elite culture in a number of countries when the force of the industrial revolution was being felt in the need for new work skills and new forms of social control.

As other countries became caught up in similar movements – through colonialism, through trade, through various kinds of international contact and competition – they were not slow to recognize the utility of formal schooling and formal assessment procedures, not least as an acceptable means of regulating entry to different levels of job. In so doing, they helped to preserve and disseminate an approach to learning and curriculum organization based on the traditions and conditions of a very different age and newly forced into the divisions of school subjects by the exigencies of the assessment system (Eggleston 1977; Hammersley and Hargreaves 1983). The persistent inability of many developing countries to realize a curriculum centred on relevant and useful practical skills, rather than high-status academic knowledge, provides clear testimony for this tendency. Even in highly developed societies there has been, at least until recently, the persistence of what is essentially a nineteenth-century elite school curriculum embodied in highly competitive academic examinations. Hargreaves (1982a) argues that this mismatch between what is provided and what adolescents need can only grow worse as the pace of social change accelerates. Although radical challenges to existing definitions of curriculum content and organization are currently being mounted in many developed countries in the form of negotiated programmes of study, cross-curricular skills and broadly based records of achievement, such challenges have as yet done little to erode the power of the status quo as embodied in formal, subject-based and examination-oriented curricula (Broadfoot 1991).

Assessment criteria within education still tend to be based on certain academic and particularly linguistic achievements, although in the wider world they may often still include the traditional status criteria of speech, dress and other social behaviour as well. The difficulty of making any sustained assault on the dominance of formal academic assessment and certification, rather than, for example, achievement in personal and social skills[1] – ostensibly at least as relevant to the majority of prospective members of society and to employers as academic skills – shows the relative insignificance of moves to foster more competency-oriented assessment compared to the political fear which is typically associated with any move to change existing ideas about 'standards' and equally the mechanisms concerned with controlling and legitimating competition.

To understand how this emphasis on academic knowledge at the expense of skills and on regulating competition rather than attesting to the possession of competence came about, it is necessary to consider the early history of the mass use of educational assessment procedures. It has been suggested (Broadfoot 1979a) that the institution of formal assessment procedures in education tended to be contemporaneous with the institution of mass educational provision *per se*, itself associated with the social changes brought about by industrialization. Indeed, it may be argued that assessment procedures have typically been directly instrumental in rationalizing educational provision into a system. So comprehensive has this process been that it now seems scarcely credible that the type of national educational provision and organization characteristic of developed societies and aspired to by developing countries is little older than the memory of the oldest members of such societies.

It is now as difficult to imagine schooling without assessment as it is to imagine society without the state-provided, compulsory, mass education it heralded. It would have been equally difficult for pre-nineteenth-century society to have envisaged these developments, for apart from isolated historical examples – such as the civil service entrance examinations instituted in Imperial China and the widespread vocational assessments used to regulate access to particular craft guilds – the notion of specifically educational assessment and, hence, educational qualifications on a mass scale finds its roots in the combined growth of political democracy and industrial capitalism of the nineteenth century.

One of the most important influences on the development of assessment procedures in the nineteenth century was a new concern with competence. In England, for example, this concern was reflected in the institution of qualifying examinations for entry to particular professions or institutions at this time. The pressure of numbers, together with the need for comparability (Hoskin 1979), meant that such examinations were normally formal written tests. But the effects of the institution of such assessment procedures went much further than straightforward quality control. In the first place, the use of a written, theoretical test for entry into high status professions invested the assessment technique itself with a similar high status – a status it still retains.

Second, the institution of formal examinations reflected a more profound change: the notion of a syllabus or curriculum; the systematization of a body of knowledge and its rationalization into a form which made it at least partly susceptible to teaching and learning in the classroom, thereby greatly enhancing the importance of schooling.

Third, it signalled the decline of the almost feudal 'whole man' concept of apprenticeship (Montgomery 1965) in favour of an increasing emphasis on educational qualifications and a change to contractual and impersonal employment. Studies of apprenticeship (for example, Ryrie and Weir 1978; Gleeson and Mardle 1980), as well as the rapidly increasing significance of national vocational qualifications in many countries at the present time (Broadfoot 1992), confirm this trend away from 'on the job' training in favour of the acquisition of more adaptable and 'portable' qualifications in educational institutions of various kinds (Ball 1992). This formalization of training provision masks a major break with the interpersonal

contract associated with traditional apprenticeships and is a powerful expression of the increasing dominance of formal certification in
hitherto less formal realms of educational provision. Fourth, examinations embody the idea of merit and the movement to a situation in
which the allocation of occupational roles was ostensibly at least
more the result of individual achievement.

As Chapter 4 sets out, this move away from the simple ascription
of occupational roles was made possible by the earlier major social
upheavals in religion, knowledge and politics which found expression in the Reformation, the Enlightenment and the French
Revolution, for in these three movements can be traced new rational,
egalitarian, meritocratic and individualistic ideologies which, incu-
bated in the industrial revolution, soon found their expression in the
explosion of practices requiring formal demonstrations of competence, and thus paved the way for the kind of relationship between
education and society, mediated by assessment, which has now
become the norm.

Assessment for regulating competition

Certification and the associated process of selection has arguably
long been the most commonly recognized function of educational
assessment, since it involves students demonstrating their achievements in relation to the goals of the educational system. Their
performance in apparently fair and objective tests is more or less
formally evaluated by 'experts'. The subsequent ranking of candidates in comparison with their fellow competitors against predeter-
mined criteria allows further and higher educational institutions and
employers to select those whom they consider to have 'performed'
the best.

Such performance thus involves elements of both competence and
competition. The extreme importance of certification as an influence
both on educational practice and on the wider society emerges from
this 'gate-keeping' role, by which it can open and close doors for
individuals to future life chances. The certification process is indeed
the epitome of the apparently meritocratic basis of contemporary
society, since in theory it allows free competition based on academic
ability and industry and thus is regarded as the fairest basis for the
allocation of opportunities for high status or remunerative careers.

Although there is considerable evidence that such a measure cannot be a neutral measure of 'merit' alone, there is still no obvious alternative which seems likely to be more fair.

One of the reasons why the domination of examinations has not been seriously challenged is their association with the crucial concept of 'innate ability', which came to dominate educational thinking during the period when the use of examinations was developing rapidly. As the idea that individuals are born with a given level of ability of 'intelligence' came to be widely accepted in many countries in the early part of the twentieth century, so the burgeoning apparatus of certification and selection devices acquired what was to prove a profoundly significant legitimating ideology. Not only were such devices taken to be a measure of a particular performance on a particular day. Their results also came to be interpreted more generally as a reflection of an individual's innate intellectual capacity. It thus became acceptable to use such results to predict likely future performance and, hence, to legitimate selection. In this respect, the concept of intelligence and the tests which were developed to measure it provided for a fourth and crucial role for assessment – that of controlling individual aspirations.

Assessment for individual control

No other assessment technique so far devised has so perfectly combined the two principal legitimating ideologies of industrial societies: the liberal democratic principle of fair competition and the belief in scientific progress. Yet, just because for many decades such tests were believed to be the most accurate way of measuring innate intellectual capacity, this need not in itself have led to a policy of educational provision based on such different capacities. The explanation of the commitment to providing different educational routes for different sorts of children which dominated educational policy in most European countries at least from the 1920s until the early 1960s can only be found in the social pressures which prevailed at the time such tests were first devised.

So great were the social and economic changes of the nineteenth century and the associated developments of social and geographic mobility, urbanization, bureaucratization and economic expansion in many of the industrialized countries that pressure on all the various rungs of the educational ladder increased rapidly. The scholarship and certification systems based on selection alone would very soon have ceased to be an adequate way of regulating access to educational and vocational opportunity, had not another mechanism of legitimating selection been found to disperse the accumulating popular frustration.

The pressure from those anxious to climb the rungs of the ladder was reinforced by pressure from those espousing the developing educational ideologies at the time. In England, for example, Williams (1961) has identified the differing perspectives of the 'industrial trainers', the 'old humanists' and the 'public educators', but whether their concern was to make the maximum use of 'the pool of ability' by the institution of what Beatrice and Sidney Webb termed a 'capacity catching' machine or whether it was to promote social justice and social order, the effects were the same – a search for an apparently accurate and thus fair way of identifying talent and of discriminating among pupils on purely educational, rather than, as had previously been the case, social grounds. Above all, there was a need for a procedure which would be widely acceptable.

Such ideological and pragmatic pressures rapidly elevated the notion of 'ability' or 'intelligence' to a position where it came to dominate educational thinking at all levels. For teachers, the process of categorizing their pupils into 'bright' and 'dull', 'able' and 'less able' became and remains a taken-for-granted feature of professional discourse even though it cannot be linked with any objective evidence of performance (Claxton 1994).

The search for some means of measuring 'intelligence' fairly was not a protracted one. The solution, like the problem, was found in the new individualist emphasis in education. A growing interest in individual achievement had led many nineteenth-century psychologists to study the determinants of various personal characteristics. Gradually, there developed a conviction among psychologists that the determining factor in an individual's scholastic achievement was his or her innate ability or 'intelligence' – a quality that was both fixed and measurable. In addition, studies arising out of Binet's early twentieth-century work in France with 'slow learners', such as Burt's (1912) article in England, 'The inheritance of mental characteristics', and the widespread and apparently effective use of such tests by the United States Army in 1918, quickly convinced academics and lay people alike not only that it was possible to measure 'intellectual ability' objectively, but that from these measurements future academic and occupational performance could be accurately predicted.

By the mid-twentieth century, so firmly established had 'intelligence' testing become that it dominated educational thinking. Sir Cyril Burt was for many people merely stating the obvious when in 1933 he wrote:

> By intelligence the psychologist understands inborn, all round, intellectual ability. It is inherited, or at least innate, not due to teaching or training; it is intellectual, not emotional or moral, and remains uninfluenced by industry or zeal; it is general, not specific, i.e. it is not limited to any particular kind of work, but enters into all we do or say or think. Of all our mental qualities, it is the most far-reaching; fortunately it can be measured with accuracy and ease.
>
> (Burt 1933: 28–9)

It is not hard to account for the rapid establishment of intelligence testing. It must indeed have been seen as an answer to a prayer that, by means of a simple test, children could be readily and justly identified as 'bright' or 'dull'; their future could be predicted and, on this basis, they could be categorized into different channels of the educational system. Not only that, but the scientific, 'objective' nature of such tests, their proven predictive power (Kamin 1974) and their measurement of a characteristic believed to be as inborn as eye colour, meant it was almost impossible for the recipient to reject the diagnosis. Thus intelligence testing, as a mechanism of social control, was unsurpassed in teaching the doomed majority that their failure was the result of their own inbuilt inadequacy.

The significance of this now almost intuitive discourse is well illustrated by contrasting those countries where it prevails, such as the United Kingdom and the United States, with a country like Japan where it does not. Arguably, the Japanese assumption that achievement is the result of *persistence* rather than innate ability, and hence that *all* can succeed if they try, is one of the secrets of the phenomenal success of its education system (White 1987).

However, the concept of 'merit' involved another dimension as well. In his famous equation

$$\text{ability} + \text{effort} = \text{merit}$$

Young (1971) highlighted a second crucial dimension in the

legitimating ideology of assessment – that of motivation. Another major reason for the proliferation of assessment procedures as a means of individual control is their capacity to motivate pupils. While the constraining effects of selection and certification examinations on the educational process itself may have been deplored, such examinations and the less significant tests and assessments associated with them are widely welcomed as an important source of motivation, and thus of control. Today, for many pupils, passing examinations is the only purpose of being in school (Broadfoot 1979b; Buswell 1983; Turner 1984). Any proposal to abandon competitive assessment meets with an outcry among politicians and even parents, who fear that standards will fall as a result. The converse of this situation is, of course, also true: the increasing lack of motivation among those pupils who are not taking external examinations, whose assessments are rarely positive enough to motivate them to try harder, and for whom no very tempting bait can be offered in an educational system that recognizes in its assessment procedures only one kind of ability – the kind which, by definition, they do not have. It is this problem, and the need to 'warm up' potential students to carry on learning rather than 'cool out' the majority as in the past when the economy did not need such a highly educated workforce, that partly underlies the growing tendency at the present time to make formal assessment more comprehensive.

In the earlier stages of the development of mass educational provision, many pupils were typically denied even the opportunity to participate in educational competition, since they could not pass beyond primary or elementary schooling and had no 'ladder' to the opportunities provided by extended secondary education (Higginson 1981). But in developed countries the enormous expansion of educational provision at all levels during recent decades has resulted from a widespread belief in 'human capital' theory combined with popular demand for greater equality of educational opportunity, and has led to a situation in which forms of control based on exclusion have operated at successively later stages.

The consistent trend for the number of statutory years of schooling to be extended has meant that more and more of what were previously 'elite' examinations for a minority of the age cohort at the end of compulsory schooling or for university entrance are becoming the target for the majority of pupils – this trend is well illustrated in France where there is a very public commitment that 80 per cent of the age cohort should achieve the baccalaureate university entrance qualification.

Assessment for system control

Before the institution of state-funded education, schools played little part in the lives of the majority of the population and so the issue of control hardly arose. In many countries the church's influence was virtually unassailable. With the advent of industrialization and its associated political and social upheavals, governments were typically unwilling to rely on voluntary agencies, and in particular the church, to provide schooling in societies in which so many of the old social codes have been swept away and in which new employment skills were needed. Indeed, many such tensions are still to be found in developing countries. Industrialization also led to privileged sections of society being more and more forced to resort to schooling as the new means of perpetuating the elite status that land and money could no longer ensure. Thus it was necessary that a means be found of carefully controlling the nature of an ever-expanding state educational provision, and of regulating the newly emerging basis for social differentiation.

Perhaps one of the earliest, and certainly one of the clearest, examples of the combined need to control the content of mass education and to ensure standards which reflect a good return on investment was the nineteenth-century payment by results system in England, in which school grants, and indeed teachers' salaries, depended on the standards achieved by their pupils in certain basic curricular areas as measured by HMI (see Chapter 7). However, recently, equally telling and crude attempts to use testing to ensure school and teacher quality as well as minimum competencies among pupils have been widely introduced in the United States (Stake 1991). Though it has long been normal for education systems to support a large army of local and national inspectors as testimony to a continuing concern that schools should be accountable to society for the investment in them, as measured by the achievements of their pupils, and their conformity to accepted practice, moves to use formal testing for this purpose have been relatively rare until recently. Indeed, provision for accountability can take many forms depending on the ideological and institutional traditions of a particular national system.

Where there is a strong central authority, control has, in the past, tended to be focused on provision. Where this has been lacking control has tended to be exerted very indirectly through the existence of various kinds of assessment and particularly public examinations. Arguably this distinction is now changing in favour of a more common emphasis on assessment as represented by various forms of quality assurance and control (Harlen 1994). Whether the control in question is that of legal or bureaucratic accountability to superiors or concerns a moral element of responsibility to clients, it is the language of assessment that increasingly provides the currency of communication.

Accountability

Accountability may be regarded as a two-stage process involving first the identification of the performance of the education system in relation to its goals, as defined at any one time, and second the response by educational institutions brought about through the mechanisms of system control in response to any perceived shortfall between performance and goals. Although conceptually distinct, these two stages are frequently simultaneous in practice. As well as these bureaucratic accountability relationships, education systems are also likely to be characterized by other patterns of informal accountability in the form of the constraints and responsibilities that actors in the education system set for themselves as part of their 'professional standards'.

Where accountability has emerged as an explicit issue – typically in systems where there is weak central control – the focus has tended to be on student gain: the results of the system. The assumption is that the supply of information and knowledge about the system is the basis for various forms of control: the sanctioning of individuals, the allocation of resources and more general exhortation including occasionally explicit coercion, although, as Chin and Benne (1978) point out, it is rarely effective to run organisations on a power-coercive basis.

Educational control is thus much more commonly exerted through attempts to colonize professional attitudes and other 'normative re-educative' strategies. Rarely do specific proposals for action follow directly from the provision of information (Kirst and Bass 1976). Rather, it is the act of assessment itself which is crucial, for the way in which information is gathered and the content of that information itself embody prevailing values. Thus, the responsibility to give an account or to be accountable acts in itself as an important force of control. This argument is discussed at more length later in the book. It is sufficient at this point merely to introduce the important argument that whether or not there is extensive provision for bureaucratic central control, the key to effective control lies in the power to generate the evaluative criteria which inform the content and style of educational discourse and to impose these as the basis of both formal and professional accountability.

A CHANGING
ASSESSMENT CULTURE

An analysis of developments in educational assessment procedures reveals more clearly than perhaps any other aspect of the education system the irreconcilable demands which education must fulfil in contemporary society. From the outset assessment procedures were a crucial part of the process of opening up routes to social mobility and the institution of a more rational basis for the allocation of social roles. On the other hand, it is important to recognize the role of assessment in limiting such mobility and, even more crucially, in legitimating what are essentially still education systems strongly biased in favour of traditional privilege. For this reason and as a result of new social and economic imperatives, recent decades in many developed countries have witnessed growing disillusion with many traditional forms of assessment. This chapter explores the rationale behind the changes currently taking place and, in particular, the gradual erosion of the two traditional bastions of the formal assessment edifice – public examinations and intelligence tests – and discusses the significant new developments in assessment policy and practice which are now occurring.

Dissatisfaction with traditional psychometric approaches is now widespread, explicit and clearly articulated. This dissatisfaction includes the emphasis on comparison between students rather than on description of specific and changing levels of attainment; the frequent mismatch between curriculum and test content; the pressure to test in a relatively limited number of aspects of a programme of instruction; and the assumption that students learn in a linear fashion and that therefore they must learn and be assessed on the 'basics' before going on to more complex intellectual processes. There is a growing feeling that the traditional preoccupation with differentiation and reliability as the most important features of assessment has led to an emphasis on quick, economic and often multiple-choice achievement tests that can be shown to have acceptable psychometric properties and are easy to mark, rather than assessment procedures that provide a useful picture of what students can do. A second important reason for increasing dissatisfaction with more traditional approaches to student assessment is that, as a now very substantial body of research testifies, the tests can be shown not even necessarily to do what they aspire to do – to provide objective, reliable evidence of the attainments measured (Ingenkamp 1977; Raven 1991; Lee-Smith 1990; Satterley 1994). A third related reason for dissatisfaction with traditional testing approaches concerns what is perceived to be their undesirable 'wash-back' effect on instruction. It is also increasingly being recognized that where there is a gulf between what is covered by formal assessment techniques and desired learning outcomes that are not the subject of such techniques (such as higher-level skills). This has major repercussions in the emphasis given in what is taught.

A number of other studies (see Crooks 1989 for a comprehensive review) have revealed just how important assessment is in defining the attitude students take towards their work, their sense of ownership and control of their own learning: the strategies they employ in learning and their confidence and self-esteem, all of which impact profoundly on the quality of learning achieved. Thus there is now growing recognition of the limitations of traditional approaches to assessment, which is centred on a greater concern with validity (Nuttall 1987; Gipps and Murphy 1994). There is concern about the influential but potentially quixotic role of 'personal' assessment. Above all, there is now a desire to harness the powerful impact of assessment to *promote*, rather than *inhibit*, learning. It is these desires which have fuelled the search for new types of both formative and summative assessment and which are associated with a number of new international emphases in assessment policy.

The review that follows highlights the main elements of this newly evolving assessment culture. Once again it is structured in terms of the four generic purposes of educational assessment: competition and control, content and competence.

Competition

One of the most marked educational policy developments of recent decades in many countries has been the bringing together of the traditionally separate higher elementary and secondary schools into some more 'comprehensive' form of provision. Thus, increasingly, it is 'elementary' education that now extends up to the statutory school-leaving age. Where such education is provided in comprehensive schools this makes overt, formal selection before this stage unnecessary. This trend is particularly marked in Europe, where post-Second World War school organization typically reflected a clear system of 'sponsored' mobility (Turner 1960).[1] Where once the majority of children would be allocated at around eleven to a non-selective secondary school which they would expect to leave at the statutory leaving age with few or no formal qualifications, while for the minority there was the extended secondary school, catering for perhaps a small minority of the year group and geared to university entrance, opportunity to compete is typically now greatly extended to the point where higher education may well become available to the vast majority.

Just as the origins of this system lie in the social and economic forces of the nineteenth and early twentieth centuries, so similar common social and economic forces are effecting a change in this structure, although national ideals of educational practice are sufficiently powerful to account for important and distinct national differences in the rate and form of such change. The trend is by no means uni-dimensional. But typically now, selection is deferred at least to fifteen or sixteen or the end of compulsory schooling and increasingly to eighteen or nineteen when those continuing with their education divide once more into academic and technical/vocational routes, a third group entering straight into the labour market (Ranson 1984). Even in those European countries where selection for secondary school still takes place, such as Germany, Italy and the Netherlands, this is now typically a protracted, teacher-based process of 'differentiation' rather than selection (Nisbet 1993).[2]

The social and ideological forces underlying the move towards comprehensive reform, which is defined by the OECD as the 'postponement of differentiation', are immensely complex. It is possible though to identify several specific influences which both arise from and in turn affect assessment practices in particular. One such is Dore's (1976) concept of 'qualification inflation'. The increasing expansion of educational provision, he argues, allows more people to gain those qualifications which traditionally led to high-status jobs. Without an equivalent expansion in the number of such jobs, the result is a devaluation of qualifications and a raising of the 'rate for the job' on the classic 'supply and demand' principle, with consequent pressure on the education system as students seek to obtain ever higher level qualifications. Staying-on rates in advanced industrial societies clearly testify to more and more pupils achieving qualifications at each level of schooling, with the likelihood that these qualifications will have less and less value as selection instruments.

The postponement of the crucial point for selection is clearly evidenced by typical changes which have taken place in certification procedures – the formal expression of assessment at the termination of a particular stage of schooling. Although the primary school-leaving certificate is likely to be still critical in developing countries, certification at the end of compulsory schooling or even at the stage of university entrance is changing both its form and its primary purpose.

Another reason for this change is the more or less explicit recognition that mass primary and secondary education require a very different ethos for the education system from when it was basically geared to university selection if the university is not to determine the curriculum right down to the level of the lower primary school.

The practical pressures facing advanced industrial societies at the present time make these developments readily understood as a pragmatic response to the pace of technological change, which puts a premium on the preparation of future workers who will be adaptable and equipped with a range of generic social and technical skills, rather than on the possession of any particular body of knowledge *per se*. Equally, such technological change has substantially reduced the demand for unskilled manual workers and replaced it with a growing need for technicians (Cassels 1990).

The rapid escalation of staying-on rates at school after the age of statutory schooling which is currently a feature of most developed societies in Europe and Australasia, where there was previously considerable attrition at this stage, is thus the result of a combination of factors. These include: an ever increasing demand for formal qualifications as discussed above; the need of the economy for more highly skilled entrants; and the widespread problem of unemployment which has tended to close off alternative routes. Underlying these very clear features of current developments, however, is the less obvious but equally important issue of control.

New forms of individual control

The control procedures that provided for the typically highly selective, differentiated forms of school provision characteristic of the early stages of mass schooling systems have now become so problematic that alternative selection and certification procedures are being instituted which draw on rather different sources of legitimation. 'It is still certainly the case', as Eggleston (1984: 32) argues, 'that success in competitive examinations, is for most people, an essential prelude to the legitimate exercise of power, responsibility and status throughout modern societies. Lack of accreditation constitutes a severe limitation and there is abundant evidence that the examination system, despite its technical and ideological critics, still enjoys widespread public acceptance.' Now, however, the regulation of that competition is increasingly achieved by more informal forms of selection. Indeed, the boundary between 'formative evaluation' and 'summative assessment' is increasingly blurred in this respect. Although there must be a form of 'summative' assessment when there are decisions to be made about alternative routes in the educational system, these decisions may be increasingly in the form of qualitative differentiation between different educational courses rather than a simple pass/fail selection system, and be based on informal discussion between teacher, parent and pupil.

This distinction between formal assessment and informal evaluation is an important one. As already suggested, teachers are continually assessing their pupils. Likewise, pupils are continually assessing themselves and each other. Although such assessments may not appear to be significant in societal terms, they are highly influential for the individual learner, and are 'one of the most potent forces influencing education' (Crooks 1988). Such assessments will indirectly feed into the more formal, 'summative' processes of certification and control and the limitations these provide to future opportunities. The significance of any assessment procedure thus depends on a combination of its selection and legitimatory currency – its power to determine and justify the allocation of life chances and its power to influence learning itself. Whether teachers' classroom evaluations are confined to the learning process and the associated effect on the pupil's self-concept and aspirations, or, as in the current tendency, are formally incorporated into the process of certification and selection, where they became a great deal more significant, the result of long-term, in-depth, positive evaluation will provide a powerful contemporary basis for the legitimation of selection.

Thus, although the expansion of educational provision may have postponed the point of formal selection and the ensuing 'qualification inflation' is tending to postpone it still further, even to the point where universal tertiary education is beginning to figure on the policy agenda of some countries, it is not safe to assume that this postponement of selection has in fact created any greater equality of opportunity in relation to differences in social background than existed under the former selective education system. Bourdieu and Passeron (1977) argue that in France during the growth in higher education provision in the 1960s, the structure of the distribution of educational opportunities relative to social class did indeed shift upwards, but remained virtually unchanged in shape. The increased enrolment of 18–20-year-olds was distributed among the different social classes in proportions roughly equal to those pertaining before. Bourdieu and Passeron also argue that a similar pattern of development of educational opportunity, combining increased enrolment of all social classes, can be identified in European countries such as Denmark, the Netherlands and Sweden. Halsey *et al.* (1980) and Goldthorpe (1980), among others, have shown that in England too there was little significant change in the relative achievements of social classes following comprehensivization.

Bearing in mind the foregoing arguments about the postponement of selection it is logical to predict that assessment during the compulsory, comprehensive stage of schooling will take on a different form and function. This has indeed proved to be the case with assessment procedures that are concerned with motivation, diagnosis and accountability rather than selection, and applied to all pupils in a routine way, now becoming the norm.

Associated with this trend, as suggested earlier, is a significantly increased measure of responsibility for teachers in many countries. Indeed, examinations at the end of compulsory schooling have typically given place to a regular series of standardized tests, routinely administered to all children at certain points in their school careers (Broadfoot 1994b). The extension of formal assessment to all the members of a year group is less a reflection of a new principle of certification than the extension of earlier certification procedures.

One reason for this development is the increasingly 'low stakes' character of at least some of the apparatus of certification as qualification inflation has led to lower levels of qualification becoming devalued. Equally important, however, is the necessity of involving teachers in any assessment that concerns skills and competencies as well as knowledge, since these latter cannot be assessed by the more traditional 'paper and pencil' approach. Thus from Europe to Australia and the Far East, there is a growing tendency for the earlier stages of certification at least to involve, if not to be completely handed over to, teachers (Broadfoot *et al.* 1991). Elsewhere, such as anglophone Africa and India, teachers are playing an increasingly important role in the setting and marking of examinations (Njabili 1987; Pennycuick 1990).

Thompson (1974) explained this trend towards teacher-based certification as the result of an increasing level of public trust and confidence in schools. Recent concern in many countries with standards and the provision for greater accountability based on performance indicators suggests that this is no longer, if indeed it ever was, the explanation. A more likely explanation seems to be in terms of legitimation. If there is only a single route to success in the education system and the examination is of crucial importance as the gate-keeper within that system, it must be invested with as much apparent objectivity, ritual and formality as possible so that the results and the failure which they imply for many candidates are accepted. As qualifications become progressively differentiated, reflecting both the availability of different accreditation tracks and the accreditation of multiple competencies within each of those tracks, they become less significant in the allocation of life chances. Then they can, and in some cases must, be left to the informal observation of the teacher. Given the need to maintain the balance between the various different social purposes of educational assessment that were identified earlier, any such move, which involves a reduction of the control of competencies, content and competition embodied in the public examination system, is likely to be accompanied by the institution of increasingly systematic expressions of accountability in the shape of national assessment systems in order to redress the balance and ensure continuing central control over curriculum and pedagogy.

Content

The democratization of secondary schooling and the associated inflation and differentiation of qualifications is linked to another current trend towards more broadly based assessment within which a significant feature is the re-emergence of affective characteristics for inclusion in formal assessment.[3] The shaping of an individual's character, attitudes and values was formerly a central aspect of schooling, particularly for those who were at either the top or the bottom of the educational ladder, being moulded for leadership and acceptance respectively. However, formal assessment of such aspects was, for the most part, eclipsed in the late nineteenth century by the meritocratic movements towards the apparently more objective, and therefore defensible, cognitive measures already described. The re-emergence at the present time of such assessment may be explained in terms of both content and control. For, given the contemporary importance of assessment in the allocation of career opportunities, whatever is assessed will be reflected in both the formal and informal curricular activities of the school. Thus, it is argued, if pupils know, for example, that certain personal qualities or attitudes are likely to count towards their final assessment, they will tend to try to develop and be encouraged by teachers to show such attributes. By so doing they are reinforcing the process of socialization.

Another reason behind this development is the attempt to

overcome the problem of the lack of realistic targets to motivate the whole range of pupils. Where it is possible to broaden the basis for assessment and widen the range of rewards so that virtually all pupils can find a reason to participate in the assessment competition, this is likely to lend support to the prevailing social order.

The increasing use of informal descriptive records such as 'records of achievement' and 'portfolios' during the compulsory schooling stage, containing both cognitive and non-cognitive information (Weston 1991), may be explained too by the orientation to a different kind of school-leaver than was traditionally the case with 16-plus assessment, when it was aimed typically at the top, academic end of the year group. This accords with the views of some scholars who have argued the primacy of the school's role, not in encouraging intellectual development, but in developing appropriate non-cognitive qualities and self-perceptions which will 'correspond' with the pupil's future occupational situation (see, for example, Bowles and Gintis 1976; Willis 1977). Employers repeatedly stress that they seek an appropriate level of formal qualifications but that often workplace and personal skills are even more important (Cumming 1982; Institute of Personnel Management 1984). Corporations looking for potential management trainees may rate personal qualities – especially capacity for commitment – higher than intellectual achievement alone. By the more overt inclusion of non-cognitive assessment in certification, the inculcation of appropriate attitudes and behaviour, which has always been one of the informal effects of schooling, is reinforced.

In many countries the attempt to move from selective and matriculation examinations towards descriptive school-leaving certificates, and, associated with this, a more explicit link between general education and vocational training, is a direct result of the problems caused by traditional examination procedures. Where there is a marked shortage of places in higher education, and consequently large numbers of qualified students unable to find a place, who at the same time lack any more vocational qualification, a considerable threat to social order may be built up. One of the principal ways of reducing the massive increase in applications for formal higher education, which otherwise would result from the expansion of secondary education which has taken place, is the extension of 'differentiation' to higher education to embrace different forms of vocational training, or even 'preparation for leisure', within a more comprehensive tertiary system. The 'old' model of school certification was typically a grouped certificate in which candidates had to pass in five or so subjects to 'matriculate' and gain the qualification which was both necessary and sufficient qualification for university entrance. Formerly, when selection had already largely taken place before this stage, certification at this higher school stage was more concerned with the attestation of achievement than discrimination. Now, where such examinations still exist, it is no longer sufficient merely to pass; you must pass well.[4]

Competence

International trends towards qualification 'frameworks' herald a return to an emphasis on assessment for competence rather than competition. Arguably they may be seen as the beginnings of an attempt to redress the balance in terms of the most long-standing and fundamental social purpose of educational assessment, which is associated with the need for a valid basis for the accreditation of occupational competency. It has always been the case, and remains true, that in a rational society demonstrated competence in a particular skill or role should be an essential prerequisite for individuals to undertake a given occupation. In the mid-nineteenth century in the industrializing world, however, the social imperative to provide an acceptable basis for competition in a situation of scarce options for occupational mobility led the regulation of *competition* – and the assessment procedures which this called forth – to become vastly more important. Thus, just as psychometrics and norm-referenced assessment generally were the reflection of this emphasis on selection, so competency-based and criteria-referenced assessments (Burke 1989) are a reflection of the economic characteristics of contemporary 'post-industrial' societies in which there is a pressing need to encourage more and more, rather than reduce to fewer and fewer, learners at every level of the education system. Furthermore, the increasingly international character of the labour market reinforces the need for *explicit* descriptions of the level of competency associated with particular qualifications since, in a highly mobile and diversified international economy, the possession of specific skills and knowledge *within* a given level of qualification is likely to be as important to have accredited as the simple fact of *achieving* a particular level was in the former highly stratified and selective education systems.

Thus, to the extent that it is possible to generalize about curriculum and assessment developments during the stage of compulsory schooling, the trend must be seen as being towards a greater homogeneity or rationalization of curriculum provision within a detailed framework of sequential targets rather than the provision of curriculum guidelines in terms simply of courses of study or subjects to be covered. This emphasis on criterion referencing and the expression of curriculum objectives in assessment terms is also in evidence in the post-compulsory phase, although paradoxically it can take quite a different form in reducing, rather than increasing, curriculum choice. There are several reasons for this. One of these undoubtedly reflects the reasons why more and more students are staying on at school and their expectations of what the courses of study they are provided with should be like, such that the traditional, highly academic and formal upper secondary courses are no longer appropriate. Consequently, there have been changes in many countries in both the content and the mode of delivery of courses aimed at non-traditional senior secondary students. Such courses have a vocational emphasis and are structured around more collaborative active learning styles. In particular, however, what characterizes many such developments is the breaking down of the competencies to be acquired into discrete units or modules and the provision of considerable choice for learners as to the path taken and the speed with which they negotiate their particular learning route.

In the most extreme cases, with the accreditation of prior learning, it is possible to assemble a dossier of evidence to be accredited with particular competencies or levels of competence, without a formal course being undertaken at all (Evans 1992). Thus the return to an emphasis on the assessment of competence is changing, once again, the characteristic features of educational organization that the growth of examinations concerned with *competition* called forth – in this case the organization of specific courses of study and syllabuses. Although the trend towards modularization and competency-based qualifications is far more widespread in vocational qualifications, it is also beginning to become quite firmly established in more formal traditional courses, such as the French Baccalauréat or the English A level, despite the fact that in the latter case at least, it has encountered strong resistance.

Implicit in the breaking down of tight boundaries linking long courses of study with prestigious end-of-course examinations is the related possibility of integrating vocational and academic qualifications into a single framework or currency. There are many problems with this, not least the emphasis in vocational qualifications on assessing competency as against the continuing norm-referenced emphasis of many academic qualifications. Another problem is breaking down the traditional discrepancy in status between academic and vocational qualifications. It is possible to find evidence, in a number of countries where such examinations have been dominant hitherto, of the uneasy coexistence of a new qualifications framework which emphasizes the accreditation of *competence* at different levels as a reflection of the need to democratize and differentiate post-compulsory school qualifications, and the continued existence of the norm-referenced, academic, high-status university entrance examinations in which the emphasis is still on *competition*.

Related to the above, and perhaps the clearest expression of the changing character of post-compulsory secondary school education, are the attempts to introduce into formal certification procedures attestation of what are known as core skills or 'key competencies'. In England, for example, where the government has identified literacy, numeracy, information technology, possession of a modern foreign language, problem-solving and personal and social skills as essential aspects of competence, these are now to be incorporated into all post-16 qualifications. A similar list is being developed following the work of the Finn, Meyer and Carmichael committees in Australia, where work on 'key competencies' and their embodiment in the curriculum frameworks is going forward (Curtain and Hayton 1995). Equally, the new 'Standards Project' within the United States, which involves 19 states in developing shared standards and a system of portfolio assessment aimed at encouraging the inculcation of those standards through assessment-led curriculum development, can be seen as another manifestation of this trend (Resnick *et al.* 1995).

An equally telling reflection of the growing preoccupation with the attestation of competence rather than the regulation of competition as the principal focus for assessment – and of the continuing tensions between these two traditions – is the international trend towards the institution of hierarchical, criterion-referenced curriculum and assessment frameworks as the basis for the organization of the *compulsory* stages of schooling. Many countries are now in the process of overhauling their traditional curriculum guidelines and reorganizing them in terms of the provision of a sequential framework of learning targets and attainment levels, which embody a commitment to the philosophy of criterion-referenced assessment. From the start to the end of compulsory schooling and beyond the curriculum is mapped out in this way accompanied by a parallel assessment framework providing for reporting to parents and, in some cases, to the public as a whole at various stages in relation to progress through the curriculum levels. Thus, for example, in Canada, the Toronto benchmarks programme provides descriptions of appropriate levels of achievement at grades 3, 6 and 8, and assessment examples illustrate the curriculum goals. Moreover, 'minimum levels of learning' have been laid down in India since 1986 for classes I to IV. The New Zealand curriculum framework, which is currently being developed, is again paralleled by an assessment framework with assessment objectives at each stage. Teachers are provided with diagnostic tests which they must use to find out the standards of their students at the beginning of each new phase of schooling. In Australia, a curriculum framework of 'subject profiles' is now being developed, which will provide a common basis for the individual curriculum of each of the states. In this radical departure from tradition teachers will be provided with sample descriptions for each level of the curriculum as expressed in detail for each state, coupled with sample assessments that they can use to guide their practice. The English national curriculum and assessment framework is similar to this, with once again teachers carrying substantial responsibility for the national assessments in terms both of their own continuous assessment, which will be reported to parents annually, and of the periodic assessments at the end of each key stage, based on standard assessment tests.

Thus the philosophy, priorities and practices underpinning assessment activity at every level of educational provision and in many different countries are currently in a state of considerable flux and development. Perhaps the most characteristic feature of the assessment policies currently being developed in most of the advanced countries is the scale of change and development. Countries where, for decades, the same assessment apparatus has continued virtually unchanged and unchallenged are now typically subjecting every aspect of their assessment and certification procedures to extensive scrutiny in an effort to reconcile in the best possible way the often contradictory pressures towards, on the one hand, widely based certification which involves targets that are meaningful and realistic for an ever-expanding student population, and, on the other, providing for assessment procedures which retain the same level of confidence in the standard being achieved as that associated with highly selective and elite-oriented examinations. Where traditional emphases in assessment and certification centred on the idea of passing and failing, fixed and narrow notions of intelligence or ability, and a restricted range of assessment techniques, these are increasingly being replaced by inclusive approaches – qualifications based on the assessment of actual performance, enhancing validity through comprehensive coverage of learning goals. Associated with this emphasis on validity is the generation of clearly-defined, hierarchical criteria of achievement as the basis for both reliability and transparency, so that those being assessed understand the criteria being applied and thus can internalize the relevant standards and direct their learning appropriately. Qualifications are increasingly being designed to address both specific and general learning goals, both short and long term desired outcomes, to combine knowledge, skills and personal competencies, to reflect a range of potential performance contexts, verbal, symbolic, physical and social, and to take account of idiosyncratic, unanticipated learning as well as instructional goals (Torrance 1995).

As Chapter 7 sets out, England seems to be finding it harder to come to terms with these pressures than many other similar countries, including Scotland. Although there are signs of a movement towards more descriptive, teacher-based assessments, particularly in the widespread support for records of achievement now institutionalized in the National Record of Achievement, and although considerable prominence is now being given to specific and general vocational qualifications by means of the introduction of National Vocational Qualifications (NVQs) and General National Vocational Qualifications (GNVQs) there is also a powerful lobby in favour of retaining and indeed strengthening traditional pass/fail certificate examinations, evidenced by recent government moves to reduce coursework assessment and modular courses and to make national assessments more like formal examinations. As such, English procedures provide a good example of the way in which the general pressures affecting individual societies are articulated within the idiosyncratic traditions and prevailing politics of particular national states, thereby producing quite wide variations in practice.[5]

Thus, despite marked national variations in the rate and form of the changes taking place, which reflect the need for individual countries to find the optimum balance between the selection and control functions of assessment in line with national differences in the institutional and ideological context, it is possible to identify consistent international trends in assessment policy at the present time. These are: changes in the nature of the assessment competition, which involves an ever later key point of selection, with a concomitant decline in the formality and significance of assessment for certification prior to this stage; a broadening of the content of assessment to include skills and qualities as well as knowledge; and a growing emphasis on the assessment of competence at every level of provision. All these trends may be attributed to powerful and common pressures resulting from a changing employment structure and the need generally for a more highly educated workforce (Nisbet 1993).[6]

Associated with these changing assessment priorities are developments in the way in which assessment is conducted. These include, for example: attempts to improve classroom assessment practices; attempts to strengthen the links between assessment and learning; providing for more continuous records of student progress and achievements; the increasing devolution of responsibility for assessment to teachers and schools; and, hence, more explicit training in assessment for teachers.

Thus, for example, in an attempt to improve the quality of teachers' classroom assessment practice, some countries (such as Scotland) are providing national tests or item banks which teachers can draw on as and when they wish, to help them in their identification of student achievement and future learning needs. In the Netherlands, diagnostic tests are now nationally provided together with the crucially important 'help books', which advise teachers on how they can deal with the learning needs identified by the tests. The approach in France, although motivated by a similar concern, is slightly different and characteristic of another common approach. This involves imposing compulsory blanket testing at key points of the school career. In France, students do national tests at the beginning of each new stage of their schooling, in order to provide teachers and their parents with diagnostic information which is intended to improve the ability of teachers to respond to individual learning needs (Broadfoot 1992, 1993).

Another illustration of the increasing devolution of responsibility for assessment to teachers is the growth in more continuous records of student progress and achievement. Though such records vary considerably from country to country in their emphasis and format, there is embodied in them a commitment to a more broadly based, positive and collaborative approach to recording achievement. Thus, in much of the record of achievement development work that has gone on in the United Kingdom over the past two decades and in the rather similar initiatives in terms of portfolio assessment in the USA, the emphasis has been on recording to empower students as more effective learners. In other countries the emphasis has been rather different, being focused sharply on the end product itself, the provision of a record of achievement, which will serve as a more comprehensive form of documentation for a student to take into the outside world. The English National Record of Achievement, in which students and their teachers and trainers can record the full range of academic, vocational and personal achievements during secondary school, tertiary education and employment, is more characteristic of this emphasis, as are several of the Australian initiatives aimed at providing records of achievement. A third variation is embodied in the use of such records as the basis for orientation and selection during the course of schooling – as is the case with the *livret scolaire* in France.

However, all these initiatives reflect the broad assessment trends already identified – a new emphasis on validity in the assessment process, and on assessing a much wider range of skills and achievements than can be addressed in conventional written examinations, which necessarily involves an increasingly explicit role for teachers in the more formalized kinds of assessment. Thus, for example, in contrast to the situation in a country like Germany, where teachers have long played a central and unchallenged role in assessment at all levels of the system, including the generation of exam papers and the marking of the prestigious *abitur* exam (Broadfoot 1994a), even in a country like the United States, where there has in the past been almost total reliance on so-called objective tests, there is now a powerful trend towards teacher assessment in the pursuit of more 'authentic' evidence of student achievement. The reason for this trend is the recognition that a great deal of important information about student competencies has not in the past been recognized because of the limitations of objective tests (Resnick *et al.* 1995). Thus there is a growing trend towards handing over responsibility for certification to teachers at the end of compulsory schooling, as, for example, in Sweden, in Germany, in a number of the Australian states (Meadmore 1995) and in the proposals for the reform of the education system in Spain (Nisbet 1993). An increasingly typical pattern at the present time is for some combination of teacher assessment and an external test or examination which operates more as a moderation device than as a contribution to assessment itself.

Checks and balances in change: new approaches to system control

Progress towards such goals is regulated, however, by both technical and political issues, involving the generation of suitable assessment techniques and the rendering of these techniques as acceptable to those concerned. In this respect it is necessary to turn to the fourth element in assessment functions as identified at the beginning of this chapter, assessment for system control.

The international trend towards greater delegation of control of the content and form of assessment to teachers, and perhaps before long to pupils, raises problems of control. Although it has been argued that such delegation may enhance *individual* commitment to the education system, it leaves increasingly problematic the state's apparatus of control over the system itself. Thus it is necessary to add another dimension to the foregoing discussion, which identifies the growth of a different kind of assessment in direct relation to the decline in external school assessment. This parameter is accountability – the means by which the controlling interests in society monitor the operation of the education system as a whole and make it responsive to the needs of society as they define them.

The range of new assessment techniques discussed above all relate to the various purposes of regulating competition, attesting competence, controlling content and providing for individual control. Perhaps the most prominent of all the current assessment changes internationally, however, is that concerned with the provision of more information about the functioning of the education system as a whole: the search for so-called performance indicators that will reassure politicians and the public of the quality of individual schools and teachers and, often, of the system as a whole. In this very brief and necessarily selective analysis of developments in assessment procedures, it is possible to show how the form of such procedures tends to change in response to new demands upon the education system, while the underlying functions remain unaltered. One would expect to find changes of emphasis in assessment practice with the ebb and flow of events in a particular country. These changes would typically be oscillations within the limitations provided by ideological tradition, and institutional inertia, and thus they would typically reflect the characteristic ethos of a particular national system. Countries faced with very similar pressures, such as France and England, as explored later in this book, might respond in quite different ways to the changing balance between the competence, competition and control requirements of assessment procedures. But it is the function of system control which ultimately gives form and content to all educational assessment. It is therefore a central theme of this analysis, and the justification for the systemic case studies, which follow in Part II. Meanwhile, this part of Chapter 3 explores this argument in a little more detail in order to provide an analytic framework for the more detailed studies that follow.

Accountability

The 1960s saw an international trend against elitism and towards the expansion of opportunity for all in education. In many countries they also witnessed a liberalization of discipline, the increasing impact and radicalism of youth sub-cultures and a fashion for 'progressive' education. The effect of all these social forces was a major onslaught on the school's function as a socialization agency – as a mechanism for social control. Although the subsequent debates of the 1970s were ostensibly about 'falling standards' in terms of academic achievement, as Burstall and Kay (1978) point out, the real concern was a much broader one, being about the extent to which the educational system was successfully meeting the present and future needs of society. Public discontent focused on both 'standards' and 'behaviour'.

It is thus certainly arguable that concern over supposedly 'falling standards' in England, for example, particularly in view of the steady *rise* in public examination passes in recent years, was merely the tip of the iceberg of a much larger concern: that the decline of external examinations and the corresponding increase in the power of teachers to determine their own curricula and try out new 'progressive' methods during the 1960s had the effect of making the education system appear increasingly autonomous of any external control. Furthermore, the cold wind of economic crisis that began to blow in the mid-1970s meant renewed pressure for education to be geared as closely as possible to the needs of the labour market. Thus it can be argued that the international trend towards internally set school examinations discussed earlier in this chapter, which was made possible by their declining importance for selection, brought with it unforeseen problems of system control for countries that had long depended on examinations for this purpose. To the extent that teachers could decide what they wanted to teach, how they wanted to teach it and whether they had been successful, with little reference to any outside authority, the dominant interests of the state were losing control of their most powerful agency of social reproduction.

To the extent that the school emphasizes responding to the needs and interests of the child, awakening critical awareness, informal pedagogy, liberal discipline and flexible curricula, it will be conflicting with employers' needs for recruits to the lower levels of the labour market equipped with basic, yet flexible, skills and appropriate attitudes, such as meticulousness and persistence in tasks (Neave 1980). Thus, in the United States, national efforts to define and assess educational standards date back even to the halcyon days of 1964 when the tide of public opinion first began to flow strongly against liberal and progressive practices in education and in favour of more traditional pedagogy, discipline and 'minimum-competency' testing. There are echoes in this policy of the worst traditions of the typically European practice of children endlessly and often futilely repeating 'grades' they have not adequately mastered – a practice still common in many countries.

Another effect of the closer monitoring and control of educational standards is that the attribution of responsibility for pupil achievement may come to be seen increasingly in terms of the school rather than the individual pupil. Focusing once again on the English and American experience, since these two countries have taken some of the most overt measures in this respect, it is possible to trace a move away from the concentration on the environmental influences affecting the performance of certain class and ethnic groups which so preoccupied the Newsom and Plowden generations in Britain and the Coleman generation in America. This preoccupation has, in these two countries at least, faded in significance relative to the emphasis on school responsibility for pupil achievement and school effectiveness more generally.

Although the sampling of national standards that began to be undertaken in both countries in the 1970s was designed to preclude comparisons between schools as much as between pupils, the underlying ideology of judging schools by pupil attainment has directly contributed to the contemporary development of assessment programmes explicitly designed to provide information with which to judge the quality of individual schools and teachers. Since that time, mandatory 'minimum competency tests' have mushroomed in the USA and are now used in many states. Some are 'low stakes', aimed at identifying pupils who need additional classroom teaching. Others are 'high stakes', which means that they have important consequences – for the individual or the institution or both.

Thus, for example, many states publish information about individual school performance within and across districts in order to encourage 'market accountability'. The 'higher the stakes' of such testing the greater the impact would appear to be (Corbett and Wilson 1988). To some extent these effects appear to be beneficial in clarifying curricular targets and in raising levels of student performance in some areas (Stake 1991). However, increasing concern over the validity of the tests and curriculum narrowing have shaded into quite profound misgivings that the emphasis on 'getting the scores up' is often at the expense of sound educational practice (Corbett and Wilson 1988).

It seems clear that the impetus behind the testing centres on social and economic issues is value-laden (Airasian 1987). Almost no attention has been paid by the protagonists and implementers of testing to the impact of such tests on the system as a whole and on pupil learning (Elwein *et al.* 1988). Rather the passion for measurement continues unabated, with the National Assessment of Educational Progress (NAEP) surveys recently coming under pressure to be redesigned to allow for inter-state comparison (Koretz 1991). Ferrara and Thornton (1988) argue that this is effectively the beginning of a 'national curriculum' in the United States brought about by testing.

In England, the 'light' sampling used to monitor national standards by the Assessment of Performance Unit avoided some of the problems of 'blanket testing' condemned in the American National Association of Elementary School Principals' book *The Myth of Measurability*. Nevertheless, the institution under the 1988 Education Act of standardized assessment and reporting for all pupils at ages 7, 11, 14 and 16 as a basis for judging standards and, by implication, school quality and teacher competence is clear evidence that American policies are very attractive in England in the current political climate. This kind of emphasis on accountability and system control, now to be found in many countries, is likely to have a third very significant effect in allowing the state a much greater influence on educational content and standards.

Arguably, what is happening is a return to a more utilitarian emphasis in education and what Johnson (1976) has called, in the context of nineteenth-century English education, the 'cul-de-sac of skills': education geared to the competencies and labour requirements of a technological society and the development of appropriate attitudes rather than free expression and personal development. External control of the content and practice of schooling in this form helps to mould professional standards in the same image. The introduction of national curriculum frameworks and, for example, in England, Australia and New Zealand, assessment frameworks as well, which were discussed above, coupled with policies in these countries designed to give parents increased consumer choice, are likely to reinforce this trend since the publication of pupil achievements against predefined standards will encourage pupils and parents to espouse the same goals for education as the system planners. Given the importance of assessment as a means of regulating life chances, the likelihood of parents and pupils emphasizing alternative goals to those implicit in informal assessment procedures is not very great. Thus it may be argued that in co-opting parents and pupils – who are often for this reason some of the more conservative participants in the education system – into the accountability process, the mechanisms of control over the education system, and teachers in particular, are in fact strengthened.

Underlying these more or less explicit concerns at the present time, however, is a much more fundamental, if rarely acknowledged, crisis of values. Although the provision of mass education has always reflected a range of motives – national development, personal fulfilment and social control being the most prominent – there was, until recently, a surprisingly uniform belief in the power of education to liberate the individual while at the same time helping to provide a nation of committed and skilled workers, from among whose number selected individuals could be rationally chosen for positions of power and privilege. A complex concatenation of factors, including economic recession, affluence and its associated anomie, changes in the capitalist mode of production leading to new modes of working and new skills being required, and an increasingly schooled and yet not noticeably better trained workforce, has resulted in growing disillusionment with the cost of education and an erosion of confidence in its value. Not only parents and politicians, but even teachers and pupils, may be found among those who no longer know what school is for. The widespread institution in recent years of technical rationality as the prevailing ethos for policy-making, of corporate management techniques at various levels of the education system, may be seen not just as part of the pursuit of greater efficiency, but also as part of the more or less conscious desire to hide this crisis of values under the self-justifying demands of efficiency.

Conclusion

This chapter has explored some of the ways in which assessment procedures are mediating the relationship between education and society at the present time. Some common trends have been identified which illustrate the constant themes in this relationship: the attestation of competence, the regulation of competition and content and the control of individuals and the educational system itself. There is a good deal of evidence to support the identification of similar trends at this time in many industrialized countries: towards the certification of more industrially relevant competencies; towards a decline in formality in individual pupil assessment as it becomes more the responsibility of teachers and selection imperatives give way to more inclusive priorities; and, at the same time, a corresponding increase in other external forms of system control, such as national monitoring and centralized curricula.

Equally, it is important to stress that national education systems are each uniquely situated in a historical and contemporary social context which determines the particular assessment techniques chosen at any particular time. To some extent a concept of oscillation may be helpful to explain the actual practices of assessment at any one time within the constant parameters of the functions of school assessment in an era of mass education. It is these same constants which are the continuing themes of this book:

- that assessment mechanisms develop to operate as a series of checks and balances on the education system in order to ensure its major function of perpetuating the social, economic and political status quo;
- that some of the changes in assessment procedures in recent years have been only superficial changes in response to changing legitimating ideologies;
- that these changes have come about to defuse potential conflict and frustration while at the same time enabling schools to continue their traditional role of selecting and channelling pupils to different levels of the occupational and social hierarchy;
- that assessment mechanisms are used to control the form and content of schooling, ensuring the preparation of youngsters in the necessary skills and attitudes for their various roles in advanced industrial societies.

It is also the case, however, that some contemporary assessment developments represent more fundamental trends in the character of the social order. The gradual replacement of the psychometric assessment culture by more idiosyncratic, learning-oriented approaches to assessment arguably embodies more than just new modes of social control. Rather these may be read as a reflection of the beginnings of a new conceptualization and mode of execution of education in tune with societies which are changing their industrial culture and hence the social forms, including the mode of educational delivery, characteristic of that phase.

It was argued in Chapter 2 that education systems as we currently know them were the creation of post-Enlightenment industrializing societies and that the characteristic features of educational provision before that time were quite different in both content and delivery. It was also argued that assessment procedures played a central role in shaping and operationalizing the characteristics of education systems in industrial societies. This role centred on the four purposes of attesting competence: the rationalization of curriculum content, the regulation of competition and provision for both individual and system control.

As such societies move from the advanced industrial phase into what has sometimes been characterized as the post-modernist era (Rust 1991), they are developing new political, economic and social features. In particular, the information society seems set to transform both the purposes of education and its mode of delivery. In place of the emphasis on knowledge acquisition and the associated emphasis on didactic teaching approaches, the beginnings of a quite different emphasis on education as the facilitation of skill acquisition is already apparent. The emerging psychopedagogic assessment culture, with its emphasis on equipping even the smallest children with the skills and attitudes to be self-regulating, independent learners pursuing their own educational targets, is arguably a reflection of these fundamental changes.

Running alongside such developments in practice are similarly post-modernist ideas in which the integrity of individual and group values and the possibility of more democratic relations between the powerful and the powerless are beginning to be realized in the individualized assessment dialogue between teacher and pupil which increasingly characterizes active learning strategies. With the proliferation of courses and qualifications in the post-primary years, the blurring of the boundary between education and training and between education and work, and the growing international commitment to life-long education, the mentoring role of the teacher as guide and counsellor rather than as provider of information *per se* is likely to become increasingly central. To the extent that this is so, it is likely that the social purposes of assessment will need to be conceptualized in rather different ways even if the fundamental functions do not change. It remains to be seen whether the two principal dimensions of current assessment developments – comprehensiveness and pervasiveness – do bring about a permanent change in the prevailing assessment culture.

At the same time that the beginnings of fundamental changes in the expression of content, competition and competence imperatives are taking place, there would appear to be unilateral developments in the control dimension of assessment which are also a reflection of the increasingly fragmented cultures of post-modernist society and the information revolution.

Centring on the generation of more and more information in the form of 'performance indicators' at every level of the system, the new rationality of the information society is that embedded in the concept of total quality management: the generation of both targets and accounts about performance in relation to those targets. Underlying such procedures is the assumption that the generation of the account *in itself* will ensure the desired effect. Thus while more conventional forms of assessment and control are manifest in the recent explosion of interest in the punitive imposition of performance indicators, through, for example, 'high stakes' testing, other forms of quality assurance such as 'quality audits' and institutional reviews are likely to become much more characteristic in a society increasingly conditioned to individual and collective target setting and review; that is, to internalized forms of control.

Neave (1989), for example, explains the growing convergence of policy strategies in French, English and other European education systems in terms of this profound change of accountability procedures. In an article entitled 'On the cultivation of quality, efficiency and enterprise: an overview of recent trends in higher education in Western Europe, 1986–88', Neave identifies the rise of the evaluative state. This is, he suggests, an attempt to insert a particular form of externally defined 'competitive ethic' as the prime driving force for institutional, and thus system, development. What were originally developed as an empirical, short-term response to financial difficulties at the start of the decade have now assumed a long-term strategic thrust. Crucial to this strategy is a growing emphasis on *a posteriori* evaluation: working through the control of *product* rather than of *process* (Neave 1989: 9).

Thus, in systems based on decentralization, the 'evaluative state' appears as a step towards greater central control and, in those based on a higher degree of centralism, it is perceived as giving rise to greater flexibility and hence greater decentralization. To the extent that this is so it renders obsolete the traditional distinction between centralized and decentralized systems in the study of educational policy-making.

Much of the above analysis is necessarily theoretical at this stage, based on an extrapolation of trends which are only now emerging. Most of what follows is couched in more historical terms and explores in more detail what has already passed, in terms of the growth of mass educational provision in the nineteenth and twentieth centuries and the way in which assessment procedures have simultaneously helped to expand opportunity and, at the same time, to reproduce an apparently meritocratic status quo. In so doing it describes how assessment procedures have also been instrumental in elevating particular forms of knowledge and particular ways of reproducing it.

The ways in which assessment procedures perform these functions in any one education system depend upon the ideological and historical foundations of any one national context and the developments referred to briefly here are taken up in more detail in subsequent empirical chapters. The intention of this more general chapter has been to demonstrate and, to some extent, account for the central role that assessment has come to play in the educational provision of industrial societies and so justify an analysis of the similarities and differences between such societies in these terms.

4

ASSESSMENT AND THE EMERGENCE OF MODERN SOCIETY

Introduction

Chapters 2 and 3 set out to examine in detail the part played by educational assessment procedures in helping to shape the organization and ethos of the provision of mass schooling as this has emerged in response to the major changes in the economic and social order brought about by industrialization. This analysis was based on an identification of general trends in assessment procedures in education systems with very different ideological and institutional traditions. The aim was to demonstrate that the determinative role of educational assessment is a feature of the *common* social and economic pressures such systems are facing at any given time, rather than simply an institutional feature of a particular kind of educational system. However, it is necessary to extend and deepen the analysis beyond simply *describing* aspects of the relationship between assessment and mass educational provision. There is a need to explore at a more fundamental level the common characteristics of the societies in which formal educational assessment procedures have evolved and, in particular, why it is that educational assessment has so conveniently been able to achieve such incontrovertible legitimation. Thus the analyses of this chapter evoke some of the central themes of sociology in their attempt to identify those characteristics of the transition from feudal to industrial society that may be associated with the rise of educational assessment procedures.

The complex and wide-ranging analysis that follows is directed at an understanding of some of the deepest societal characteristics that underpin the now widespread use of educational assessment procedures in all societies with mass education systems. An attempt is made to understand the role of educational assessment in representing the demands of the instrumental order and of the prevailing ideological basis for social control, and to understand the source of its dual role in opening up avenues for personal liberation and occupational mobility while at the same time playing a key role in social reproduction. The intention is to draw, eclectically, on the common and relevant insights of often contradictory perspectives in addressing a specific question, rather than to undertake the inevitably vain project of seeking to reconcile fundamental divisions in sociological perspective or, equally undesirably, to ignore many valuable insights in seeking to maintain the coherence of a unitary perspective. In particular the analysis focuses on the work of four leading sociological theorists – Weber, Durkheim, Bernstein and Foucault – whose work is taken to be most centrally relevant to the issues in question.

Despite what are often profoundly conflicting perspectives, a number of central issues emerge from the various theoretical perspectives reviewed as the basis for an understanding of the growth of educational assessment. These may be summarized as follows.

1 *Individualism*: instrumental and expressive social functions are now organized on the basis of the individual. Thus both instrumental and expressive legitimating ideologies, the whole basis for social integration and control, are now defined in terms of the individual.
2 *Rational authority*: traditional, coercive authority is replaced by a rational and impersonal (scientific) basis for hierarchical control. This authority increasingly takes the form of hierarchical observation and normalizing judgement (i.e. evaluation), which, with the growing dominance of a technological rationality, the individual is increasingly powerless to resist.
3 *Contradiction and legitimation*: despite the carefully concealed

power relations underlying the institutions of rational authority, the fundamental irreconcilability between the need to provide for social integration (by 'buying' commitment, through economic growth, by 'moral socialization', by the arguments of scientific rationality or by disciplinary mechanisms) and the need to maintain inequality leads to a continuing tension, not to say crisis, within capitalist society.

It is because educational assessment is central to all three of these characteristics of capitalist societies that it has become so central to contemporary social organization. In education, as in other areas of social life, the advent of 'normalizing judgement' makes possible the idea of fixed definitions of competence. This normalizing judgement combines with the idea of 'hierarchical observation' to provide the 'rational authority' for competition and selection. It will be argued that this Benthamite notion of 'panoptic' surveillance, in which individuals learn to judge themselves as if some external eye were constantly monitoring their performance, encourages the internalization of the evaluative criteria of those in power, and hence provides a new basis for social control. Competence, competition and control will be traced as the characteristic themes of the new disciplinary power that education provides in industrial societies. At the same time, the possibility of individuals and institutions using these same assessment mechanisms to empower creative social action through a more conscious awareness of their own strengths and weaknesses will also be traced as a reflection of the equally profound potential for liberation embodied in the change to a more individualistic society.

The characteristics of industrial society

Assessment has become integrally connected with teaching and learning as we know it in contemporary educational practice simply, yet fundamentally, because in its broadest sense of evaluation – to make reference to a standard – assessment is one of the most central features of the rationality[1] that underpins advanced industrial society itself. Assessment procedures are the vehicle whereby the dominant rationality of the corporate capitalist societies typical of the contemporary Western world is translated into the structures and processes of schooling. As Cherkaoui (1977: 162) suggests, the system of assessment that emerged with mass education systems must be understood as 'organically connected with a specific mode of socialisation' – a mode of socialization in which preparation for a division of labour, bureaucracy and surveillance were dominant characteristics.

Sociologists have been much concerned to conceptualize the difference between 'traditional', 'pre-modern' and 'industrial' societies. Although varying widely in their perspective on central issues such as the basis for social order, social divisions or the scope for creative social interaction, sociologists spanning the whole range of order versus control and system versus action perspectives (Dawe 1970; Bernstein 1977; Banks 1978) find substantial areas of common ground in their discussion in general terms of the changes in the basis for social institutions which characterized the transition from 'traditional' to 'industrial' societies. Such changes included a number of different social institutions, notably the legal, the religious, the economic, the political and the familial. But, while it is relatively easy to identify associations between the changes that took place in these different social institutions, the attribution of causation is necessarily a good deal more problematic since the emerging nature of industrial society was reflexively related – as both cause and effect of the changing nature of social life.

The changes made necessary by the changing economic order of the industrial revolution were both 'practical' and 'ideological'. Under 'practical' would be included the necessity for a mobile workforce in which individuals – not the family or the community – would take responsibility for a particular unit or stage of production, the whole process of which they might not even be able to conceptualize. This was in marked contrast to the hitherto prevailing work organization, in which one individual was typically responsible for the whole task. Given the cost of any long term use of 'power-coercive' control strategies (Chin and Benne 1978), it was a 'practical' imperative that these new workers should come to accept as quickly as possible the legitimacy of a system in which they were paid a money wage which was only a proportional return for their contribution to a system they were powerless to control.

These changes in the nature of work – its increasing fragmentation and alienation for some, expanding entrepreneurial activities for others – offered and required a degree of geographical and social mobility which brought about associated changes in the family's economic and educational role (Coleman 1968). This increase in flexibility and mobility was also increasingly apparent in the ascendancy of Protestantism over Catholicism in many industrializing countries, and in legal innovations based on the right of the individual before an impersonal law which came to replace the old feudal system of reciprocal obligation. Associated with legal developments of this kind were political movements which also had at their centre the idea of liberal democracy: the right of individuals to self-determination (Smith 1980).

These changes reached their apotheosis in the major scientific, religious and political movements which marked the end of the Middle Ages: the Enlightenment, the Reformation and the French Revolution respectively. Herein lies the link between associated changes in social forms, between the economic base and the social and ideological superstructure.[2] Although the profound changes that took place in every aspect of life at this time were legitimized and reinforced by the challenge and, later, the hegemonic domination of a new entrepreneurial class, the most central theme in the changes taking place went far beyond class relations in both its origins and its implications and, for this reason, cannot be neatly categorized as either cause or effect. This was the theme of individualization.[3]

The change from a predominantly communalist basis for social integration to a more individualist orientation is of crucial importance since it was this new orientation that made possible changes in the whole range of social institutions and legitimating ideologies in the newly industrializing societies. The key to these changes was the growth of a particular kind of rationality. This is the rationality of science, of logic, of efficiency and of individual rights and responsibilities.

The nature and significance of these changes is a central theme in sociology and particularly in the work of Weber, Durkheim and Marx, whose very different approaches to the study of post-feudal society are characteristic of the range and significance of attempts to understand these changes within sociology. Clearly there is a monumental volume of writing now available on this subject and of necessity the discussion of it here is confined to those aspects of the work available which bear centrally upon the question being explored here – the origins of educational assessment.

Weber and the rise of rationality

Weber's analysis of the transformation from feudalism to capitalism is dominated by a preoccupation with the rationality that informed the scientific-technical progress of the age, together with the associated bureaucratic and institutional structures which also developed at this time. Durkheim's very different social system perspective nevertheless emphasizes the same ideas of the rational, individual, hierarchical and specific allocation of roles in his fundamental distinction between mechanical and organic solidarity. Building on this Durkheimian tradition, Parsons (1951) conceptualized the distinction in terms of 'pattern variables' with 'affective neutrality', 'universalism', 'achievement' and 'specificity' replacing the 'affectivity', 'particularism', 'ascription' and 'diffuseness' of 'traditional' or 'simple' societies.[4] These distinctions enunciate very clearly some of the key characteristics of the modes of social organization which emerged. Actors were increasingly required to perform specific, defined roles in a whole range of social institutions, notably the division of labour. They were increasingly chosen on the basis of their demonstrated competence as measured by some rational criterion. In this process – assessment – in one form or another – would henceforth be central.

The Protestant ethic

To offer such a brief description of the changes in the social order which accompanied the rise of capitalism is very much simpler than any attempt to explain the source of these developments. An over-simplistic reading of the Weberian perspective[5] suggests that capitalism was brought about by the associated rise of Protestantism despite the fact that specific instances can be found where both capitalism and Protestantism have flourished independently of the other.[6]

In fact, Weber's analysis suggests a more limited attribution of causality. Weber is careful to be historically specific, linking particular stages and types of capitalism with other specific social formations. Thus his account of the transition from feudalism to capitalism in Europe refers to the significance of the traditional European distinction within the peasant household of the functions of ownership, production and consumption – a relationship further specified in, for example, England by the existence of the market which was at least partly owing to the nature of state institutions and the rational legal system imposed by the Norman conquest (Marshall 1982). Even the notion of rationality itself is not used as a blanket term but as an historical specific.

Although it would be inappropriate to go into the details of Weber's wide-ranging analyses here, the general thrust of his argument is central: that there is an important, empirically documentable, relationship between a particular world view and a particular form of economic relations, between superstructure and substructure, but that the direction of causality between economic, political, legal and religious factors is not generalizable (see also Chapter 5).

Weber's refusal to descend to determinism in this respect is a product of his sociological perspective: his respect for empirical reality and for detailed historical study and his lack of sympathy with deductive approaches which refer to the concrete merely to substantiate general theories. Weber's distrust of abstract theorizing is based on his ideas of social action. For Weber, ideas can exert an independent influence on social conduct; understanding of the world can change independent actors' views of their material situation.

> I would like to protest the statement . . . that some one factor, be it technology or economy, can be the 'ultimate' or 'true' cause of another. If we look at the causal lines, we see them run, at one time, from technical to economic and political matters, at another from political to religious and economic ones, etc. There is no resting point. In my opinion, the view of historical materialism, frequently espoused, that the economic is in some sense the ultimate point in the chain of causes is completely finished as a scientific proposition.
>
> (Weber 1923: 456, quoted by Marshall 1982: 151)

Thus, as Marshall (1982) suggests, Weber avoids any attempt to formalize his implicit theory of the relation between substructure and superstructure because he denied all forms of necessary determinism in the social sphere. 'Empirical research alone can establish, in each instance, whether ideas exert a direct and independent influence on social action' (Marshall 1982: 155).

Marshall argues that Weber was insistent that ideas became

significant in history and are causally effective in shaping social conduct because, at certain points, a class or status group with specific material or ideal interests takes up, sustains and develops these ideas, and is influenced by them. Weber, he suggests, was insistent that ideas are shaped by and in turn help to shape interests and action, though accepting too, as a general principle, that the 'inner logic' of their development does not proceed independently of all other spheres of social reality.

Thus Weber's analysis is important because it emphasizes general themes in the development of capitalism while in no way denying the significance of specific social forms in mediating the precise effect of such movements. It therefore points the way to the kind of approach being adopted here, which seeks to understand how educational assessment procedures relate in general terms to education under capitalism by a study of the specific *and different* forms it takes in individual systems. Weber's emphasis on the independent contribution of interest groups in the process of 'structuration' (Dallmayr 1982; after Giddens 1976) justifies the detailed attention given to national educational politics in this book, both in theoretical terms (Chapter 5) and in empirical terms (Chapters 6, 7 and 8).

This balance between 'the general' and 'the specific' is similarly reflected in Weber's analysis of the characteristics of protestant mentality as expressed in the dominant social form of bureaucracy – 'the institutional prototype of the emerging rationalised society' (Wilson 1977, quoted by Salaman 1981: 188). While the institution of bureaucratic organization is common to all industrial societies in some degree, there is also clearly a good deal of variation between societies in the extent to which this mode of organization is predominant. In the provision of mass education, for example, elements of Weber's 'ideal type' of bureaucracy are necessarily manifest in every national education system, but there are equally significant variations in bureaucratic style, so that notions of hierarchy, general rules, continuous and impersonal offices and the separation between official and private life must be interrelated with historically specific social situations (Gouldner 1952).

Thus there are different styles of bureaucratic provision just as there are significant differences in all the other social institutions in countries which nevertheless share a common history of capitalist and industrial revolution.

Bureaucracy

It is this emphasis on bureaucracy which forms one of the major distinctive features of the Weberian perspective. Although Weber shares with other sociological theorists, and Marx in particular, an emphasis on the economic interests arising out of the ownership of property as the key to social conflict and change, the Weberian perspective includes other important sources of social power. These other sources include the control of organizational resources especially in state and private bureaucracies and control of cultural resources, notably religious ones initially, but increasingly in secular terms through, for example, the education system. Thus from a Weberian perspective, interest groups and their associated struggles reflect the whole range of economic, cultural and political divisions in society, divisions institutionalized in terms of Weber's well-known distinction between status and party. Collins (1979) argues that the education system embodies all three of these struggles in its economic concern with the production of appropriately skilled workers, its cultural concern with social integration and the maintenance of prestige and its political concern with the legitimation of control through certain formal organisations. Collins (1979: 282) argues, following Weber, that

> education, which has arisen as part of the process of bureaucratisation, has been shaped by the efforts of elites to establish impersonal methods of control; the content of education here is irrelevant but the structure of grades, ranks, degrees and other formal credentials is of central importance as a means of discipline through hierarchy and specialisation.

It is this Weberian emphasis on the form or mode of control, as well as its purpose, that is crucial to the attempt to understand the origins of educational evaluation. The Weberian emphasis on social action, on multiple sites for struggle, on bureaucratic organization and on scientific rationality are themes which dominate the emergence of mass schooling while allowing for all its variety. In particular, it provides a specific rationale for the developing significance of formal evaluation and qualifications as a logical and integral part of this process – a theme which is taken up in similar vein, if in much more detail, in more recent post-structuralist work, notably that of Foucault.

Although there are many similarities here with Marxist perspectives on the capitalist state, there is clearly a fundamental distinction to be made as to whether primacy is given to economic determinants. Marxism locates forms of struggle other than the economic in the determined superstructure in which the battle to legitimate the power relations of the economic and social status quo is waged through the ideological domination of various forms of false consciousness. It would seem, however, that most Marxists, as well as many non-Marxists, would want to concede 'some measure of genuine interaction between the spheres of production and other spheres of social life ... and, at the level of individual actors, a "dialectical" relationship between class interest and ideological representation' (Marshall 1982: 145). For the purpose in hand, it is less necessary to adjudicate between these fundamental distinctions than to recognize their common identification of the importance of the new forms of essentially ideological control in the changing basis of social organization which characterized industrial society.[7]

Thus the characteristics of the social order associated with the emergence of capitalism as the dominant economic system were neither simply causes of, nor caused by, this economic development. Rather they must be regarded as mutually dependent and reinforcing developments, the lack of either of which would have inhibited the development of both. It is certainly true that the central themes of this chapter – rationality and individualism – are deeply integrated with both the economic and the social order, finding their origin and their expression in both arenas.

In the Western world individualism has emerged as both the necessary practical basis for the rational allocation of roles and the necessary source of legitimation. As the dominant ideology it allows classes to be reduced to individual persons who are then reorganized into various imaginary and non-antagonistic unities such as the 'nation' and the 'community' (Poulantzas 1973). Taking up this point, Larson (1981) argues that this allows the principle of equality between atomized individuals to be the cornerstone of the new inequality which appears to be based only on the rational criteria of will, competence, drive and, more recently, choice. In particular the existence of state education systems which apparently provide for meritocratic competition on the basis of equality of opportunity and, increasingly, the discipline of the market deflect the criticism of professional elites and allow them to legitimate their own position.[8]

If some conflict theorists like Poulantzas and Larson emphasize the strategic importance for the maintenance of social order of the ideology of individualism as a major way of fragmenting and thus deflecting self-conscious class action, others have taken a more pessimistic view of it. From this dependence on individualism it is possible to identify a profound contradiction between the instrumental and the expressive order, between public and private life, between general and particular interests. This contradiction is particularly evident in education, since this plays a crucial role in the process of allocation to social and occupational roles and in that of social integration.

> There is a fundamental contradiction within the heart of education: while embodying and reproducing a system of domination based on hierarchical control, the *form* of the discourse – and hence content – in education is that of the liberal discourse of the state, according to which rights are vested equally in all members of the community. This contradictory position of education explains its dual progressive/reproductive role promoting equality, democracy, toleration, rationality, inalienable rights on the one hand, while legitimising inequality, authoritarianism, fragmentation, prejudice and submission on the other.
>
> (Gintis 1980: 2)

This contradiction is not new; it is, as Habermas (1976) suggests, the perennial 'legitimation crisis' arising out of the fundamental contradiction of capital – the necessity for wealth to be socially produced while being privately appropriated. 'Because the reproduction of class societies is based on the privileged appropriation of socially produced wealth, all such societies must resolve the problem of distributing the surplus product inequitably and yet legitimately' (Habermas 1976: 96).

Thus the education system embodies a constant contradiction between the need to *differentiate* pupils on the basis of an order of merit which ultimately serves to legitimate differential chances in the labour market and the contradictory need to *integrate* pupils, parents and teachers in a way which enables the school to be seen as serving commonly conceived purposes. While the need for the former is conceived by teachers in terms of a relatively fixed distribution of basic 'abilities' which pupils, as individuals, may be identified as possessing, the need for the latter is a social imperative which has to be worked for in terms of desirable *general* social attributes based on principles that may be accepted as legitimate.

This fundamental contradiction between the need to divide and yet unite, to create inequality and, at the same time, to promote social cohesion is a problem that goes well beyond a Marxist interpretation framed specifically in terms of class struggle, to the heart of the division of labour itself and the problems of social order.

As suggested earlier, the contradiction is essentially between the 'instrumental' function of education – the training of people for jobs in terms of the requisite skills and knowledge and through anticipatory socialization, in terms of appropriate personal expectations and behaviour – and the 'expressive' function of education, aimed at fostering at least a minimal level of social integration despite the inevitable and disintegrative effects of the prevailing individualist 'instrumental ideology' and the potentially even more divisive tendencies of the associated inequality. Although class-based inequality is central here, it is the form of social organization and legitimation characterizing the current basis for inequality – namely individualism – which gives rise to this distinctive problem. Unlike other more explicitly coercive forms of economic exploitation – as found under feudalism or tribalism, for example – capitalist society is a manifestation of the change in the nature of social bonds which has at its heart rationality and individualism. This latter point is clearly made by Durkheim, for whom 'capitalism' is essentially an 'abnormal form' (O'Connor 1980) and for whom the issue of individualism and the consequent problems of social integration were fundamental.

Durkheim and the problem of social control

The theme of Durkheim's *The Division of Labour in Society* (1947) is the source of social solidarity and social order. He argues that the increasing occupational specialization which characterizes a division of labour replaces the 'mechanical' solidarity of pre-market societies based on homogeneous social and occupational roles. With occupational specialization comes 'organic' solidarity based on people's mutual interdependence. The political and social upheavals of nineteenth-century France eventually forced Durkheim to modify his earlier analysis to argue in *Moral Education* (1961) that new forms of social solidarity do not occur spontaneously but require new social institutions to be set up. He envisaged that these institutions would be a sort of occupational 'guild' which would bind individuals into special interest organizations and hence to the state. Durkheim saw a key role for schools in this – preparing and socializing individuals for their place in the division of labour and, at the same time, providing the basis for communalism and true organic solidarity.

Durkheim's distinction between social divisions arising from anomie and social divisions arising from egoism is also useful here since the former refers to a lack of 'system integration' – the weak integration of social functions – and the latter to the integration of people themselves into such social functions. From this distinction, Durkheim's work offers an implicit critique of the ideology of egalitarianism, as expressed in strategies for income redistribution and equality of opportunity; for, although such strategies may militate against egoistic social division, far from ending anomie, where self-interest becomes a defining social principle, anomie is increased. The recent rise of New Right ideologies in many Western countries provides a contemporary graphic illustration of Durkheim's analysis. What would be required to counteract it, in Durkheim's view, would be 'moral' regeneration and a fundamental change in the nature of social relationships.

Clearly there are important parallels here with the emphasis in Marxist theory on the necessity for a change in consciousness, as well as economic relations, as the precursor of a genuinely socialist society. Durkheim is not specifically concerned with class struggle and his work provides important general insights into the basis for social order and particularly the contribution schooling has to make in this respect.

In the search to understand the associated question of the origins and significance of assessment as a social and educational characteristic, this Durkheimian emphasis is likewise valuable. In Chapter 2 it was suggested that the institution of formal evaluation procedures within education was directly instrumental in rationalizing educational provision into a system and, in particular, emphasized three themes which became dominant in the provision of schooling, namely the attestation of competence (including the rationalization of syllabus content), the regulation of competition and provision for individual and systemic control. The first two themes may readily be associated with the *instrumental* role of education in providing and selecting individuals for specific slots in the division of labour. The third, control, is associated with the *expressive* order. This control may be mediated through one or more of the following: the apparently objective testing of individual potential (intelligence tests), assessing individual performance (e.g. continuous assessment, guidance and examinations), the evaluation of teaching or school performance (inspection and accountability) and the evaluation of the system and performance as a whole (national monitoring).

The operation of these forms of control depends upon the dominance and consequent legitimacy of an individualist rationality of personal talent, personal responsibility, personal endeavour and personal reward. It is the unquestioned acceptance of the individualist ethos (Mills 1979) that permits social integration and control to be mediated in this way, since such judgements and their more or less pleasant consequences are seen to be a legitimate, rational basis for the inequalities associated with a division of labour. Thus assessment plays a central role in making the education system responsive to larger social pressures, and it plays an equally important role in helping to minimize the effects of the contradiction between the instrumental and expressive functions of education by providing for the legitimation of the necessary inequalities.

This contradiction is that between the training and allocation of people for different jobs (both in terms of the requisite skills and knowledge and in terms of appropriate personal expectations and behaviour) and the need for social integration to be maintained despite a hierarchical division of labour and diverse pressures towards individualism (Durkheim 1947). Both these aspects of school functioning – the 'instrumental' and the 'expressive' – are informed by the dominant individualist rationality.

To explain how this change came about, Durkheim goes back to the major historical transformations which immediately preceded industrialization. To begin with, Durkheim (1947) protests that:

Even the most cursory historical survey is enough to make us realise that degrees and examinations are of relatively recent origin; there was nothing equivalent in classical antiquity . . .

the word and the thing only appear in the Middle Ages with the university.

(p. 126)

The explanation Durkheim offers for this invention is that the system of degrees and examinations derives from the corporate organization of educational provision. He suggests that the existing feudal model of the series of initiations or stages which must be gone through before penetrating to the heart of any organization – such as page, squire and bachelor before becoming a fully armed knight – was a natural model for educational 'stages' to be introduced once the teachers, 'instead of teaching separately, formed themselves into a corporation with a sense of its own identity and governed by communal laws' (Durkheim 1947: 130). That is to say, the advent of certification depended on the institutionalization of education in the form of schools and colleges. From this it was but a short step to the institution of some organized course of study or curriculum (see Hamilton 1981).

At this stage the function of assessment was almost entirely ritualistic: a *rite de passage* (as described in Chapter 2) modelled on traditional concepts of initiation, which served the purpose of demarcating those who had reached a level of scholarship and commitment that justified their entry to the next level. The assessment itself was in practice a legitimation device – a public relations exercise which confirmed a selection that had already been undertaken, informally, by the teacher. But although the French universities Durkheim was describing have kept this manifestation of their corporate existence almost entirely unchanged in its essential structure until the present day,[9] one element that did change fundamentally was the use of assessment for motivating and controlling students.

Durkheim describes the situation of the young arts student in the Middle Ages, who at between 13 and 15 years of age was accorded almost complete freedom from supervision or exhortation:

> We are so accustomed to believing that emulation is the essential motivating force in academic life, that we cannot easily imagine how a school could exist which did not have a carefully worked out system of graduated awards in order to keep the enthusiasm of pupils perpetually alive. Good marks, solemn

statements of satisfactory performance, distinctions, competition essays, prizegivings; all these seem to us in differing degrees, the necessary accompaniment to any sound education system. The system that operated in France and indeed Europe, until the sixteenth century, was characterised by the surprising fact that there were no rewards at all from success in examinations. What is more, any candidate who had assiduously and conscientiously followed the course of studies was certain of success.

(Durkheim 1947: 159)

Until the end of the fifteenth century, pupils were treated like autonomous adults. Then, in France at least, the status of pupils gradually changed. They became minors, shut off from the world in educational institutions in which they were powerless to resist the authority of those put in to teach and regulate them. Although the timing of this process was particular to the educational history of France, the link between the advent of institutionalized education, organized around substantial, monastic-style disciplinary powers, and the advent of educational assessment is a more general one (Broadfoot 1991). 'Academic discipline implies a system of rewards no less than a system of punishment' (Durkheim 1947: 159).[10]

Nowhere was this more clearly seen than in the education practices of the Jesuits from the mid-sixteenth century. The Jesuits placed equal emphasis on the power of competition.[11]

Not only were they the first to organise the competitive system in the colleges but they also developed it to a point of greater intensity than it has ever subsequently known . . .

Academic work involved a kind of perpetual hand-to-hand combat. Camp challenged camp, group struggled with group, supervised one another, corrected one another and took one another to task. It was thanks to this division of labour between the teacher and the pupils, that one teacher was able without much difficulty to run classes which sometimes numbered as many as 200–300 pupils. In addition to such methods of chronically recurring competition there were intermittent competitions too numerous to enumerate . . . Thus an infinite wealth of devices maintained the self-esteem of pupils in a constant state of extreme excitation.

(Durkheim 1947: 261)

One effect of this policy, Durkheim suggests, was that the genuinely intensive activity which it fostered was flawed by being expended on the superficial rather than the profound, still a major criticism of the effect of exam-motivated learning.

The reason for this sudden shift from the extreme of no assessment to that of extreme competition, Durkheim suggests, was the advent of individual self-consciousness that characterized the Renaissance. Thus education too had to become individualized, no longer a uniform and homogeneous activity: the teacher must get to know pupils and be able to provide differentially according to their diverse needs. In the same way, 'the individual cannot be motivated or trained to act in the same way, as an amorphous crowd, he must be convinced and moved by considerations which are specifically appropriate to him' (Durkheim 1947: 264) – notably, competition.

Not only did the institution of formal assessment procedures encourage the growth of individual competitiveness in education, it also helped to change the quality of the teacher–pupil relations to one which emphasized a more personal, 'formative-evaluation' in teaching in place of the older, more impersonal style.

Durkheim's analysis evokes an important general question in relation to assessment, concerning the currently widespread view that a more individualistic emphasis in assessment is desirable, as found, for example, in the Records of Achievement initiative and the corresponding fear among other people that such approaches also have the potential to lead towards new, more intrusive modes of 'surveillance' and hence social control (Broadfoot 1992). Certainly it can be argued that it is the political dimension to such assessment, and the way in which such procedures covertly delineate a particular set of values, which is likely to be of critical importance. However, in a very real sense, the desirability of identifying individual character-istics[12] has always been an informing principle of educational assessment, a *sine qua non* that attracts unquestioning commitment from scholars and practitioners.

Durkheim's analysis is applicable more generally than to French history alone. It is possible to argue that the various ideologies of schooling that have developed – the developmental, the child-centred, the moral and the meritocratic (Hargreaves 1979) are all options within an individualist rationality which emphasized per-sonal needs, personal responsibility, personal reward and even personal fulfilment. Furthermore, all of them are predicated on both the concept and the practice of educational assessment. It is therefore necessary to draw on some more recent sociological theory – notably that of Bernstein, whose work is strongly influenced by Durkheim – to consider the more contemporary manifestations of these concepts within formal educational provision.

Bernstein and the significance of educational codes

Bernstein is one of the very few sociologists of education to have attempted to conceptualize the relationship between the constant requirements of education systems in capitalist societies and the particular variations in the way in which those requirements are fulfilled in particular national systems. In a now well-known quotation, Bernstein asserts:

> How a society selects, classifies, distributes, transmits and evaluates the educational knowledge it considers to be public, reflects both the distribution of power and the principles of social control. From this point of view, differences within and change in the organisation, transmission and evaluation of educational knowledge should be a major area of sociological interest.
>
> (Bernstein 1977: 55)

The Durkheimian echo in this quotation is not accidental. Bernstein is preoccupied with questions of social order, social control and social reproduction. He sees the education system as a major determinant of both the strength and the nature of that order in that it regulates (a) the kind of worker produced (with all that that implies for economic efficiency and industrial relations), (b) the kind of social integration upon which social order will be based and (c) which individuals will accede to positions of power and privilege (i.e. control). Implicit in his theories is the need for the circle of control to be made complete, in that society must possess the means of determining and controlling the education system because it is to a great extent determined and controlled by it. However, Bernstein does not take 'control' in a Durkheimian, structural-functionist sense, despite the fact that Durkheim's categories of social order are used; rather the education system is seen as working in the interests of particular, dominant class groups. It accomplishes this by being slow to change from traditional modes of enshrining privilege (e.g. the collection code), but at the same time incorporating new control techniques which allow the education system to respond to new social and economic conditions or to establish its legitimacy (public confidence) if inequalities or inefficiencies inherent in it seem likely to become too glaring.

Thus, as Chapter 3 sets out, the pressure of population, the values of traditional humanism, the requirements of democratic equality and the needs of a sophisticated industrial economy are among many powerful social and economic trends which during recent decades have led to international pressure for educational change. Particularly notable initially was a trend towards the structural reorganization of schools, the abolition of internal school divisions, the institution of a common curriculum and the democratization of assessment procedures (Neave 1980). All these dimensions of change involve a breaking down of educational barriers in favour of a more flexible, open and democratic basis for educational competition. More recently, the emphasis has become more explicitly a reflection of the prevailing economic imperatives resulting from intensifying international competition and the new skills sought as a result of changing working practices (Organization for Economic Cooperation and Development 1989). Assessment is central to such changes, for the shift in the basis of social order that Bernstein identifies as being reflected in such policy development is integrally bound up with the way in which educational assessment procedures represent the changing characteristics and requirements of the social context within the provision and process of schooling.

Employing Durkheim's categories of social order, Bernstein identifies a tendency in contemporary society for there to be a transition from a social and economic order based on overt mechanical solidarity and covert organic solidarity to one of overt organic solidarity and covert mechanical solidarity. One outward sign of this change in education systems is a trend towards invisible pedagogies and integrated codes represented by more student-centred teaching and cross-curricular approaches. The latter are presented by Bernstein as a movement towards weak classification and weak framing, in which subject boundaries are broken down and teachers enjoy considerable freedom over what and how to teach. The reason for this trend, Bernstein argues, is developments in technology which have given rise to the need for a more flexible, inner-directed labour force (which may be envisaged as the likely outcome of an education system that develops pupil, rather than teacher, control of learning and seeks to inhibit the development of specific subject identities). Although there is by no means a consistent development in this respect in any society, since any such change comes up against a whole range of powerful sources of resistance which are rooted in traditionalist ideologies and vested interest (as in the current backlash against 'progressive' educational ideas in the United States and the United Kingdom), international evidence concerning the changing shape of educational qualifications and thus courses would nevertheless appear to demonstrate a continuing trend (Broadfoot 1992).

Such a development, Bernstein argues, may challenge *society's* basic classifications and frames (for example, assumptions about job identities, authority structures and status) and *therefore* its structures of power and principles of social control (which of course include social reproduction). He suggests that if the integrated code is successful – if in producing its less specialized outputs it is successful in perpetrating effectively and implicitly an ideology which is explicit, elaborated and closed – then order based on mechanical solidarity will follow. This is exactly the same situation as that facing a team of teachers seeking to implement an integrated course in a school in which the traditional standards and controls provided by individual subjects have disappeared and hence the curriculum can only be successful to the extent that the mechanical solidarity of a common ideology and situation is adhered to by the teachers concerned. If integrated codes are not 'successful', Bernstein suggests, social order, in all its forms, is immediately made problematic.

Little of Bernstein's work is directly concerned with evaluation. Nevertheless, his emphasis on the *interrelationship* of curriculum and pedagogy – classification and frame – is highly relevant to an understanding of assessment practice. Although Bernstein has not produced a concept equivalent to classification and frame for his third message system – 'evaluation' – he makes many references to changes in such procedures associated with the shift from visible to invisible pedagogies and from collection to integrated codes. Fundamentally, Bernstein argues, there has, in recent years, been a change of emphasis from overt to covert assessment and from specific to diffuse evaluation criteria. In visible pedagogy, the 'objective grid' for evaluation is based on clear criteria, delicate measurement and standardization, which can allow comparison between schools so that pupil, parent and teacher can all make an apparently objective assessment of a child's progress. This very objectivity, this recourse to scientific rationality, lends to the assessment a legitimacy which makes it hard to refute. (Outstanding in this respect are, of course, intelligence tests and public examinations.)

In invisible pedagogies, evaluation procedures are multiple, diffuse and not easily subject to apparently precise measurement, so that it is difficult to compare pupils or schools. The tendency of invisible pedagogy to be associated with weak classification and framing means that there are few traditional criteria for evaluation, and there is little standardization of curriculum content or pedagogy between teachers and schools. Thus assessment comes to be part of the pervasive and private personal relationship between teacher and taught. Bernstein suggests that in visible pedagogies, assessment will be in terms of those dispositions of a child which become candidates for labelling by a teacher and, given that in such visible pedagogies the attention of the child is focused on the teacher, the teacher will tend to compare children in terms of motivation and interest, attentiveness, cooperation, persistence and carefulness. The judgements will usually be short, stereotyped, unexplicated and public. By contrast, the invisible pedagogy is likely to be associated with a dossier covering a wide variety of the child's internal processes and outer acts and the teacher's explanation of the relationship between the two. Recent research into the impact of National Assessment requirements in English primary schools bears out Bernstein's more theoretical analysis. It documents teachers' preference for intuitive, idiosyncratic assessment strategies rather than the more 'categoric' assessment requirements of the National Curriculum, which they see as producing only 'dead data' for reporting purposes (Pollard *et al.* 1994; Broadfoot *et al.* 1996). Teachers' preferred assessment mode of a private 'diagnostic discourse' concerning individual children is arguably more likely to provide educational experiences which are of maximum benefit to the learner. Alternatively, they can be argued to allow a much more subtle and pervasive discrimination and control, because they make assessment harder to challenge and hence raise the teacher's power. The current emphasis on 'student-centred assessment' and 'person-centred schools' (Munby 1989; Broadfoot 1991) in some of the more radical literature concerned with assessment certainly seems to support this latter argument.

This part of Bernstein's analysis was made before the current fashion for the concept of accountability and this is evident in his writing, since he does not draw out here the implications that his analysis of invisible pedagogy and its accompanying informal assessment are likely to have for maintaining confidence in the education system as a form of control and legitimation. It is clear from English and American experience that trends in the 1950s and 1960s towards invisible pedagogies in basic schooling together with the decline or abolition of the external control exerted by public assessment procedures has been a direct source of worry about standards and thus of associated calls for more 'categoric' measures of accountability (control). In England at least, such measures have helped to restore the legitimacy of more traditional educational transmissions, in Bernstein's terms: strong classification, strong framing, visible pedagogy and formal, 'categoric', overt assessment.[13]

In his more recent work, Bernstein (1982) has revised his theory to associate weak classification and weak framing with economic expansion, strong classification and strong framing with economic contraction. This suggests that Bernstein's analysis is now more in line with current 'crisis' theory in associating educational codes with changes in the legitimating context rather than in the mode of production itself. Equally, his more recent work gives a more explicit role to evaluation as part of the 'pedagogic device' which is 'the condition for the production, reproduction and transformation of culture and which, in turn, provides the intrinsic grammar of pedagogic discourse through distributive rules, recontextualising rules and rules of evaluation' (p. 21). Bernstein further suggests that the realization of the pedagogic device, the conceptualization of which he traces back to Durkheim, carries the contradictions, cleavages and dilemmas that are generated by the power relations underpinning such realizations (p. 64). Bernstein thus stresses the need to conceptualize 'evaluation' as a separate, albeit determined, variable of pedagogic practice. However, it could be argued from contemporary evidence that because assessment procedures are so closely bound up with the legitimation of particular educational practices, because they are the overt means of communication from schools to society and, to a greater or lesser extent in different societies, the covert means of that society's response in the form of control, assessment may be the *most* important of the three message

systems. Assessment procedures may well be the system that determines curriculum and pedagogy and, hence, social reproduction.

As Bernstein (1982: 98) further suggests, 'The public examination
system is based upon a visible pedagogy as it is realised through
strong classification and strong frames.' As such it must be regarded
as the mediator of 'symbolic property' – educational goods ex-
changeable in the educational market. 'Knowledge under collection
is private property with its own power structure and market situation' (p. 97): the traditional order of capitalism which still retains
ideological legitimacy.

The significance of this issue of the nature and origin of evaluative
criteria has already been touched on in Chapter 2, where it was
suggested that those who are in a position to define such criteria are
also in a position to regulate entry to the elite and so provide for
social reproduction. The current trend away from narrow, academic, externally imposed certification procedures towards broader,
more continuous, teacher-based certification procedures (Nisbet
1993) means that the criteria of successful performance are increasingly being left to teachers to decide. Even where the criteria for
such assessment are externally agreed, the breadth of such assessments can make any effective moderation of the *application* of the
criteria almost impossible (GNVQ 1994) leaving teachers very significant power in determining life chances.

More recently, many of the countries which veered towards more
school-based assessment in recent decades have tended to encounter
a reassertion of externally imposed assessment criteria as, at best, the
credibility of school-based assessment has diminished in the face of
pessimistic views about educational standards and pupil achievement, and, at worst, there has been widespread abuse and cheating,
as in, for example, Sri Lanka. Tests are perceived as symbols of order
and control in the midst of diversity, chaos, competition for dwin-
dling school resources, and the need for external verification of
educational standards (Airasian 1988: 307). Thus Airasian echoes
Bernstein's emphasis on *symbolic control* as increasingly the central
problematic and one in relation to which testing and assessment has
grown rapidly to become of critical importance. School-based assessment continues as a powerful grassroots movement in many
countries, however, leading to an interesting dualism in assessment
paradigms, the implications of which are returned to in the conclud-
ing chapter of this book.

But although changes in the power of different parts of the education system are of considerable significance in themselves, the power relations involved in the definition of such criteria are very complex and go considerably beyond any simple dualism involving central government and teachers. Bernstein himself has recognized both the significance of the issue and its extreme complexity in an analysis in which he tries to provide a model for the highly complex and reflexive articulation between central government rhetoric, actual and perceived constraints and professional ideology in the formulation of educational 'modalities'. Bernstein (1982: 351) has attempted to conceptualize what he terms the 'discourse of education' in terms of the 'primary' context, 'where specialised discourses are developed, modified or changed', and the 'secondary' context, where various types of educational agencies engage in the 'selective reproduction of educational discourse'. Such discourse, he argues, relates the context for primary contextualizing – that is, the 'positions, relations and practices arising out of production' itself – with the recontextualizing involved in the generation of 'pedagogic theory, research and practice'.

Assessment procedures which provide the language of accountability are a vital element in this reflexive process, since the assumptions and the priorities they ensure may be regarded as the code which is translated into the appropriate forms of discourse at each stage of the recontextualization. How this process actually works in practice is a highly complex, empirical question which resurrects the theme of this book, namely that the fundamental role of assessment procedures in advanced and, indeed, post-industrial societies is a constant but that the institutional expression of that role will vary according to the social context and over time.

The extent to which such variations are essentially determined – the different institutional mediations of a common economic order – and the extent to which such variations represent real differences in the actual content of educational messages is again an empirical question. That is to say, are the apparent differences in the organization and provision of education systems of different capitalist societies simply reflections of different *instrumental* legitimating ideologies or are they at least to some extent reflections of differences at the level of the expressive order itself – of the fundamental value systems of each society?

Part of the answer to this question is embodied in the rationale for the move towards more 'invisible' evaluation – the increasing difficulty of identifying educational objectives and, hence, criteria of achievement which will command support from all sections of the community. The conflict of aims which has always been implicit in educational provision between the 'old humanists', 'new industrialists', 'public educators' and 'state bureaucrats' (Salter and Tapper 1981) has recently been greatly exacerbated by economic recession, youth unemployment, technological change and other, equally fundamental, changes in the social order.

Following Habermas and Marcuse, among others, it may be argued that the potential 'crisis' that this diversity of educational aims produces is largely kept in check by the elevation of the pursuit of rationality – always a characteristic of industrial society – from being merely the *means* of providing for efficient social organization (the instrumental ideology) to being the *end* itself (the expressive ideology). There is considerable disagreement among sociologists as to whether this trend is but one element in the hegemonic domination of a particular class and is thus still part of the instrumental order or whether the growth of scientism and technical rationality has been such as to render increasingly anachronistic traditional definitions of class struggle. The changes currently taking place in assessment procedures strongly support this latter argument, which is taken up in detail in Chapter 8. Before we proceed to such a substantive analysis, however, it is necessary to clarify the general issues involved in identifying one final theme in this review of educational assessment in industrial society, that of technological rationality.

Rationality and legitimation

This emphasis on the form of social life and its significance for social control is dealt with at length in the writing of the German philosopher Jürgen Habermas. Although some kind of distinction between the instrumental (normally economic) order and the expressive (normally social) order is common to a wide range of sociological theory from both conflict and functionalist perspectives, Habermas's distinction between the 'practical' (*praktisch*) and the 'purposive rational' (*zweckrational*) is particularly relevant to an understanding of the role of educational assessment.

Habermas defines the 'practical' as the basis for symbolic inter-action within a normative order – the level of feeling, consciousness and volition and the associated level of ethics and politics (loosely, 'superstructure'). The 'purposive rational' is action which is directed towards specific purposes (loosely the economic and administrative 'base'). Habermas's *zweckrational* links closely with Weber's concept of rationality, which he used to define the form of capitalist economic activity, bourgeois private law and bureaucratic authority. Habermas (1970) argues that as social labour is increasingly in-dustrialized, the criterion of rationality penetrates ever further into other areas of life through such developments as urbanization and the technification of transport and communication. Indeed, it may be argued that the growth of rationality has been of more importance than that of capitalist production itself and that the story of modern history is essentially that of the growth of bureaucracy: 'apart from the opaque line of technological rationality, social life is drift and habituation' (Gerth and Wright-Mills 1952: 165).

There is a clear Weberian legacy here. In *The Theory of Social and Economic Organisation*, Weber draws a distinction between: the simple, undifferentiated society accepting the traditional authority which embodies prevailing social values; the charismatic leader able to inspire the kind of collective value consensus to which Durkheim attached such importance; and the 'routinization' of that value consensus into institutional structures and practices. Weber argues that such an active 'moral consensus' is a temporary phenomenon inevitably to be replaced by the much more enduring and essentially impersonal authority of institutional process and bureaucracy (Weber 1947).

But there is equally a Durkheimian legacy in Habermas's concep-tion. Durkheim describes the gradual change from 'humanism' to 'realism' in the content of education from the seventeenth century onwards, a change in the legitimating ideology of education which has endured until the present day. Humanism in one or other of its forms, Durkheim argues, was the guiding spirit of all education in the Christian era until the early seventeenth century, or in France, where change came later, the eighteenth century. In this perspective, he suggests,

Things were not intrinsically interesting: they were not the object of a special study carried out for its own sake, but were

> only dealt with in connection with the human beliefs to which
> they had given rise. What people wanted to know about was not
> how the real world actually is but rather what human beings
> have said about it . . . Between the things of the world and the
> things of the mind falls the text, which acts as a partial veil
> between them.
>
> (Durkheim 1947: 279, author's emphasis)

The traditional, humanist paradigm, Durkheim suggests, resisted the
incursion of any form of science, of finding out about the real world,
into the curriculum. By contrast, the new perspective that Durkheim
describes as being inspired by writers such as Comenius is designed
to create good and useful citizens. It is 'realist', concerned with the
study of things, with preparing men [*sic*] for every possible action
and giving them insight into the world in which they live.

Although a complex and confused tradition, subject to many
reinterpretations and changes of emphasis, it is still essentially the
educational 'realism' of Comenius, Montaigne, Rousseau and others
which provides the contemporary legitimating rhetoric of 'scientism'
and hence of assessment. At the same time, Durkheim suggests, the
alternative, humanist tradition of the study of people, their interpretations and creations has never been eclipsed, the struggle between
the two perspectives constituting a persistent theme in educational
theory and educational policy.

Thus, the progression from feudalism to capitalism and, in
particular, from entrepreneurial to corporate capitalism may be seen
as one in which the ever increasing power of technical-scientific
rationality not only structures the ideology and organization of
production, but is more and more pervasive in the ideology and
organization of social life as a whole. Reimer (1971: 19) puts the
point with some force:

> School has become the universal church of a technological
> society, incorporating and transmitting its ideology, shaping
> men's minds to accept this ideology and conferring social status
> according to its acceptance. There is no question of man's
> rejecting technology. The question is only one of adaptation,
> direction and control. The role of the school teacher in this
> process is a triple one combining the functions of umpire, judge
> and counsellor.

As institutional life becomes more hierarchically and pervasively ordered, social life becomes correspondingly fragmented. High rates of social mobility serve to transform group conflict into individual competition, so that it is increasingly difficult for common interests and values to be identified as the basis for informal, democratic, collegial (that is, horizontal) forms of organization (Bates 1980a,c).

Habermas also suggests that, in advanced capitalist societies, deprived and privileged groups no longer confront each other *as* socio-economic classes. Although class distinctions still persist in the form of subcultural traditions, lifestyles and attitudes, the scope for normative activity – political initiatives, debates about the nature of the 'good life', the capability for conscious action as a class – are increasingly drowned in the technocratic consciousness.

> Today's dominant, rather glassy background ideology, which makes a fetish of science, is more irresistable and farther-reaching than ideologies of the old type. For with the veiling of 'practical' problems it not only justifies a particular class's interest in domination and represses another class's partial need for emancipation. but affects the human's race's emancipatory interest as such . . . technocratic consciousness reflects . . . the repression of 'ethics' as such as a category of life.
>
> (Habermas 1970: 112)

The legitimation for this process, according to Marcuse, is the constantly increasing productivity which keeps individuals living in increasing comfort.

> In the universe, technology also provides the great rationalisation of the unfreedom of man and demonstrates the 'technical' impossibility of being autonomous, of determining one's own life. For this unfreedom appears neither as irrational nor as political, but rather as submission to the technical apparatus which enlarges the comforts of life and increases the productivity of labour.
>
> (Marcuse 1964)[14]

What is being described here is the phenomenon of 'one-dimensional man' – the logical development of the process of individualization and rationalization associated with the development of capitalist economic relationships. As capitalism has itself become more and more institutionalized, into various kinds of state and corporate capitalism, its ideological legitimation has equally moved from the hegemonic domination of a particular class to the predominance of a common prevailing rationality *per se*, where science and technology are both base and superstructure. If, earlier, ownership and control of the means of production were crucial to effective domination, increasingly it is the bureaucracies of production and of administration which have become both controlling and self-determining. In this sense, class is not a tangible entity but rather the *form* of relations between interests and individuals (Hogan 1981). What started as a desire to understand and, hence, harness the material/natural world for the means of production is increasingly being extended by technocrats and bureaucrats alike into an attempt to extend 'technical' control into the realm of social life itself. This takes the form of new and more pervasive techniques for the surveillance, monitoring and control of both individuals and organizations.

> The economic take-off of Western Europe began with techniques that made possible capital accumulation, methods for the accumulation of men made possible a political take-off, as the traditional, ritual, costly, violent forms of power were superseded by a subtle calculated technology of subjection . . . The establishment of a coded, formally egalitarian constitution supported by a system of representative government. But this 'Enlightenment' politics had its dark underside in the ever-proliferating network of disciplinary mechanisms.
>
> (Foucault 1977: 201)

Foucault suggests that the 'scientific method' of observation and evaluation was related to a growing post-enlightenment preoccupation with rules and normality. It was this tradition, heralded by earlier, more extreme attempts to impose a norm, as found for example in the Spanish Inquisition, which has also come to underpin the acceptability of making judgements on others in relation to prevailing norms and hence the acceptability of educational assessment.

More significant even than the evaluation of individuals according to some arbitrary social standard, disguised in the language of apparently objective science, is the bureaucratic style of administration that this makes possible. In practice, this means that issues which are in reality questions of alternative values are perceived as technical problems to which a 'right answer' – an 'optimum solution' – exists, waiting to be discovered.

Foucault and the power relations of discourse

Foucault's theories have much in common with the emphasis of Marxist theory on the crucial role of false consciousness in the ideological legitimation of capitalism. Foucault differs strongly, however, in his identification of unequal power relations as the inevitable feature of any social intercourse, rather than a particular manifestation of capitalism (Donald 1981). His structuralist perspective is located between the freedom of interactionism and the determinism of much macro theory, as represented in the following quotation:

> Structuralism, then, involves deconstructing the subject. Certainly the individual remains at the centre of the analysis: what he or she 'knows' is the starting point. However, the subject is not seen as a free agent, centre of his own self creating and conferring meanings on the social world around him. Rather the approach effectively 'deconstructs' the subject, explaining meanings in terms of a structure which lies beyond the individual's comprehension and control . . . this necessitates a perception of the individual act as a representation of the underlying structure . . . a node through which language and the social formation speak.
>
> (Webster 1981: 6, 7)

One of the main strengths of Foucault's analysis in this respect is his commitment, like Weber's, to empirical study and his attempts to map in detail the outcomes of specific human actions. Straddling the normal boundaries of history, philosophy, politics, sociology and the history of science, Foucault's work grew in significance during the 1980s partly in response to the vacuum created, in France at least, by the discrediting of both Marxism and 'reformism'.[15] There is no conspiracy theory in Foucault's work. His essentially phenomenological approach argues that all types of social form, from sexuality to penology and the law, are relationships of power. He thus locates power not in particular social structures, but as an effect

of the operation of social relationships between groups and individuals. Hence power cannot be located as emanating from any particular point, such as 'the state', since Foucault sees the state as a composite of a multiplicity of centres and mechanisms of 'micro-powers', such as hospitals, schools and factories. The strategic aims of the state apparatus, in particular, must be understood in relation to these 'micro-powers'. Far from being the currency of the ideological superstructure in relation to the economic base, power and the political transformations it informs 'are not the result of some necessity, some imminent rationality but the responses to particular problems combining not in a totalised, centralised manner but by serial repercussion' (Sheridan 1980: 218).

> Political power from this perspective, is not the possession of a social class, but a proliferating, anonymous force which cannot be attributed to the ideological self-expression of a unified economic group . . . disseminated through many and varied discourses and institutions, power possesses no single determining centre and cannot be identified with a monolithic state apparatus which it largely outstrips . . . his [Foucault's] work invites a radical rethinking of such notions as the neutrality of scientific truth and the progressive acquisition of knowledge through trial and error, just as it challenges us to re-examine the idea that political power is increasingly centralised within the state and that power emanates from ideological oppression and ownership of the means of production.
>
> (Hill 1981: 7)

These now familiar arguments have proved extremely influential in recent years. Following the theoretical work of Foucault and others it is now widely accepted that power and knowledge are two sides of the same process; knowledge cannot be 'pure' but is necessarily political, not because it has necessarily political consequences or utility but because 'knowledge has its conditions of possibility in power relations . . . knowledge is not true or false but legitimate or illegitimate for a particular set of power relations' (Sheridan 1980: 20).

Thus, Foucault's work challenges the very basis of modern rationality and science, which have, according to this argument, the same ignoble origins as the lunatic asylum – one of Foucault's favourite subjects of study. People are only mad and in need of containment when they lack the power to assert the legitimacy of their version of reality, their knowledge, over that currently prevailing.

In Foucault's work there is no conception of historical determinism or of 'false' as opposed to 'true' consciousness. Although for him history is not simply the product of human interaction, it is nevertheless incomprehensible except as the outcome of human projects.

Clearly there are strong links here with Giddens's notion of 'structuration' (Giddens 1976), in which he conceives structures as existing 'out of time and space and impersonal for purposes of analysis but structures which (nevertheless) only exist as the reproduced conduct of situated actors with definite intentions and interests' (p. 127). Indeed in Volume 1 of his *Contemporary Critique of Historical Materialism* (Giddens 1981), he explicitly pursues Foucault's emphasis on covert domination as the basis for social control, identifying two of Foucault's principal themes – the commodification of time and the use of surveillance as a form of social control – as central in his own analysis of the characteristics of modern industrial society.[16] It is the centrality of these themes to a sociological understanding of the specific topic of educational assessment which justifies the foregoing rather abstract discussion and the more specific analysis that follows.

In his *Two Lectures* (Foucault 1976) Foucault argues that one of the great inventions of bourgeois society and of industrial capitalism was that of disciplinary power. In *Discipline and Punish* (1977), he describes the emergence in France of a whole range of new 'disciplines' between 1760 and 1840 as an army of technicians – warders, doctors (and later), psychiatrists and teachers – came to replace the executioner, whose crude retribution is replaced by processes of assessment, diagnosis and normative judgement covering not only explicit offences but the 'whole range of passions, instincts, drives and desires, infirmities and maladjustments' (Sarup 1982: 15).

These new tactics of disciplinary power involve two principal techniques. The first, 'hierarchical observation', involves a 'permanent and continuous field of surveillance'. The second, 'normalizing judgement', involves the novel concept of a norm which serves as the basis for categorization. The initial, negative role of these emerging disciplines, which was simply to protect society, rapidly gave way, Foucault suggests, to a more positive emphasis on 'socialization' to reinforce the norm.

Foucault's analysis of the way in which 'delinquency' is 'neutralized' and deprived of any potential political content by the operation of total institutions, such as prisons, has some common ground with the work of Durkheim, who also stressed the significance of the public identification of deviation not so much for the protection of society but crucially for the reinforcement of social norms among the majority of the population. The two French scholars share a common interest in the techniques evolved by industrial society to provide for the division of labour and, at the same time, for social order. They have both been criticized for not distinguishing adequately in their analysis between the specific social configurations of France and its more general applications (O'Connor 1980; Sarup 1982).

Nevertheless, Foucault's preoccupation with the micro-processes of power as they emerge from the whole range of interactional discourse separates him fundamentally from Durkheim's statist and benign view. Although based on the specific micro-politics of France, Foucault's arguments offer insights which are generally applicable to societies undergoing an equivalent transformation of the social order to that of France. His description of the features of industrializing societies, which include the way in which the new 'disciplines' rapidly become attached to the new class power which developed with industrialization, the latter's central concern with reproducing national security and the power relations of the status quo through the maintenance of the expansion of production and the provision of a docile and appropriately skilled workforce, would appear to be valid for all such societies.

Crucially, though, Foucault rejects analyses which locate power within the economic relations of capitalist society. He explains the emerging disciplinary mechanisms through the technical requirements of mass production in industrial society *itself* (Sarup 1982: 24). His work is thus more in line with that of other more recent scholars, such as Marcuse, who, despite his Marxist orientation, emphasized the characteristics of social life under capitalism and the implications of these, which in his view transcend questions of class struggle and inequality. Thus Foucault argues, like Marcuse, that there is a:

Proliferation of 'judges' who take the form of technical experts – teachers, doctors, psychologists, guards, social workers. As they operate in a sphere well protected from judicial or popular intervention, an antithesis has developed between discipline and democracy. Disciplinary power co-exists with democratic forms and undermines them from within. The roots of discipline are so deep in the organisation of modern society that the subordination of discipline to democratic control is increasingly difficult.

(Sarup 1982: 24)

It is this emphasis on the significance of the form of social life itself, rather than on the specific balance of power relations, which makes Foucault's work so central to the exploration of the social roots of assessment. More particularly, Foucault has himself identified educational examinations (i.e. assessment) as one of the more significant disciplinary mechanisms to have emerged. For Foucault what might appear to be only a harmless technique of knowledge is in fact, simultaneously, a technique of power. By combining the two principles of hierarchical observation and normalizing judgement, the examination becomes one of the major instruments for locating each individuals place in society. In arguing that examinations both help to establish the 'truth' and deploy the force to maintain it, Foucault's work thus echoes the fundamental rationale for educational assessment given at the beginning of this book. The student is controlled through a system of 'micro-penalties', the constant giving of marks which constitutes a whole field of surveillance.

Foucault's own analysis of the nature of this discipline is drawn predominantly from French examples. He describes a school of drawing for tapestry apprentices in 1737, emphasizing the detailed ordering of every minute of time, the regular, individual and carefully graded exercises, the supervision, assessment and subsequent allocation of individuals. The essentially monastic model of elaborate and detailed prescriptions for curriculum and pedagogy for each minute of the day is, and has remained, characteristically French.[17] Although it made a significant, if relatively brief, appearance in England under Bell and Lancaster's tightly structured monitorial system,[18] England has not typically provided generalized rules for such detailed curriculum structuring. More generally the commodification of time is, as Hargreaves (1989) has shown, an important apparatus of educational control which resonates with the core themes of technical rationality and individual control as these are addressed in this chapter.

Drawing on Jeremy Bentham's architectural concept of the 'panoptican', in which the isolated individual is constantly visible to a central authority, Foucault extends Bentham's idea that the perfection of surveillance makes the actual exercise of power unnecessary: the visible and unverifiable power will make the individual 'self controlling' as he is conscious of being observed, assessed and classified.

Very few individuals, except perhaps those in some prisons or mental hospitals, are now subjected to an explicit 'panoptism'. Although 'open-plan' schools were, arguably, a brief resurgence of the panoptic idea which characterized much of eighteenth- and nineteenth-century school architecture,[19] the panoptic function is now largely symbolic, carried out pervasively and efficiently with little real opposition – not least by examinations and various other forms of assessment and accountability.[20] As Foucault suggests, the age-based organization of the school, the graded curriculum, the marks for performance, produce an ensemble of compulsory align-ments, some physical, some mental, by means of which individuals replace each other in a space 'marked off by aligned intervals' (Foucault, quoted by Sarup 1982: 18). The examination is the fixing, at once ritual and 'scientific', of individual differences.

Hoskin (1979) sets out in detail one example of how Foucault's theory may be applied to the empirical reality of the development of examinations in England. The advent of print and the explosion of knowledge was associated with the development of examinations based on individual questions, marks and syllabuses. The giving of marks for individual questions constituted a major step towards establishing a *mathematical* model of reality, a step which was in Hoskin's view arguably as important as the invention of the alphabet in that 'the science of the individual was now feasible, for the principle has now been articulated that a given "quality" could be assigned a quantitative mark' (p. 144). It was therefore possible to weigh up individuals and compare them to others.

Hoskin argues that the new technique of disciplinary power emerging from the fusion of traditional rationality and authority into 'rational authority' finds its archetypal form in the examination. It is the examination which lies at the heart of the control function of schooling. Equally, it is clear that the principles of examination –

quantitative, particularistic, pseudo-scientific evaluation for specific purposes – are not confined to education, their growth in that sphere being reflexively related to a developing 'rational authority' in Western capitalist society as a whole. However, the recent trend towards hierarchical curriculum and assessment frameworks arguably represents an even more powerful manifestation of such symbolic control, in which the learner's identity is continuously defined by a series of categoric levels.

But, as well as being central, assessment is also necessarily flexible as an allocation and legitimation technique. Indeed, it is shot through with contradictions not only at the level of practice concerning the incompatibility of means which serve equally important ends (Eckstein and Noah 1993), but also at the fundamental level of purpose since, as has already been argued, it embodies the potential to be both liberating and controlling. That this is so is best demonstrated by illustration from the wide range of empirical practice. Before we turn to this part of the analysis, however, it is necessary to complement the foregoing general discussion of the social role of educational assessment with a conceptual analysis capable of addressing the issue of systemic variation. This is the subject of Chapter 5.

Overview

This chapter has delved into some very different sociological theories in its attempt to explain the origin and significance of the very concept of educational assessment. The analytic themes identified at the beginning of the chapter – individualism, rational authority, contradiction and legitimation – may now be seen as characteristic features of modern societies which together give rise to the necessity for, and the possibility of, a set of procedures based on certain defining principles which we recognize as assessment. But if it is the prominence of individualism and rationalism which has made *thinkable* the concept of assessment as we know it, it is to contemporary theories of power relations, notably structuralist and post-structuralist perspectives, that we must look for an explanation of the significance of the *practice* of such assessment in terms of the realization of particular forms of social division and relations of control.

ASSESSMENT AND THE
NATIONAL CONTEXT

Chapter 4 explored the general reasons behind the way in which
assessment techniques have evolved in the education systems of
advanced industrial societies. These reasons were closely related to
the need to provide for the complex socialization and training made
necessary by a division of labour and the breakdown of the social
homogeneity and traditions which had formerly provided the basis
for social order and control. It is readily apparent, however, that
despite institutional similarities, there are major differences in the
provision and practice of education in such societies. At the level of
educational process, there are different emphases in relation to both
the form and the content of the curriculum, pedagogy and evaluation.
At the level of provision, too, there are differences in the organization
of educational institutions and the power and associated budgetary
structures which link central, local and institutional functioning.

Working at the beginning of the 1980s, Archer took the view that
'the single most neglected question in the vast literature on education
concerns is the educational system itself' (Archer 1981a: 261). In
particular, Archer (1981a: 261) suggested, 'The defining characteristics of a *state* system are in it having both *political* and *systemic*
aspects.

While the term education system is not necessarily synonymous with the national level – since it is possible to distinguish separate systems at institutional, regional, national and international levels – these are not strictly independent systems but are more or less autonomous interaction 'sites' of the practical outworking of national provision. Thus, while in empirical terms they are an essential part of the conceptualization of the 'relative autonomy' of individual actors and sites within the overall system, which has received so much sociological interest in recent years, such analyses must take into account the backdrop of national educational provision and the state as the principal determining context for economic, political and social institutions and hence for cultural tradition and legitimating ideology.

For many years the questions that arise from this relationship, and specifically from the articulation between general and nationally specific social trends, received little attention. In 1980 Ramirez and Meyer were able to write: 'Questions both of the origins of structural variations and of their consequences for educational effects and other social variables remain relatively unexplored' (Ramirez and Meyer 1980: 380).

During the 1980s, however, sociological interest in the role of the state rapidly increased, fuelled at least in part by a rapid and substantial escalation of state intervention in educational policy especially in countries such as Britain and the United States with decentralized education systems where such intervention flew in the face of tradition. The growth of 'policy sociology' (Ball 1990), in recent years had done much to rectify the neglect that writers at the beginning of the last decade were deploring. However, the growth of policy sociology has arguably been in the form of a pendulum swing away from macro theory. The associated preoccupation with middle-range analyses has led in turn to a relative neglect of attempts to situate specific national policy developments in the context of more fundamental and international social, economic and political trends (Broadfoot 1991). There is still arguably a dearth of carefully focused comparative national studies which can provide the empirical basis for an analysis of the way in which broad general trends in late capitalist societies are articulated in countries as different as the United States, Japan, Australia and France. Not only are such studies essential to an adequate understanding of the salience of specific policy developments in any one national system, they are also the necessary starting point for more generalized explanations of current social change.

This argument may be readily clarified by a reference to the substantive topic of this chapter – assessment. Perhaps more than any other aspect of educational policy, assessment issues have grown during the past decade from relative insignificance into one of the most prominent features of many governments' educational strategy. In North America, Australasia and the United Kingdom a substantial and rapidly growing literature on assessment policy (e.g. Stake 1991; Gifford and O'Connor 1992; Torrance 1994) reflects the measured scholarly attention that this particular policy issue is now attracting, and much has been written to try to explain both the causes and the significance of specific assessment policy initiatives in individual education systems.

Comparative studies which compare and contrast such initiatives within different national contexts are much rarer, however, although some are now beginning to emerge (for example, Eckstein and Noah 1992; Vedder 1992; Nisbet 1993). Attempts to build on such empirical policy studies to create analyses at a more theoretical level concerning the evolving social role of educational assessment (such as Neave 1989) are still an almost totally neglected field in the sociology of education.

It is in the light of the pressing need for studies in the sociology of assessment to be conducted at this level that this chapter has been written. Its purpose is twofold. First, it provides an elaboration of the argument set out briefly above concerning the importance of articulating comparative, system-level analyses with broader attempts to understand those common trends currently impacting on many different societies, which are mediated through a range of different national policy responses. Second, the more specific goal of the chapter is to draw up a conceptual framework on which to base an analysis of the relationship between one particular social formation – assessment – and the more general characteristics of education under capitalism as they too are expressed in assessment practices.

These analyses are necessary, for two reasons. First, they avoid an over-deterministic perspective. They allow the particular events of national educational history to be interpreted as manifestations of more general developments in the contemporary social order but *not subsumed within them*, thereby retaining a vitally important voluntarist dimension in the analysis, a dimension which allows for the creative effects of the interaction of individual actors. In so doing it also guards against the more obvious dangers of 'armchair theorizing' and forms a rich inductive basis for examining and developing a more general analysis of the role of educational assessment in modern education systems. These points are, once again, well made by Archer, a leading exponent of this perspective:

> imputation dispenses *with analysis of social interaction* and the interests actually salient in it at the time. For these are the real processes which drive the system – which are responsible for structuring it and for its re-structuration . . . to deal only with abstract interests (e.g. parents seek the best for their child, the State has an interest in a minimum level of civil disobedience within the total population) prevents interests from a) ever being seen as *vested interests* in a *particular structure* that is firmly anchored in time and space and conditioned by that specific educational reality and b) as elements whose results depend exclusively upon *interaction* taking place in that *context*.
>
> (Archer 1981b: 213, emphasis in original)

Archer also suggests that over-theoretical perspectives endow educational development with excessive rationality and artificially absolve it of the accumulation of unintended consequences.

Hargreaves (1982a: 117) makes a similar point in his criticism of ' "macro" level statements about dominant patterns of social relations, forms of hegemony, features of the capitalist mode of production . . . ambitious explanations of the nature and effects of capitalism in a search for "deeper underlying forces" . . . without in any way specifying how these broad social structural forces are filtered down to the school level.' What such theories lack, Hargreaves suggests, is an extra *political* dimension – in particular an analysis of educational policy, the state and capitalism, as important providers of the context in which teachers and pupils do their work.

In arguing against mechanistic models of the relationship between capitalism and education, Dale (1983) invokes the concept of 'relative autonomy' to explain the independent life of educational systems; that despite the constant demands that capitalism, patriarchy, racialism and tradition make upon education, they are not defining. 'Education systems are to be seen rather as the arenas, with their own boundaries and historical specificities, and housing their own set of interests within which the separately and collectively contradictory sets of demands are mediated into educational practice' (Dale 1983: 187). Durkheim (1977: 42) had earlier put a very similar point with some force:

> When one studies historically the way in which education systems have been formed and developed, it is apparent that they depend on religion, political organization, the degree of scientific development, the state of industry etc. If one detaches them from all these historical causes, they become incomprehensible. Educational institutions are social institutions.

Whitty (1980: 8) has succinctly summed up the issue by suggesting that 'theoretical issues cannot usefully be considered independently of studies of ideological practice within historically specific conditions of existence.'

To establish the importance of such a perspective, in which attempts are made to explain why particular educational practices emerge and are maintained, does not in itself suggest how this might be done, however. Any consideration of the relationship between general sociological insights and the substantive realities of a particular social world raises in an acute form the central debate within sociology itself between determinism and voluntarism, structuralism and interactionism, system and action, macro and micro perspectives.[1]

The intention here cannot be to resolve these issues but is rather to discuss briefly those theories which are most concerned with the constituting and reconstituting of organizational structures and educational systems in particular. Assessment procedures must be seen as part of the dynamic articulation of major changes in the social context, and their associated changes in individual consciousness and volition. In this respect it is the relationship between *system and society*, as much as that between *school and society*, which is worthy of study.

The relative neglect of the system in recent decades as a separate focus of study has recently given way to a general recognition of the need for comparative sociological studies couched within a theoretical framework which is sensitive to *both* action and system, as these are related at institutional, national and supranational levels. Such studies combine the best of the comparative education methodology,

with its emphasis on empirical research and its refusal to countenance any unilateral transferability of concepts and institutions
between national systems, with the powerful theoretical perspectives
of sociology and the latter's insistence that an educational system
must be understood as a dynamic whole which is substantively
different from the sum of its component parts.

Thus, while analyses such as those of this book, which are couched
in very general terms in an attempt to identify and account for the
constant presence of assessment procedures in mass education
systems, are necessary, to be adequate such analyses must also be
extended, conceptually and empirically, to take account of the
detailed processes involved in the development of each individual
education system. In particular, some attempt must be made to
explain why individual societies have evolved different and, sometimes, what would appear to be counter-productive procedures for
achieving these same general goals.

In the light of these arguments, this chapter attempts to provide a
theoretical basis to link the current and historical developments in
educational assessment in two nation states with the more general
analyses of Chapters 2, 3 and 4, concerning the part played by
educational assessment in mass education systems. The aim of this is
to substantiate the foregoing general theoretical arguments about
the centrality of an evaluative rationality while demonstrating that
the institutional form of its expression may be very different.

The social construction of education systems

The dynamic functioning of education systems may be understood
as the product of three interacting rationales. First there are the
requirements imposed upon the system by the nature of the
capitalist state, as discussed in detail in Chapter 4. These may be
loosely summarized as the provision of an appropriately *skilled*
workforce and the provision of an appropriately *socialized* workforce. Second, there is the requirement for the system to legitimate
itself – a process which may be distinguished from the legitimation
the system provides for the social structure as a whole and which
may well require the toleration of practices within education that
are at best irrelevant and at worst counter-productive to the main
purposes of 'manpowering' and 'socialization'. Indeed, substantive

structures are often the results of compromises between competing ideologies.

Compromise is not confined to the level of ideology, however. 'Micro-politics' (Hoyle 1982) at the level of practice also ensure that decisions arise from a quasi-political process of negotiation. There is then, third, the creative and independent life within the system itself which can never be entirely constrained. In practice, these last two dimensions are frequently conflated. The 'relative autonomy' enjoyed by educational personnel – whether it be large or small – is thus partly the inevitable product of social interaction and partly a deliberate sacrifice to enable traditions important for legitimation to be maintained.

The distinction between those policies which are designed to meet substantive purposes and those which may have even as their primary rationale a legitimatory function is an important one. It is arguable, for example, that public examinations do not in fact fulfil their alleged purpose very efficiently (Lee-Smith 1990). However, they have an overwhelmingly important legitimatory role. The importance of the legitimatory role of assessment may be more clearly understood by refining the concept in terms of three different levels of legitimation. These may be identified as the legitimation of societal goals in the broadest sense, the legitimation of societal processes and the legitimation of the educational contribution to those societal processes. The first level is legitimated by expressive ideologies – the conception of societal goals, which, in the case of capitalist society, ranges from economic theories to theories of personal motivation such as acquisitiveness and personal responsibility. The second and third levels are legitimated by instrumental ideologies – accepted conceptions of how to reach defined goals. These latter conceptions are nationally specific and the product of a particular historical social formation. Thus although the mode of production itself – in this case capitalism – is not a specific national configuration, its existence leads to certain requirements and problems to which the potential responses are as varied as the differing national contexts.

Each of the three levels of social functioning identified above must thus be seen as a compromise between function and legitimation, whether it be the capitalist mode of production itself or the education system that is associated with it. Education's contribution to control is thus a function of this relationship between levels two and three, between education and societal process, and not at the level of expressive ideology which is above this. The state is the *context* for the educational contribution to societal process (function and legitimation) but some form of this relationship will be a constant feature of all capitalist societies.

Thus the educational codes determining the characteristics of curriculum, pedagogy and assessment are informed by, and in turn reproduce, the ideological discourse which is the basis for instrumental legitimation. Such discourse is also a reflection of the characteristics of the over-arching expressive ideology.

In this book it has been suggested that particular forms of assessment are characteristic of the expressive ideology of industrial society; that the individualism which was a defining characteristic of the advent of industrialization, and which is the legitimation of societal goals (i.e. level one), is translated into societal processes based on 'hierarchical observation' and 'normalizing judgement' (level two). This legitimating ideology finds expression at the level of educational discourse (level three) in various forms of individual and institutional assessment whose precise form varies in response to changes in the broader instrumental ideologies characterizing level two. Contrasting examples in this respect would be that of the meritocracy and the more recent ideology of the market.

The distinction that has been made between the over-arching requirements of capitalist societies and how these requirements find different expression in particular societies suggests certain inadequacies in theories which lack either one of these two defining elements. Thus Archer's elaborate model of educational systems might be criticized by neo-Marxists for its failure to address the characteristics of the over-arching capitalist order (level one). Equally, Bernstein is typical of those writers who are open to criticism for not giving sufficient emphasis to the realm of educational politics and the instrumental ideologies of level three.

Without such a theoretical perspective, it is hard to see how the very real differences in national systems could be accounted for. The many detailed empirical studies of national educational policy-making that exist underline the importance of 'institutional archaeology' in mediating such general trends, and highlight the multicausality, pluralistic conflict, administrative complexity and historical inertia which deny the validity of any simple determinism. Careful empirical documentation of these processes can reveal much more about the complex nature of educational decision-making and state policy than mysterious invocations of concepts like 'centralization', which simply tend to gloss over these differences and subtleties.

Archer's model of education systems

In her major comparative work on four national educational systems, Archer (1979) has provided one of the most theoretically and empirically developed models of this process of negotiation. Although now inevitably somewhat dated, Archer's work is particularly relevant to the discussion of this chapter since it is specifically applied to the emergence and operation of four national educational systems, two of which, France and England, are also the basis for this book. Archer focuses upon the reflexive relationship between structure and action, the social structures which shape the context in which interaction and change occur and hence result in the emergence of particular forms of educational provision.

A crucial element in Archer's perspective is the emphasis on the present as well as the past, so that the social context is, in this view, not only the result of historical interaction but also the result of the contemporary behaviour of individuals or groups who cannot or will not change these structures. This perspective enables Archer to open up the whole area of 'educational politics' and the 'internal strains' which lead to change. The focus is thus on interest groups, on the processes of exchange, negotiation and consolidation, within more general changes in the social context. It is these more general functional incompatibilities or structural contradictions that lead to strains and a pressure for change which has repercussions throughout the system because of its interdependence.

Building on what is clearly a Weberian perspective, Archer distinguishes between privilege, authority and power, which she links in educational terms to achievement, organization and curriculum respectively. Beyond this basic currency of analysis, however, Archer's focus is specific rather than general, concerned with developing a conceptual framework which can explain the historical idiosyncrasies of individual education systems within the more general pattern of their growth in post-feudal societies.

Drawing on Blau's (1964) concept of exchange theory, in which the possession of various kinds of resources allows competing groups to trade off against each other, the major distinction Archer makes between societies is in terms of their degree of centralization. Such differences are taken to be a product of whether state involvement in education was the result of a deliberate attempt on the part of a political group to gain control over education (restriction) or whether the state was historically reluctant, dragged into the educational debate by one particular interest group as provision expanded and thereafter fought over as a prized ally as its role became one of creating some kind of system out of these competing interests.

Archer argues that successful control of the emerging system depended upon monopoly ownership of educational facilities (thereby preventing others from converting financial and human assets into schools and teachers). This was achieved through convincing competing groups that they lacked the right, ability or experience to provide education. This is a combination of the operation of a legitimating ideology based on traditional charismatic or rational grounds and symbolic or coercive protective constraints. Where, as in France, the elite was sufficiently homogeneous to operate such a restrictive approach successfully, the result was a highly centralized bureaucratic system specifically designed to reproduce the culture of the dominant group. Where, as in England, no one group could establish such a monopoly, the education system was decentralized, its character changing with the shifting alliances (substitution) between competing groups.

Archer's elaborate and empirically based analysis of the common and variable characteristics of education systems highlights a number of themes already discussed in this chapter, notably those of relative autonomy, ideological legitimation and negotiation – in short the ingredients of educational politics. But it is Archer's identification of the centralization–decentralization continuum as the principal defining characteristic of educational systems that adds an important additional conceptual dimension for the analysis of educational assessment procedures, which will be discussed later in this chapter. The fact that Archer explicitly identifies national examinations as one of the crucial ingredients of central control makes her model even more relevant. But in centralized and decentralized systems alike, the education system has a measure of autonomy which is the result of the social construction of its participants and the processes of interpretation and action they undertake in the light of their perceived 'micro-political' interests.

One of the most significant groups of participants in this respect is the teaching profession, on whom devolves the task of carrying out the work of the system, of making a reality of its more or less explicit and contradictory objectives. The significance of teachers' 'resistance', of the possible boundaries of their professional autonomy and of their ability to mediate and transform policy initiatives is now well recognized.

The relevance of this analysis to an understanding of the social role of assessment procedures is apparent, since one of the most important 'goods' that teachers have to 'sell' is their ability to prepare candidates to acquire valued qualifications. At the present time their power in this respect is increasing in many developed countries. As a growing emphasis on skills acquisition makes a greater emphasis on continuous assessment inevitable, teachers become the direct, as opposed to the indirect, arbiters of such awards. To the extent that teachers are entrusted directly with the responsibility for assessment – rather than being employed simply as markers for a nominally independent agency – that power is increased.

The ideological context[2]

In focusing upon political struggles based upon the more obvious currencies of power, such as the law or financial resources, it is all too easy to disregard the equally important but more covert ideological forms of power struggle and social control. For if, as Larrain (1979) suggests, legitimation is the necessary instrument of power, ideology is the neccesary instrument of that legitimation.

Whitty (1980) makes a twofold distinction between ideology as 'lived existence' and ideology as 'discourse', between what may be loosely referred to as culture and the way in which the content and form of discourse works to produce meaning and structure consciousness. Thus an analysis of educational discourse is necessary to emphasize the process of negotiation and construction between rival ideologies and the extent to which 'common sense' can be made to conform to prevailing political necessities.

In this model of ideology there is room for various legitimating traditions – political, religious, moral, nationalist, utilitarian, economic and technicist – and the possibility of a series of compromises and contradictions in response to changing historical conditions, people's lived experience and the struggles that ensue. But, at the same time, this is only flexibility *within* a defining political agenda. Such 'hegemonic ideology' (Whitty 1980) defines the issues and terms of debate: it has its 'structuring silences' (Lukes 1974). What emerges is a degree of autonomy, in which ideological, political and economic policies mutually provide each other with their broad conditions of existence. Thus, although the 'educational apparatus' can be said in general terms to be geared towards the reproduction and legitimation of capitalist social forms, this 'educational apparatus' also has a complex life of its own, which is the product of the changing historical context and inter-group power relations.

This rather abstract discussion of the social construction and legitimation of education systems is usefully translated into more specific terms by Dale.

> The aims of education in any society cannot be plucked from the air, nor do they develop in hermetically sealed units . . . It is also the case that what it is taken for granted education is capable of achieving, what we might call the feasible expectations of education are not wholly the product of deliberate rational calculation but are themselves also rooted in existing ways of doing things in a society, in its existing pattern of social institutions. Hence we might expect the feasible as well as the normative expectations of education to vary culturally, to be affected for instance, by, among other things, the degree of centralisation of state activity, by the proportion and strength of various religious groups within the society, and by the existing development of educational provision within the society.
>
> (Dale 1981b: 12)[3]

But it is not just the aims of education that will express the diverse and perhaps contradictory ideologies of different sites. Institutional structures and practices such as assessment are equally affected by the ideological power of different social forces. Ideology is locked into the institutional structure itself and not just into members' consciousness. A major and often overlooked consequence of this institutional incorporation of ideologies is the degree of 'inertia' in the system to which it leads. Practices which play no obvious ideological or practical role but which are simply the more or less haphazard hangovers of tradition may result in the system being slow to change and unresponsive to larger societal pressures (Broadfoot 1994a).

Ranson *et al*. (1980) also explore this relation between cause and meaning, between determinant and voluntary in the relation of structure and action. Like Archer, they are specifically concerned with structures from a 'neo-systems theory' perspective which focuses on the interaction between meaning, power dependencies and contextual constraints. Ranson *et al*. (1980) identify five sources of change in this respect which, they argue, contribute to 'the structuring of organisational structures' through being embedded at the level of culture and ideology. Thus they suggest change is likely:

- if organizational members revise the provinces of meaning, the interpretive schemes which underpin their constitutive structuring of organizations;
- if there are contradictions between the purposes, values and interests behind the strategic implementing of structural features;
- if there are significant changes in resource availability and in other key sources of organizational uncertainty which undermine the power bases of dominant coalitions;
- if there are major changes in situational exigences such as technology and environment, which will require changes to be made in structural arrangements;
- if there are contradictory imperatives in situational constraints, which will entail change in structural arrangements.[4]

Ranson *et al*. stress the importance of locating such contradictions among meanings, power, structure and context in a temporal dimension if the determining influences are to be unravelled. Following Perrow (1967) and Braudel (1973) they distinguish between the uncertain day-to-day experience of organizations, in which the actor and interaction patterns are dominant; the medium term, in which the emergent regularities of size, technology and environment are more apparent; and the long term, in which meaning, value and belief, 'sedimented' into institutional structures, provide for the dominance of a cultural system. 'In short, the closer the "horizon" the more visible the actor but constrained by his context. In the longer time perspective, actors become less "visible" but their frames of meaning, the product of their structuring, more determinate: constituted structures have become constitutive' (Ranson *et al*. 1980: 17).[5] Thus it would be quite wrong to anticipate any neat correspondence between systemic requirements, cultural norms and educational practice. Rather what is required is a reflexive theory capable of conceptualizing the articulation between action, system and context over time.

This is the rationale for the empirical chapters that follow, which trace the social role of assessment procedures in two different national systemic settings. Taking the very general theoretical framework outlined in Chapter 4 of the defining characteristics of industrial societies and the more detailed analysis in Chapter 2 of the different parts assessment procedures play in making schooling responsive to the needs of such societies, Chapters 6, 7 and 8 set out to trace the different elements of this relationship in two contrasting substantive contexts.

The organization of the analysis follows that already identified in Chapter 2 in distinguishing the themes of competence, content, competition and control, the last being further divided into its individual and systemic, micro and macro aspects. But there the resemblance to the approach of Chapters 2 and 3 ends, for the analyses of Part II are also informed by the arguments of this chapter, which stress the need to avoid any simple determinism in accounting for the development of assessment procedures. Thus Chapters 6 and 7, if Chapter 8 rather less so, are accounts of educational politics and of the way in which the emerging state apparatus of assessment in two very different societies reflected both the common pressures experienced by all industrializing societies and nationally specific cultural norms which combine to form the context for micro-political struggle.

Although analyses couched at the level of educational systems typically address the whole range of educational politics, no attempt is made here to provide such a comprehensive study. The aim is rather to provide an understanding of the characteristic part educational assessment plays in such systems rather than to provide an understanding of the system *per se*. But even this limited remit requires quite a substantial excursion into the realms of culture, control and pressure group politics. Much of the argument that follows is not directly concerned with the question of assessment procedures as such, but will be concerned with the more general question of the articulation between action, system and context over time, as these determine the development of specific assessment procedures.

The arguments of this chapter underline the need to understand the evolution of assessment procedures in terms of a prevailing legitimating rhetoric and the way in which the various interest groups involved in education succeed in defining the values and ethos of institutional practice through their influence on the language of accountability. The study of such discourse reveals that while the attestation of competence and the regulation of competition – the 'selection and certification' functions of assessment – are informed by a common legitimating rhetoric of education which is a product of the individualization and rationality on which all industrial societies must be based to a greater or lesser extent, the 'control' function reflects a much more idiosyncratic legitimating rhetoric which is bound up with political, rather than economic, exigencies and the specific national traditions of government.

Thus, for example, while the provision in both England and France of a national inspectorate may be read as a reflection of the assumption of normalizing judgement and hierarchical authority which accompanied the increasingly powerful expressive ideology of individualism in both societies, the nature and function of that inspectorate varied considerably at different times both within and between systems. Not only have French inspectors always been concerned with individual teacher quality while their English counterparts have been charged with inspecting schools, the character of each inspectorate has itself changed radically over time in the ebb and flow of educational politics. It was only recently, for example, that HMI in England began to think of itself as a national service concerned with standards in general as much as the rolling inspection of individual schools,[6] and even more recently that government has stepped in to alter radically HMI's role yet again, so that as 'Ofsted' it is now the manager of an inspection 'market'. Similarly, in France, the impact of educational policies on the National Inspectorate may be traced in its increasingly conciliatory and benign stance, in which 'animation' rather than judgement takes precedence.[7]

Why these and other changes in the character of assessment procedures in the two systems should have come about are questions addressed in detail in Chapters 6 and 7. Before we move to such a substantive level of analysis, however, it is necessary to provide a more theoretical framework to justify both the *need* for such an approach and how it may be operationalized. The final part of this chapter focuses more specifically on the role of assessment in attempting to provide a conceptual framework with which to approach the *different* parts played by assessment procedures in advanced industrial societies. As such, the analyses of Chapter 5 complement those of Chapter 4, which were concerned with the common and constant part played by educational assessment in such societies and lead into the empirical accounts that follow.

Modes of system control

It has been suggested that much of the variation between educational systems can be understood in terms of the different patterns of power relations that characterize them; that the complex interaction between ideological tradition, institutional inertia and changing social pressures produces a unique mediating context for determining how education will be provided. At the same time, however, it is also possible to categorize at least some of these differences systematically. Often this is done in terms of a particular variable, such as patterns of social mobility (Turner 1960; Hopper 1968) or stages of development (Beeby 1966). One of the most common categorizations used in this respect and one of the most significant for understanding the social role of educational assessment (Lauglo and Mclean 1984; Lauglo 1995) is the centralized–decentralized dichotomy. Thus, in order to link the more general discussion of the need for policy studies with the particular issue of assessment, this more focused analytical filter provides the theoretical framework for the final section of this chapter.

In systems categorized as 'centralized', power to control educational provision and process is taken to reside in central government. In systems categorized as 'decentralized', such power is taken to be dispersed among various competing interest groups, including local government, the teaching profession, other interest groups and local communities.

In Chapter 2 it was suggested that such power to control is ultimately bound up with assessment procedures to the extent that it goes beyond mere coercion, since any rational authority depends on a two-way flow of information. Not only does it require 'accounts' of how far policy is being achieved, it also needs to inculcate criteria of self-accounting on a 'normative–re-educative' basis. Indeed, given the difficulties of enforcing bureaucratic control, it is this latter sense of 'moral' accountability which is likely to be the more important source of constraint. Thus, it was argued in Chapter 2, the critical influence on the identification of educational goals and practices is likely to be the interest group that has the power to determine the criteria for self-imposed, 'moral' and 'professional' accountability. In a strongly centralized system this is more likely to be central government. If goal-setting is not enforced by some form of evaluation, however, the mere articulation of priorities is likely to be largely a rhetorical exercise.

It would seem logical that where a strong central bureaucracy closely prescribes the form and content of education and yet does not monitor whether its directives are being followed lower down the hierarchy, the demand for information about such activities to be produced is reduced and, with it, the control that the need to give an account provides. Although nominally it may still be correct to regard teachers in a centralized system as closely controlled employees where their colleagues in a decentralized system are autonomous but accountable professionals, this distinction does not necessarily reflect the reality of control.

Thus, despite the long-standing assumption that in 'centralized' education systems, such as those of France and Sweden, teachers' practice is more closely controlled than in 'decentralized' systems, such as those of England or the United States, this is misleading.

The equation of strong control with a high degree of centralization fails to take into account less obvious and generally much more powerful sources of control and constraint, notably that of assessment – the collection and evaluation of information about the system. Indeed, Archer (1979, 1982) stresses the key role of assessment procedures in this respect, arguing that in centralized systems the ideological homogeneity of the prevailing legitimating ideology allows the dominating elite to design a system of centralized control procedures, including a variety of assessment procedures such as public examinations, inspection and bureaucratic accountability based on 'performance indicators', which carry the legitimating rhetoric on which that status is based. In so doing it also reinforces it. To the extent that reality falls short of this ideal type of central control, as in decentralized systems, there is likely to be conflict between the substantive interests of different social groups, one expression of which will be a struggle to influence the legitimating rhetoric and hence not only the content of education but the criteria for determining quality against which schools and teachers will be held accountable.

Thus, it is possible to argue that in both decentralized and centralized systems assessment procedures have a different, but equally central, role to play in providing the explicit articulation of this legitimating rhetoric; that there is typically an ongoing struggle between the different interest groups involved in the education system who seek to establish control of the content of education, one crucial element of which is control of the public assessment apparatus in its several forms. It follows that a crucially important way of identifying differences in control in different types of education system is in terms of the different assessment procedures employed within those systems, since, in any sort of mass education system, assessment procedures act as one of the greatest constraints on classroom practice. In this sense, much of the variation between systems in terms of their dominant patterns of control can best be understood in terms of the particular *form* that control by assessment takes in each case. Such differences in control cannot be reduced simply to differences between centralized and decentralized systems. Assessment procedures vary on grounds other than this. They may, for instance, be informal or formal, school-based or external.

This does not mean that the importance of assessment factors makes the centralization issue *per se* irrelevant to the study of control. Indeed, a centralized, government-controlled, external assessment apparatus possesses great power to enforce the pursuit of a centrally determined curriculum. But the distinctions between different forms of assessment are much more subtle than this; more than a dichotomy between school-based (decentralized) and external (centralized) procedures of assessment. For where a number of more or less independent institutions like the English examination boards provide for external assessment, control can be both tight *and* uncentralized.

It is therefore important to distinguish between the *degree* of assessment control on the one hand (strong or weak), and the *source* of that control (central or local) on the other. This distinction is crucial, for the tendency to conflate *strong* control with *central* control within the concept of centralization has led to an over-preoccupation with administrative variables in the study of differences between educational systems and a consequent disregard for how that control is actually mediated and ultimately experienced by teachers in the schools.

Thus apparently different education systems such as those of France and England, which are often taken to be classic instances of centralized and decentralized systems respectively, may, despite initial appearances, be characterized by a remarkably similar *degree* of systemic control. At the same time, differences between the systems in the *form* that control through assessment takes and *where* power over those assessment procedures is located is likely to be significant (Rodmell 1977). In so-called centralized systems, there has traditionally been a great emphasis on assessment by 'process evaluation', by the exertion of control through the bureaucratic relationships of accountability to which teachers are subject. This is essentially the control of inspection of the quality of the educational process itself. By contrast, within the very strong traditions of curricular freedom and professional autonomy which have charac- terized decentralized systems, control over teachers' behaviour and the basis of their accountability has, in the main, been via 'product evaluation' – by evaluation of educational products as expressed in various forms of measurable pupil achievement.[8]

On the question of *where* power over assessment procedures is located, this too is associated with the form of evaluative control – process or product. In process evaluation, power over assessment procedures resides in that part of the education system which controls inspection – usually central but to some extent also local government. In the case of product evaluation, power is located more within those institutions which control the design and administration of assessment procedures – usually in central govern- ment, together with local government authorities to whom some limited power has been devolved, and also, in decentralized systems, in a large number of other non-statutory bodies such as examination boards and their clients (notably parents, pupils, employers and, of course, teachers themselves).

A consideration of the nature and amount of control over their practice experienced by teachers in terms of assessment procedures demands a more complex conceptualization than the traditional centralized–decentralized dichotomy. In particular it requires a theoretical model which is based on the way *in which the education system actually works* rather than on its formal administrative arrangements alone (Zeldin 1973). Only such a model, which takes

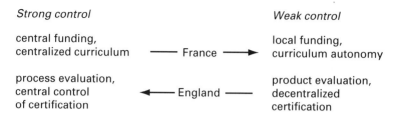

Figure 5.1 Model of assessment control in France and England.

the form and location of assessment procedures as determining criteria, can explain the increasing convergence in the form of control between societies at the present time, a convergence which, as the following section sets out, cannot be explained simply in terms of movements along the continuum between centralization and decentralization.

Control by assessment: a model

It is widely accepted that education systems in advanced industrial societies are becoming increasingly similar in their organization and objectives (Sutherland, M. 1977; Neave 1989). The reason for this increasing similarity, it is usually suggested, is that the central governments of countries like England are exerting ever-more centralized control on a whole range of educational provision, most notably on curriculum, assessment and finance, while countries such as France are moving in the opposite direction towards decentraliz- ation (deconcentration) in finance and administration. Figure 5.1 offers a diagrammatic representation of this argument.

This model of systems which are the polar opposites of one another gravitating towards a mid-point of similarity is misleading, however. For, in many respects, the systems are not polar opposites at all. In reality, the movements towards a common pattern of centrally directed control by product evaluation have commenced from very different starting points, which cannot be identified simply on a centralized–decentralized continuum. The traditional associ- ations between decentralized control and product evaluation on the one hand, and central control and process evaluation on the other, misrepresent what tends to occur in practice. Thus, it is possible to

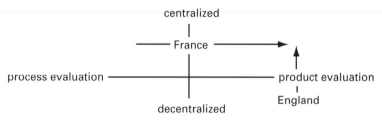

Figure 5.2   Representations of changing patterns of assessment control.

maintain a traditional emphasis on product evaluation within a context of increasingly centralized control. Alternatively, it is possible for a system to change its traditional pattern of assessment towards an emphasis on product evaluation, but without lessening its central grip upon the education system (see Figure 5.2).

As Figure 5.2 shows, it is no longer sufficient to conceptualize control over education in terms of its strength or weakness (as in Figure 5.1), because control cannot be equated with centralization. Rather, what appears to be important in determining patterns of educational control is the relationship between the two variables mentioned earlier: *the form of assessment control* and *the location of power over assessment procedures.*[9] Thus, it is not the gravitation of centralized and decentralized systems towards some educational mid-point that has produced the growing convergence between education systems, but the particular way in which these two variables, the *form* and *location* of assessment control, are tending to intersect in such countries.

In England, for example, there has been something of an oscillation between a more 'free market', decentralized approach to assessment control mediated by the semi-autonomous examination boards and the links they in turn have with the universities at times of plenty, and more directive, centralized strategies based on the tighter control of public examining and institutional accountability when economic and social problems dictate a more utilitarian direction for educational activity. In France, by contrast, the development has been from what was in fact the relative freedom of a highly centralized system in which assessment control was vested in national, government-run selective examinations and personal teacher inspection.

In both countries, there is now a move towards a nominally more decentralized, positive control based on a reflexive relationship between teacher-conducted continuous assessment according to nationally prescribed norms, and an increasingly technicist approach to educational administration, provision and control. The information thereby generated provides an increasingly powerful means of both directing the careers of individual pupils and directing the educational system as a whole. By the same token, the institution of continuous assessment based on national norms now not only exhorts teachers – as the system has always done – but makes that exhortation effective as these norms relate directly to the assessment of pupil progress and simultaneously provide for the national statistical monitoring of educational standards within the system (Broadfoot 1992).

If in some ways such developments can be seen as, in England at least, steps towards greater equality of educational provision, they are just as much a step towards greater control. As such they represent yet another reflection of the liberation–control dilemma in assessment procedures already discussed. In the past, where autonomy was safeguarded by the lack of central curricular prescriptions, the very powerful control exerted by the emphasis on 'product evaluation' still left considerable room for individual teachers, pressure groups and semi-autonomous bodies such as examination boards to influence the *content* of that control.

Similarly, in other systems, in the past autonomy could be safeguarded by the relatively minor role of 'product evaluation' despite the existence of a highly centralized, bureaucratic education system in which every aspect of pedagogic activity, and especially curricular objectives, was tightly controlled. The increasing similarity at the present time between England and France, as documented in Chapters 6 and 7, reflects the fact that each is tending to institute the aspect hitherto lacking to ensure effective control.

Perhaps even more important than this increasingly effective control, however, is the growing association of educational administration in both countries with a corporate management approach. Such an approach is likely to disguise the essentially political nature of educational goals – in an ideology of scientific rationality. In this event, value judgements appear as merely administrative decisions dictated by rationality and the goal of maximizing efficiency. It seems probable that effective educational control implies the existence of a social order ready to concur in educational goals. The way in which assessment procedures help to bring this about will perhaps prove ultimately more significant than their role in imposing such goals, for the requirements of mass testing are such as to require a considerable measure of agreement over educational objectives. It may well be that the testing technology overwhelms the initial, sensitive identification of educational goals, reinforcing the long-deplored tendency for assessment to reduce curricular goals to what can be measured and bringing a stage nearer the predominance of a technocratic ideal of managerialism (Airasian 1988), as set out in Chapter 8. Before we come to such a discussion in detail, however, it is necessary to establish how far the theoretical explanations for systemic similarities and systemic differences in educational assessment procedures, as set out in Chapters 4 and 5 respectively, are adequate to explain the specific assessment practices of the two countries under study.

PART II

TWO CASE STUDIES:
FRANCE AND ENGLAND

ASSESSMENT IN THE FRENCH EDUCATION SYSTEM

Introduction

Up to this point, the analyses of this book have been concerned with identifying the significance of assessment as an aspect of mass schooling in general and the different forms such assessment may take within any one education system. After the general theoretical analyses of Chapters 1 to 4, Chapter 5 explored the more specific theoretical issues which arise in a consideration of how these constant features of educational systems in modern industrial societies are mediated through the substantive reality of any particular national context. There it was suggested that the idiosyncratic blend of ideological and institutional traditions and the contemporary social, economic and political pressures that determine the nature of educational provision in any one country will be reflected in the *form* that assessment procedures take, but not in their essential importance, which is rooted in the characteristic ideology and resultant institutional structures of industrial society itself.

In this chapter and the next, these theoretical arguments are explored by means of a detailed comparative study of two national education systems: those of France and England. These two countries were chosen, as suggested in the introduction, because of their relative similarity in terms of national characteristics such as socio-economic development, size, geographical and historical context, ethnic mix and political traditions. That is to say, they share many common features as advanced industrial societies. On the other hand, they differ markedly in terms of several key aspects of their respective educational traditions, notably that of the degree of overt central government of education, and it was anticipated that the differences would help to illuminate the significance of assessment in educational provision. There is no suggestion that the empirical descriptions which follow are in any way definitive. Apart from the impossibility of such a project, the aim here is to pick out those characteristics of each system which are, or have been, significant in its development, particularly with regard to assessment and accountability procedures.

In each national case study, the first part of the discussion is concerned with all four of the principal themes identified – *competence, content, competition* and *control* – as they are interrelated in the development of evaluation procedures for assessing the performance of individual pupils within the education system. The second part of each case study is concerned with the part played by assessment procedures within the system as a whole, and is thus explicitly concerned with the very different ways in which the necessary provision for systemic control is provided for in the two countries. Although these two aspects of the part played by evaluation procedures are necessarily interrelated in practice, they are treated separately for the sake of clarity.

This book is written in English for a largely English-speaking readership. Thus while the case studies are intended to offer comparable insights, they are not similar in format. This chapter, on the French system, includes a great deal more descriptive material than Chapter 7, on the assumption that English-speaking readers will in general be relatively more familiar with the English context than the French. Equally, the two case studies are not arbitrarily matched but highlight the different historical periods and assessment practices that most clearly reveal the underlying social pressures to which they are a response.

Both chapters, however, focus on the struggle between various interest groups to gain influence within the education system so that they can establish their own value priorities in the evaluative criteria of the assessment apparatus. It is this assessment apparatus – of individual progress, of teacher effectiveness, of systemic efficiency – which is the template that gives meaning to all educational activity; it is the more or less explicit articulation of educational goals. Thus the two chapters that follow must necessarily embrace – albeit briefly – the whole range of systemic activity if they are to conceptualize the social role of assessment at all adequately. If sometimes this results in what may seem a protracted departure from the subject of assessment *per se*, the underlying theme of its role in the struggle to control education practice by defining educational goals, and thus the implicit or explicit criteria of accountability, are omnipresent. The third chapter in this section, Chapter 8, draws together these separate analyses in a consideration of those features which the two systems have in common and the significance of those more general developments in forms of assessment which may be identified as acting upon and within educational systems at the present time.

The context for growth: the pre-history of educational assessment and its effect on curriculum content in France

A long-standing theme in French education has been the struggle between church and state to control education. In this battle, assessment procedures have had a crucial role to play in helping to reinforce the pursuit of state, rather than church, inspired notions of *competence*, and, in so doing, have also had a major influence on curriculum *content*. Arguably it was not the provision *per se* of schooling for the masses which was significant. It was the changing content of that schooling. 'For long the church schools dispensed education as though it were a mystic initiation into sacred truths . . . traditional Catholic teaching was designed not to awaken the child but to teach him that desire could never be satisfied, except in the next world' (Zeldin 1973: Volume II, 101). Examinations made possible and indeed essential a different emphasis in schooling, in which, though even many liberals and intellectuals continued with the conservative and clerical interests to support 'religion for the masses and rationality for the privileged' (Vaughan and Archer 1971), the growing importance of formal qualifications during the nineteenth and twentieth centuries and their changing character belied this belief in practice. The qualifications associated with entering into teacher training and qualifying as a teacher provide a good illustration of this.

As early as 1793 the idea of formally certifying competence may be identified in the establishment of an official certificate in civic virtue as a requirement for all *instituteurs* (elementary school teachers) in the *écoles centrales*. From 1816, however, elementary teachers had to have a *brevet* qualification but the certificate in civic virtue was no longer required. Instead the model of the recently instituted Baccalauréat exam (1806) and the tenuous scholarship system set up by Napoleon in 1808 was increasingly to be the source of assumptions about what was to be taught and how it should be tested. In 1831 the demise of the *certificat d'instruction religieuse* marked a further stage in the changing content of schooling. Although pressure for this change came as much from anti-clericalism as from any explicit desire to 'modernize' schooling, the precise form of the emerging curriculum was as much a reflection of what was assessable as it was of what was relevant. Thus, assessment procedures have consistently been an important weapon in the state's struggle against clerical interests in education, since not only do they not easily lend themselves to reinforcing religious and affective aspects of the curriculum but also the very existence of coveted national certificates, over which the state has consistently held a monopoly, has forced church schools very largely to accept the state-determined curriculum.

Thus at the very earliest stages of mass educational provision, assessment procedures were already playing a highly significant part in introducing those features characteristic of schooling in an industrial society with which it is associated: the formal attestation of competence, and the replacement of the traditional, holistic concept of education as being concerned with both mind and character, with the more limited, predominantly academic, curriculum, which, being organized into subjects and levels, is amenable to formal written, and to a lesser extent oral, examination. Whereas in the late eighteenth century it was the non-cognitive criteria of character and virtue that were paramount in deciding who was fit to provide elementary education for the masses, by the early nineteenth century this emphasis had been replaced by a concern with cognitive competences as assessed in the *brevet*.

But these changes in the certification procedures for elementary school teachers did not simply reflect and reinforce changing notions of competence and the appropriate content of schooling; they also heralded a changing basis of social control. In the ideological battle between church and state, examinations were to prove a decisive weapon, not only in establishing academic rather than spiritual criteria as the paramount goal of education, but also in introducing control based on the idea of a qualification-based meritocracy rather than the ascriptive criteria of birth and breeding. One example of this process was the establishment of the Certificat d'Études Primaires as a national certificate in 1880. The London International Exhibition of 1862 convinced the French – as it had the English – of the need for new skills to be taught. It was also necessary at that time to find some means of retaining children in elementary school. Thus in 1867 the then Minister of Education, Duruy, established a primary leaving exam so that the lure of formal qualifications would meet both these needs. In so doing he also provided a significant stimulus to the idea of a qualification-based meritocracy.

For the elite, too, similar changes were taking place. The establishment of the Baccalauréat in 1806 meant that, as in England, what had formerly been primarily a residential and informal 'stage' of education for the elite became part of the bureaucratic structure of the Université which had been set up in 1808 by Napoleon as a national system of education embodying the principles of supreme central control and a state monopoly of instruction. The Maîtrise es Arts was now to mark a specific grade in the Université, regulated by an examination to be known as the Baccalauréat. As Frémy and Frémy (1978) suggest, the Baccalauréat examination which marked the first grade of the Napoleonic Université[1] was a direct legacy from the orders of chivalry of feudal times, when it marked the stage of apprenticeship before the attainment of a particular social role (Frey 1992).

> As in the middle ages, the whole of society was regulated on the basis of a feudal hierarchy, the idea for the young knight came to be applied more broadly to refer to all those about to start on a career. Monks who were not yet priests were called 'bacheliers' [bachelors!], a young unmarried man, an apprentice studying a craft and lastly a theologian or a student who had achieved the first grade of the university. The word 'bachelier' is now no longer used with this one exception.
>
> (Frémy and Frémy 1978)

This influence of feudal bases for social organization on the emerging structure of the exam-based qualifications which were to replace them in the new social order of an industrialized society is also manifest in the widespread use of the term *brevet* for lower and more applied qualifications. From 1816, prospective elementary school teachers had to sit for the *brevet* examination. The word *brevet* incorporates the same feudal idea of apprenticeship and the attestation of a particular level of competence. Traditionally the *brevet* was a royally given right to an apprenticeship embodying the kind of reciprocal contract idea which, interestingly, is currently being revived in contemporary assessment initiatives in other countries, such as the 'compacts' now established in Britain and the United States. 'An act, taken before a lawyer, by which an apprentice and a master made a mutual commitment, the apprentice to learn an art or a craft, the master to teach him, during a certain period of time and under certain agreed conditions' (Chervel 1874: 5). The ideology implicit in this choice of feudal terms to label the different rungs of the new educational hierarchy points to the way in which, during the nineteenth century, social status became increasingly bound up with educational qualifications for all but the very few remaining aristocrats whose status was still essentially of feudal origin.

In particular, in a century of social and political upheaval characterized by the growing power of the bourgeoisie, the anti-clerical movement and anti-monarchical republicanism, the Baccalauréat and, to a lesser extent, other forms of certification, played an increasingly crucial role as the arbiter of membership of the increasingly powerful bourgeois class – a new sort of elite whose status depended on academic qualifications, confirmed by attendance at the Université faculties and the more professional *grandes écoles* and military colleges.

As Vaughan and Archer (1971: 43) suggest, 'the role of the baccalauréat epitomised administrative control over the testing of merit and constituted a demarcation line between secondary and higher education. It also symbolised the social bias of the system towards the bourgeoisie.' The way in which formal qualifications continue to provide for the reproduction of the bourgeoisie has been analysed in detail by Bourdieu in terms of his concept of 'cultural capital'. Although many of the most prestigious schools in France are state rather than private, Bourdieu's work shows clearly how the internal processes of schooling, and particularly of selection, were increasingly oriented in favour of the reproduction of the elite rather than constituting a genuine meritocracy. The school system was designed to favour bourgeois 'cultural capital' and experience, so that as well as facing practical problems, such as forgoing badly needed income, the working-class child had to demonstrate a good deal more ability and tenacity to reach the same point in the education system as the child from a more favoured background. 'At every stage of their school careers the individuals who survive the system exhibit less and less the career characteristics which have eliminated the other members of the category' (Bourdieu and Passeron 1977: 82).[2] Although the French did not develop an elite, private school system equivalent to the English public schools, the success of different lycées in preparing students for the Baccalauréat and the entrance examinations for the *grandes écoles* continues to reinforce inequality in the system. Compère and Pralon-Julia (1990) provide ever more explicit testimony to this process in their unusual analysis of pupils' Latin exercises in the elite Collège Louis-le-Grand in 1720, where 'anyone who is anyone in France spent their early youth' according to a contemporary Archbishop of Paris, Christophe de Beaumont. As Caspard (1990) suggests, it is possible by means of these artifacts of teaching to trace the norms informing the curriculum: the criteria governing evaluation, indeed all the ingredients in the training of those destined to become the social elites.

The ideology of national homogeneity which was one of the first principles of Napoleon's Université meant also that the Université clung to the principle that all educated Frenchmen [*sic*] should share a common culture and was opposed to allowing pupils a choice of subjects (Anderson 1975). Attempts to introduce even a minimal degree of specialization between classics and science – for example, the creation of the Baccalauréat en Sciences in 1852 – largely failed. 'By 1912 the Baccalauréat had become the barrier which separated the bourgeoisie from the population as a whole, but it has also become the leveller which erased distinctions within that class' (Goblot 1967). It had also become of major importance both in influencing the way in which the centralized curriculum objectives were defined and in helping to make those objectives a reality in the schools.

Mass assessment and the institutionalization of competition

Gradually, however, as in England, the emphasis on examinations to provide for standardized curricula and the attestation of competence gave way during the nineteenth century to an increasing emphasis on their role in the regulation of competition for places within the new, more flexible, social order. With the expansion of educational provision in the twentieth century, it is arguably this role that now predominates. In France, by contrast, pressures for greater democracy and opportunity in educational provision have resulted in a radical restructuring of the traditionally highly selective and elitist educational system, the commitment to comprehensivization going far beyond the institution of a common school, as has largely been the case in England, to include significant changes in curriculum, internal school organization and, not least, assessment procedures.[3] Notable among these last was the virtual abolition until recently of all public examinations below the Baccalauréat level together with, officially at least, the regular promotion tests during the course of schooling and their replacement with continuous assessment by teachers. The Baccalauréat, too, while still a formal public examination, has been subject to major reorganization.

One of the most notable attempts at reforming French education in recent decades was that of René Haby in the mid-1970s when he was Minister of Education. With the explicit support of the Giscard Government, Haby's measures, in keeping with the prevailing educational ideology, were designed to make the education system more democratic and egalitarian and, less explicitly, to go some way towards reconciling this ideology with a modern economy's demand for differentially trained, vocationally oriented, school-leavers.

Previously, in direct contradiction with the strong nineteenth-century republican tradition of *égalité* the French education system had been dominated by selection hurdles: *compositions*, *devoirs 'mensuels surveillés'*, determining progress – or lack of it – from year to year and the phenomenon of *redoublement* or repeating the year; examinations for selection for various kinds of secondary schooling; and a range of formal, exam-based qualifications. During the 1960s this traditional pattern was overtaken, as in many other countries, by an apparently strong political commitment to egalitarianism which resulted in the institution of comprehensive schooling up to sixteen (*le collège*) and after 1986 with mixed-ability teaching in the first four years of secondary education.

The current goal – which represents a logical extension of these policies – is that, by the year 2000, 80 per cent of young people should be staying on at school up to the Baccalauréat stage. Such contemporary developments in curriculum and assessment, which we return to later in this chapter, are in response to the need for change which came about as a result of the pressures for greater opportunity and the disaffection caused by early failure in selection hurdles.

In common with many other countries, France is now seeking to face up to the challenge of providing education and training of an appropriate kind and level, which will ensure a sufficient pool of skilled labour to meet the needs of industry in the future. As well as the massive expansion of provision at all levels, this goal also requires a movement away from the celebrated homogeneity and central control of French education in favour of a measure of decentralization and institutional autonomy to allow for greater flexibility of response to the very different educational needs of students within the system. Current developments in the way in which educational assessment is used to regulate competition are readily understood in terms of the two main themes of, on the one hand, the need to make education more accessible to a wider range of students, and, on the other, the need to reassure the public that quality and national equality is being maintained as the accepted pattern of national direction, monitoring and control gives way to greater local variation.

Teacher assessment

Assessment of pupil learning in France has traditionally been frequent and formal. A recent survey by the National Inspectorate found that for formative assessment purposes the use of numerical marks is still totally dominant at every level, as is the use of written exercises for assessment, which take up, in the third and second classes (notional age 14–16), up to 20 per cent of the timetable (years 10 and 11 in England). In fact, such evaluation has, in practice, been largely summative, with students receiving a mark (*contrôle*) every fortnight or month, which goes into their cumulative record or *livret scolaire*. At the end of each term the *conseil de classe* meets to discuss each student's progress as the basis for a termly report (*bulletin*) and, at the relevant career points, to decide their *orientation* for the future. Although dialogue is increasingly being regarded as the keynote of student orientation such that the latter can become more continuous, educative and collaborative, its implementation in practice is slow. In addition to the usual barriers to change and the difficult challenge in the French context of achieving the necessary whole-school approach, Coqblin (1991) argues that this development is being hindered by the lack of a precise framework of achievement criteria. In the French context, the movement away from the language of marks in favour of the language of interpretation appears extremely subjective and open to differences in interpretation (Bottin 1991).

Apart from the lack of genuinely formative assessment and guidance, a consideration of the pattern of teacher assessment reveals two further issues of importance. The first concerns the predominance of numerical marks, despite widespread recognition that they are unconstructive and difficult to interpret (Bottin 1991) because of the lack of explicit objectives and criteria. The Inspection Générale de l'Education Nationale (IGEN) concludes that teachers need better tools if they are to get the maximum benefit from their assessment efforts and to be better able to tailor their teaching so that students understand the reasons for their success or failure. At present students tend to disregard the comments made by teachers about their work. To remedy this situation the inspectors recommend that there should be an improvement in the precision of assessment objectives, so that students, teachers and policy-makers can understand and use them, and an increase in the number and methods of assessment used.

Records of achievement in France: the *orientation* procedure

The second, less obvious set of issues concerning teacher assessment centre on the process of continuous guidance known as *orientation*, based on teachers' comments in the *livret scolaire*, which, as well as academic assessment, includes teachers' comments concerning application, discipline and the like. In the more highly selective parts of the French education system – the prestigious *lycées* and the preparatory classes for the highly selective *grandes écoles*, the dossier can play a role as important as the Baccalauréat in determining who 'fits' and who does not. This situation provides an important illustration of the tension between a system which has traditionally placed enormous emphasis on evaluation techniques that are as objective and impersonal as possible – as in the formal written examination (Dosnon 1991; IGEN 1991) – and one that places subtle but considerable emphasis on selecting as future members of the elite those students who demonstrate the right personal and social qualities.

The idea of *orientation* originally dates back to Jean Zay's plan in 1937, in which he appeased the powerful egalitarian interests which had been growing since the end of the First World War[4] by instituting experimental *classes d'orientation* in which pupils would be directed to 'classical', 'modern' and 'technical' streams in the first two years of secondary education, during which time they could be observed and re-directed as appropriate. As in England, the prevailing assumption at this time of fixed and innate capabilities provided a rationale for a continuing process of educational sorting while allowing the abolition of what was clearly a formally divisive system. It was not until the Fouchet reforms of 1959, however, that this idea was actually put into practice in the division, in 1963, of the junior secondary *collège* curriculum into an initial two-year *cycle d'observation* and a subsequent two-year *cycle d'orientation* (Pautler 1981). The emphasis in the reform on guidance rather than selection is well encapsulated in the following description:

> during the first cycle of secondary education, senior teachers and educational guidance specialists are required to take account of the pupils' abilities – to map out each pupil's academic career in the context of the class he attends, the whole group of classes existing at the same level, and the resources of the school, college district or educational adminstrative area.
>
> (OECD 1971: 41)

Since in practice pupils tended to continue in the stream (*filière*) in which they were initially put, this reform did little to increase opportunity or reduce disaffection in the lower streams. It only justified the vain attempt to make all three streams follow a common syllabus. In practice, 'C' stream pupils were so frequently required to repeat the year's work, they had little hope of ever 'catching up'.

Building on plans and consultations begun during the Pompidou presidency under Minister of Education Joseph Fontanet (Duclaud-Williams 1982), in 1975 Minister of Education René Haby proposed a much more subtle solution to the problem. Such streaming was to be replaced by mixed-ability classes pursuing a common core curriculum, with continuous, individual pupil orientation linked to the new structure of collaborative, democratic councils involving the whole range of participants in the educational process and, not least, pupils and parents. Thus part of Haby's reform included a proposal for *orientation* to be based on *group* recommendation, in which the vagaries of individual teachers (and hence the exposure of individual teachers to excessive pressures) would be guarded against by *orientation* based on the *conseil d'orientation*, which would discuss with the pupil and responsible personnel the recommendations of the *conseil des professeurs* (Premier Ministre, Service d'information et de diffusion 1977). This procedure required that throughout a pupil's school life vocational guidance is to be based on continuous observation by teachers, recorded in a cumulative dossier. Regular meetings were to be held between the teachers, a guidance counsellor (*conseiller d'orientation*), a school doctor, a psychologist and representatives of parents. Such meetings were to be held every year, with two major ones taking place at the end of the second and last years at *collège*, when decisions had to be made on the basis of the 'dossier' as to the type of studies the pupil would subsequently undertake.

Despite a rhetoric of partnership between home and school in the process of guidance, however, in reality it is teachers who play the determining role in pupil *orientation* through their classwork assessments and the recommendations of the *conseil de classe* and the powerful *conseil des professeurs*.[5] The *orientation* procedure was originally based on the premise that no educational path should represent failure, the paths being rather equal but different:

> What must be avoided above all is *orientation* by failure . . . No career should be seen as failure, but there are careers which correspond with diverse dispositions . . . moreover, orientation cannot be the product of the school alone. It must be the result of a collaboration between, first and foremost, the children concerned, the parents who are responsible for them, and the school.[6]

This procedure appeared to solve the dual problems of selection and the control of pupil and parental frustration at a time when public opinion was still strongly egalitarian and democratic, by instituting the idea of rational guided choice rather than selection. The reality, however, has been rather different. It is not simply that 'equal but different' is at best a naive hope, but more that this form of allocation to variable opportunities can provide for a much more pervasive and insidious form of social engineering and control than overt selection. If formal examinations are arbitrary and unreliable the results are at least open to debate, since all parties are aware that both pupil and examiner are bringing to bear their subjective personal perspectives. *Orientation*, however, is based on the idea of a norm. Berger (personal communication 1980) argues that the result is a measure of conformity to this norm as adjudicated by a corporate decision which, if it prevents the operation of individual prejudice, nevertheless disguises value judgement under a bland, objective, technocratic facade in which the individual is powerless to challenge the norm. Given the immense amount of evidence available of the bias, particularly class bias, inherent in teachers' assessment of their pupils, the *orientation* movement seems likely to provide a new and increasingly rigorous basis for the identification of an elite since, as the 1983 review of the *lycée* found, orientation towards vocational education was six times more frequent among the working class.

At the same time, it may be argued that the *orientation* procedure is also likely to ensure a relatively novel way of making central control a reality through the national provision of detailed curricular objectives which are thus translated into evaluation criteria. The coexistence of this trend with an already centralized system is doubly significant in the contemporary utilitarian climate, in that following the model of the *classes préparatoires*, tracks or orientations which correspond most to society's current economic needs can receive most emphasis; the number of places available in each type of course can thus be determined according to a *numerus clausus*, this restriction of opportunity being arguably a good deal more significant than the actual content of such courses. This is explicitly recognized in the 1983 Prost Report.

In the first place, the criteria chosen are uniform. Orientation rarely takes into account pupils' centres of interest and the diversity of their aptitudes. The two major criteria are their results in mathematics and their age (as we have already indicated). Second, *orientation* is frequently transformed into a procedure of practicality. Pupils must be divided up between the sections that exist, according to the space available in different establishments. This bureaucratic procedure, together with the rigidity of the learning programme, engenders in families a feeling of helplessness in the face of a blind technostructure. In the third place, it [*orientation*] constitutes a vast fragmented distillation which divides up pupils between streams which are strongly bounded and hierarchic as a function of dominant social models: supremacy of training in abstract science, less consideration for technical and professional training.[7]

Thus although 'the principle of *orientation* is at the heart of all the reforms of education carried out since 1959 by the Vth Republic' (Rothera 1968), and although left-dominated teachers' unions have officially been in favour of greater equality, particularly since the influx of young teachers after 1968, they fought strongly against the proposals (Stevens 1980), as they have against the similarly inspired institution of a common-core syllabus and mixed-ability classes.

Some of this hostility is simply resistance to the practical problems posed by the new procedures. Many teachers continue to resent the additional burden it places on them and their exposure to criticism as well as their almost total lack of preparation and training for this task.[8] Not surprisingly the result has been that many dossiers are not filled in with more than rudimentary information and the single *conseilleur d'orientation* in a college has neither the time nor the information to give a considered response to each child. The *orientation* is thus as often as not merely the recognition of a choice already made, often by default. Research by IGEN (1991) reveals that each pupil receives between 30 seconds and four minutes of consideration and that, of the total discussion, 50 per cent is devoted to giving general information about results, and 30 per cent is concerned with the behaviour and attitude to work of the students, meaning that less than 20 per cent of the discussion is devoted to considering how to help students make progress or to considering what would be the best *orientation* decision for each.

For many, it appears, not only is 'assessment' a finer means of judgement than exams, but that *orientation* is submitted to, not chosen. The individual is powerless to resist the identification which is the end product of a continuous and benign surveillance.

There is also a gap between law and reality over the notion of choice of educational paths since future orientation tends to be predicted by primary schooling, by social group and by teachers' decisions. In some rural areas too, organisational factors further limit the potential choice (Herzlich 1980). As the 1982 Le Grand 'Review of the Collège' put it, '*être orienté*' means to be put into a 'short' (i.e. less prestigious) cycle and a *lycée d'enseignement professionnel* for vocational training. It is rooted in failure rather than success and its image is of arbitrary manipulation.

Those who choose and are chosen to continue in the formal school system by entering the *classes de seconde* of a *lycée* are accompanied by their *dossier scolaire*, which continues to play an important role in determining the choice of Baccalauréat option available and, in many cases, eventual selection for a particular course of higher education. The Le Grand report therefore urged the introduction of a personal 'tutorial' system in the *collège* which could take over the existing guidance function of *orientation*, confining the latter to a single summative evaluation at the end of *troisième*, which would be a statement, in the form of a profile, of the objectives achieved by the pupil and would be the only point at which there would be a summative evaluation.

Although this proposal provoked considerable opposition among teachers in particular[9] and was not implemented, it provides an interesting illustration of the way in which some French educational thinking at least was moving in a very similar direction to that in England in the early 1980s, in giving increased emphasis to pastoral care and pupil–teacher dialogue in 'formative' evaluation, which would culminate at the point of school-leaving in a positive, summative 'profile' report offering a comprehensive statement of the pupil's school achievements. Continuous assessment in relation to detailed, nationally prescribed norms of performance is, nevertheless, now becoming the norm.

As can be seen Figures 6.1 and 6.2 provide extracts from a *livret scolaire* for nursery and primary school pupils which was designed by the Académie d'Aix-Marseille in response to a 1990 national decree. It embodies both a concern to provide a detailed record of progress for teachers and parents and the explicit translation into assessment procedures of national curriculum goals.

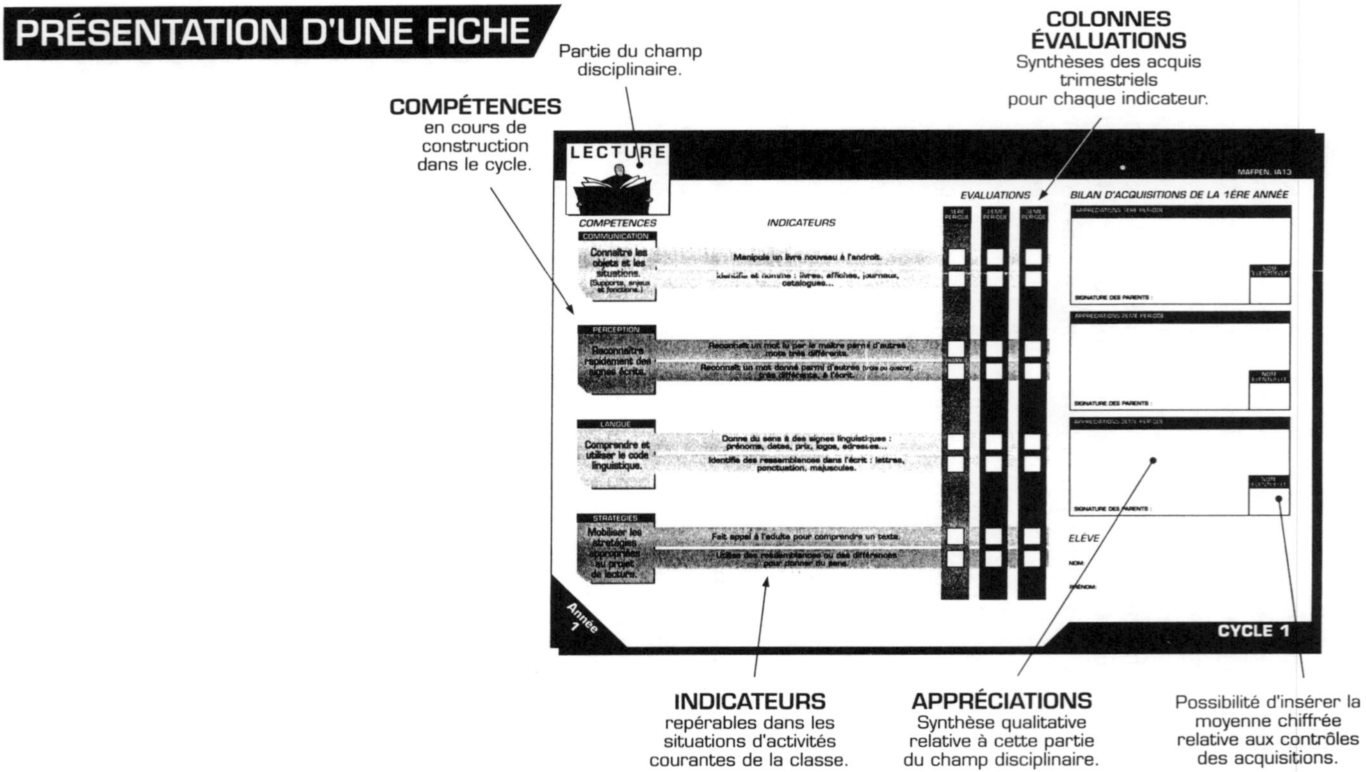

Figure 6.1 Extract from *livret scolaire* giving an explanation of the record's design and intentions.

Article 5 of Decree No. 90–788 dated 6.9.1990 relating to the organization and running of nursery and primary schools.

A *livret scolaire* is provided for each pupil. It comprises:

- the results of periodic evaluations designed by the teacher or by all the teachers of the 'key stage' (cycle) in a staff meeting;
- precise indicators of what the pupil has learned;
- the recommendations made by the teacher and the teachers of the 'key stage' meeting as a group about the period of time the pupil should spend in a 'cycle', about when a pupil should move from one 'cycle' to another, about the decision taken to keep a pupil for another year in the 'cycle' after the family has been consulted as required in article 4;
and
- it is regularly sent to parents who sign it;
- it serves as a form of communication between teachers as well as between teachers and parents;
- it goes with the pupil if they change schools.

Figure 6.2   Translated extract from the *livret scolaire* designed for the Académie d'Aix-Marseille MAFPEN Education Nationale giving the brief for the livret.

Thus the *livret scolaire* eliminates the potential injustices of the caprice of an individual teacher but is also, by the same token, an effective form of curriculum control for both teacher and pupil and is now becoming the norm. Moreover, it is also a means of making a practical reality of the tradition of imposing curricular and pedagogic norms, which was hitherto the responsibility of the inspector and thus represents a shift from 'process' to 'product' evaluation. The parallels here with both the system of continuous assessment on the basis of nationally prescribed criteria provided for in the 1988 Education Reform Act in England and the trend towards cumulative records of achievement is striking, and will be returned to in later chapters.

Thus, the assessment 'dossier' – the elaborate profile which follows a pupil throughout his or her school career – combined with a series of *orientation* decisions taken by a pupil's teachers in the periodic meetings of the *conseil de classe*, carries into the classroom the same assumptions of scientific rationality which characterize all aspects of a technicist approach to management. That is to say that the norms of performance chosen are taken to be in some sense absolute and given the pseudo-legitimacy of science and not the values of a particular group and time. As authority within the education system is thereby dispersed, control becomes a composite and increasingly impersonal phenomenon, impossible to pin down and hence to resist. If what is to be taught to whom, when, how and why can only be answered by reference to particular values, disguising such pedagogical and curricular decisions under the cloak of an apparently objective, scientific assessment is perhaps the most effective form of educational (and thus social?) control yet developed. This is because where traditionally assessment represented the personal and possibly arbitrary judgement of an individual based on the values of dominant social groups, it now tends to disguise both of these under an appearance of conformity with rational norms.

The *orientation* procedure arguably addresses several current assessment problems at once. First, it addresses the dimension of competition in providing a means of selection which minimizes potential opposition in appearing egalitarian, democratic and professional. Second, it provides for greater 'product evaluation' control of teachers by clearing away some of the traditional assessment bureaucracy and making teachers directly and visibly responsible for their actions. Third, it allows for a more technocratic, depersonalized approach to educational administration and more efficient 'process evaluation'. Fourth, it provides for the most effective sort of assessment control of teachers – a combination of 'process' and 'product' evaluation in which the central prescription of curriculum norms is linked to the formal processes of pupil assessment.

Public examinations

Le Diplôme National du Brevet

During the 1970s the long-established Brevet d'Études du Premier Cycle (BEPC), which marked the end of compulsory schooling, was transformed from a pass/fail selection device to a teacher-assessed award based on an average of class marks, and achieved by the majority of pupils (Dundas-Grant 1975). In 1980 the anachronistic BEPC was finally abolished. Several approaches to the certification of student achievement at the end of college have however been tried, including the Brevet des Collèges, which was an optional exam for those unhappy with the result of their continuous assessment. The relevant qualification currently is the Diplôme National du Brevet (DNB). With the goal of 80 per cent of students studying for the Baccalauréat, the DNB is not intended as a terminal assessment but a stage along the way. The DNB attests that the student has achieved a certain standard in his or her studies. It acts as a challenge to motivate some pupils and to give them their first experience of an exam. In the *collège* the result is based on an examination in French, maths, history and geography and on the results of continuous assessment. But while the locally set examination is rigorously standardized, there is little or no moderation of the continuous assessment awarded by the school, which tends to be over-generous in its marking. Even so, in many places the percentage of students achieving average marks is too low, so that the whole distribution is moderated up to ensure that 20 per cent of the candidates achieve an acceptable standard. This results in inequalities between different *départements* and penalization of the more rigorous, leading to widespread doubts about the value of the results (Caroff 1991).

Having taken the DNB at the end of troisième, students will continue towards the Baccalauréat Général or Technologique, which is the passport to higher education. Alternatively, they may continue in a professional *lycée* to undertake a two-year course culminating in a Certificate d'Aptitude Professionnel (CAP) or a Brevet d'Études Professionnelles (BEP). *Lycées professionelles* also offer the option of a Baccalauréat Professionel. This range of qualifications, many of which, like the Baccalauréat Technologique, are innovations, reflects the attempts that have been made in recent years to retain more young people for longer in the education system and to put more emphasis on the generation of high level vocational and technological skill. This commitment dates back explicitly to 1985, when Jean-Paul Chevenèment was Minister of Education. He published plans to reform the 'Bac' by increasing the percentage of an age group reaching 'Bac' level from 40 to 80 per cent over the following 15 years. The proposals also included the greater emphasis on scientific and technological specialization which is now being realized.

The Baccalauréat

The explicit policy commitment to wider, more vocationally oriented provision that has characterized French educational policy in the past two decades has resulted in major changes in both school and higher educational organization. The post-16 *lycées*, in which students study for the Baccalauréat examination, have been affected by the significant increase in the numbers of pupils now attending them. Given that the Baccalauréat exam still automatically provides the matriculation requirement for university entrance, universities too have been becoming increasingly overwhelmed with successful applications.

In 1900, for example, only 10 per cent of young French people obtained the Bac II or its equivalent – some 5,717 people. In 1976, by contrast, the number was between 35 and 40 per cent – 204,480 (Frémy and Frémy 1978). Numbers in higher education have increased proportionally. Where there were 20,000 students in higher education in the 1950s, in 1981 there were approximately one million.[10]

The increasing over-subscription to universities has mainly been controlled by selective examinations – notably the Propédetique at the end of the first year – during the higher education stage itself, and the creation of the now very popular Instituts Universitaires Techniques (IUT). Nevertheless, there is chronic overcrowding in the universities, prompting several desperate but ill-fated attempts by successive Ministers of Education to rectify the situation by providing for more general restrictions on entry. The public outcry and massive student demonstrations which followed higher education Minister Devaquet's attempt in 1986 to initiate such changes testify to the deeply rooted principle of the right to a university place for all Bac holders. The pressure for reform of the Baccalauréat has been building up in recent decades. There has been considerable government concern about the over-academic nature of many of the specialisms pursued and the over-recruitment to particular prestige subject areas such as maths, which in many cases have little to do with future career intentions. Associated with this has been increasing public concern over the declining market value of the Baccalauréat overall.

Recent attempts to reform the Baccalauréat examination to bring it more in line with the reality of mass secondary education date back to the Fouchet reforms of 1963, which attempted to break the hold of the university professors who had been given control of the Baccalauréat and, hence, considerable influence over the secondary school curriculum in the 1950s (Goblot 1967). Fouchet introduced a programme of 'modernization from above', in which an element of 'streaming' in secondary and higher education would differentiate between an upper stratum of modern professionals and a middle stratum of educated semi-professionals – the bulk of Baccalauréat holders. From this reform developed one of the most significant trends affecting the Baccalauréat in the past two decades – its increasing differentiation into subject specialisms of different status, referred to above.

To try to overcome this problem, in 1975 Minister Haby proposed as part of his reforms a scheme for postponing specialization in the Baccalauréat (Haby 1975). His idea was to return to the traditional model of a two-part Baccalauréat, the first, more general, part to be taken at the end of the second year in the *lycée* and the second part at the end of the third and final year, during which students would be more specialized, studying only four subjects, three in depth. The intention was to encourage higher education institutions to require passes in particular subjects and so to broaden the number of desirable Baccalauréat specialisms, emphasizing content rather than status in the subjects pursued as the important criterion for selection.

Although Haby himself was not able to introduce such a policy, the need for reform was such that 1981 saw some of Haby's ideas being implemented in the institution of a 'common core' in the first year of *lycée* study so that students could have a more broadly based course of study and keep their options open. Explicit efforts have been made to raise the status of technical studies in particular, first by the institution in 1966 of the Diplôme Universitaire de Technologie and, in 1971, of the Maîtrise de Science et de Technologie; and, in 1977, by opening access to the *grandes écoles* to holders of the Technical Baccalauréat (Pautler 1981).[11]

While these policies to 'vocationalize' the Baccalauréat bore some fruit, the more general problems brought about by the 'democratization' of upper secondary and higher education remain.

Thus, although the official standing of the Baccalauréat has not changed since the decree of 17 March 1808, which gave Baccalauréat holders the right of admission to higher education, in practice the possession of the certificate *per se* no longer guarantees the holder the free choice of subject specialism in higher education to which he or she is nominally still entitled. Apart from the fact that some universities and university institutes of technology have the right to dispense with the Baccalauréat entirely as an entrance qualification, increasing pressure of numbers has led many other *facultés* to discriminate more or less overtly on the basis of the Baccalauréat specialism pursued and the candidate's school record (Pautler 1981).

More important is the relative status ranking between subjects,[12] and, in particular, the prestige of option 'C' (mathematics and physical sciences) referred to above, the only specialization which still allows successful students access to the whole range of disciplines in higher education. Not surprisingly, there is still considerable competition within *lycées* to be allowed to take the Baccalauréat 'C' option, and many students will repeat a year in order to achieve this, particularly given the increasing tendency for universities to follow the *grandes écoles* and the IUTs in selecting on entry. Hitherto, the practice has been to allow open access and then to fail students either in the Propédetique examination at the end of the first year, or at the stage of the Diplôme d'Études Universitaires Générales (DEUG) after two years, which may be obtained by around 45 per cent of students. In some faculties, weeding out may be postponed until graduation stage itself. Universities have been increasingly losing status as a result of a growing increase in the number of unemployed graduates, since such unemployment is attributed to the universities not being sufficiently selective and not offering useful courses rather than to the state of the job market as a whole. These sorts of criticism have been a major cause of the increasing tendency to select students on entry rather than at graduation. In many popular faculties, such as medicine and pharmacy, the necessity for a *numerous clausus* policy has strengthened the faculties' hand in this respect. It is also clearly one of the reasons behind the re-establishment of central government control of the content and grading of national diplomas.

An important effect of this trend towards initial selection in all the prestigious branches of higher education has been to increase teachers' power in a number of ways. The decline in value of the Baccalauréat, which has been associated with its 'quantitative democratization' and 'qualitative differentiation' (Rothera 1968) has given teachers an increasingly important role in 'guiding' students into the different options. In addition, the devaluation of the Baccalauréat had led to an associated increase in the importance of the marks obtained in the last two years of upper secondary education and, in particular, the *dossier scolaire* based on the continuous assessment of teachers.

In the early 1980s there was growing pressure for the Baccalauréat to become an award based on continuous assessment. But the 1983 Prost Report on the *lycées* has stopped well short of abolition in its recommendations for Baccalauréat reform, suggesting instead a new, simpler organization for the exam, with largely local papers aimed at certifying 'a certain number of competences linked to *une caractéristique référential pour chaque type d'apprentissage* (p. 146), and based to a considerable extent on continuous assessment. This is the way, Prost suggested, of overcoming the well-known subject and geographical variations in the supposedly uniform Bac without provoking the hostility that would result from any attempt to remove one of the last bastions of tradition in French education.

Many teachers deplore the existence of crammers specializing in Baccalauréat preparation – *les boîtes à bachot* – and the associated practice of *bachotage*. They argue that pupils who have never faced a formal public examination before are subjected to enormous tension. Several teachers suggested in interview that the lack of marketability of the Baccalauréat often came as a surprise and consequent let-down to youngsters reaching this stage of their education (Broadfoot 1981a).

In contrast to England, where A level is still viewed as the unassailable 'gold standard' of the education system, it is widely recognized among policy-makers in France that the Baccalauréat needs changing (Ministère de l'Education Nationale 1991). It takes too long out of the school year and dominates the curriculum. There is still the problem of the arbitrary domination of maths and science specialisms. Regional variations in Baccalauréat standard since the responsibility for the Baccalauréat examination was entirely devolved to the Recteur d'Académie in 1966 have also fuelled calls for reform. Despite provision in each *académie* of a small permanent staff to run the Bac, the responsibility for setting and marking over a hundred different examination papers for more than a million candidates in a short time is proving an overwhelming task. Many senior educationists and administrators are in favour of the abolition of public examinations on the grounds of cost and teacher time alone (Ministère de l'Education). While the shortcomings of the over-crowded and impersonal *lycée* are overcome for those with the means to buy the provision of private tuition, the large number of families without such a recourse continue to fuel the pressure for teachers to update their teaching approach from lecturing to facilitating the learning of their students. Education Minister Lionel Jospin's April 1991 initiative 'for the reform of the *lycée* (Jospin 1991), which provided, among other things, for students to have three hours a week in their principal subjects for more individual work, including any particular help they may need, gave emphasis to the perceived need for students to become more active learners and, in consequence, for teachers to change their teaching approach.

Given the dominating influence of the Baccalauréat on the teaching style, subject matter and the kinds of learning outcome sought in the *lycées* and even, to an extent, in the *collèges*, the Ministry is seeking to introduce change via provision for continuous assessment – currently being used in both the 16-plus *brevet* and the more vocational Baccalauréat Professionel taught in the *lycées professionelles* (LEP). In these latter institutions, experimentation with the use of continuous assessment has been going on for 15 years. This has involved abandoning final examinations and marks and the introduction of teaching based on detailed course objectives, with evaluation checklists comprising detailed and precise criteria. Courses are modularized and there is some student self-assessment.

Teachers of the BEP and the CAP in the LEP complain that the continuing formality of their role and the return of the use of marks militates against the spirit of continuous assessment, and that the time needed for it is not recognized, so that there is now a decline in the use of continuous assessment. In relation to vocational training courses, 80 per cent of senior staff support continuous assessment as providing for more valid assessment and student-centred pedagogy as well as avoiding the end of year chaos. However, many teachers fear being vulnerable to outside pressures and being accused of favouritism. They also doubt the national value of a qualification in which teachers have a say in the result of their own students.

Given the very strong support among students, parents and teachers for the Baccalauréat as an anonymous, external examination and as a guarantee of equality against the influence of teachers' values and schools of different status, attempts at fundamental reform of the Bac continue to fail. The Baccalauréat is a *rite de passage* – any reform that does not maintain its ritual status appears devaluing.

Contemporary developments in French education concerning the assessment of individuals thus provide a very good example of the general trends identified in Chapter 3. The postponement of selection, the comprehensivization of assessment, the need to boost overall standards of achievement and the increasing delegation of responsibility to teachers are central themes at the present time. In Chapter 3 it was argued that the principal cause of such developments is changes in the social and economic context, which have given rise to the need for new legitimating ideologies that will justify selection and hence provide for both individual and systemic control. Thus, for the individual, the legitimating ideology of equality of opportunity and fair competition is being replaced by a new legitimating ideology of positive choice in which, rather than being competitors for selection, individuals are 'helped' to choose what the school decides is in their best interest. The difficulty of refuting such well-meaning advice in practice or of criticizing the assumptions on which it is founded makes this a very powerful basis for control. The second part of this chapter, which now follows, explores how this same ideology is currently replacing the more traditional bases of control at systemic level.

Assessment and system control: the French approach

Central control

From the earliest days of the nineteenth century, French educational provision was recognizably a system. In particular the early establishment of a range of national qualifications was significant in making a reality of one of the major principles of the Université: supreme central control. The decree of 1808 stated that no one could teach without a qualification from the Université or without being a member or graduate of one of its faculties. No other institution could deliver valid diplomas since '*diplômes reservées à l'État*' was one of the '*grands principes*' of French education.

Until well into this century, the Baccalauréat performed the dual functions of maintaining the social bias of the education system in favour of the bourgeoisie (Bourdieu and Passeron 1977) and of preserving the ideal of equality in education by subjecting all candidates to a common educational experience (Rothera 1968), a communality that was only made a reality in practice, given the size and complexity of the educational system, by the existence of national examinations, despite the provision of detailed curricular objectives (Fraser 1963; Anderson 1975).

Historically, despite radically different administrative traditions and associated ideologies, public examinations have played a surprisingly similar role in France and England as a means of ensuring a considerable degree of national homogeneity in educational standards and practice. In both countries, public examinations have been of central importance in legitimating the preeminent position of a liberal-classical, academic curriculum (Eggleston 1984), and in regulating access to different levels of employment.

In reality, of course, the schools were not the same either geographically or socially. Differences between one *lycée* and the next, and especially those *lycées* which had the best *classes préparatoires* for the post-Baccalauréat entrance exam for the *grandes écoles*, were marked. If 'monopoly was the first law of the system' (Crozier 1970), of its rhetoric and its organization, it cannot be taken from this that uniformity of practice ensued as a result or that where uniformity was apparent, this was its source. If there was 'a grotesque uniformity' (Aron 1969) this is more likely to have been the result of the common educational experience of teachers and administrators (Broadfoot and Osborn 1988; HMI 1989), the importance of which was clearly recognized by Napoleon in the emphasis he placed on teacher training. Second, the persistently marginal economic and social status of most teachers (except for some highly qualified *lycée professeurs*) was probably also an incentive for them to look to the state system as the basis of identity and support.

The more sensitive academic and professional commentaries recognize the illusion of centralization for what it is (Fraser 1963; Anderson 1975):

> The schools might once have been expected to study the same Latin passage at the same time, in every classroom throughout the country, but in practice there was infinite variation created by the eccentricities of the teachers and the pressures of local conditions. Centralisation gave them status; but human weakness made them what they were. No ministerial order could be enforced until it had travelled through the hierarchy; but officials, headmasters and teachers often hated, despised or feared each other, and these animosities stirred up resistance

which could completely transform the spirit in which the orders were applied.

(Zeldin 1973: 271)

The homogeneity inherent in the bureaucratic, financial and administrative *provision* of education could not, of itself, ensure an equivalent homogeneity of practice. The provision of detailed performance criteria of the expected outcomes of each stage of schooling, the close control of educational publishing (Becher and McLure 1978), the central provision of detailed timetables and syllabuses and manuals on pedagogy do not of themselves represent control. The system of inspection on which teachers' promotion depends provides a good example of the difference between theory and practice, since regardless of the assessment, all teachers will progress, more or less quickly, to the maximum salary point their qualifications allow, and only extreme *moral* corruption can overcome their security of employment as civil servants. The control exerted by an inspector who can only possibly visit once every three years and often even less frequently cannot be significant in practice. Hence Latourte could write in 1961, 'One is no longer in the country of Descartes, one is nearer to the pragmatism of the English.'

These arguments imply that central control in its pure sense is, and always has been, a logical impossibility given that the chain of command involves a whole series of personal interpretations, mediations, actions and relations that will 'flesh' the bones of the original order.

The *instructions ministerielles* give very precise suggestions on what and how to teach. In reality the true picture of teacher control is one in which teachers have far more autonomy over method than they do over content, in which they do not exercise all the freedom they potentially have but in which the extent to which they do depends on their ideology, their personality and their definition of the needs of the particular children in their care and their school situation (Broadfoot and Osborn 1987). Relatively few French teachers can even conceive of the possibility of no central syllabus, let alone seek it, and many feel that there is now too much curricular freedom.

The significance of the centralization of French education rests not in its effect on practice as such, but in the fact that an instrumental order which should in theory be highly responsive to policy decisions is constantly put at risk by the internal tensions so created. The necessity for practice to be directly responsive to both local and institutional needs and constraints conflicts with both the expressive and the instrumental ideology of bureaucratic standardization prevalent in society as a whole. Centralization in the French context may more realistically be taken as the point at which decisions are made – the formal accountability of the Minister of Education to Parliament for the functioning of the whole system (Halls 1976) – than as the degree of power any one such minister as the head of the hierarchy can effectively exercise (Duclaud-Williams 1980). The ambiguity here is partly a result of the imprecision of the term centralization, as discussed in Chapter 5, where it was argued that centralized organizational arrangements cannot necessarily be equated with strong control.

A related set of distinctions are those between 'decentralization', 'deconcentration' and 'democratization', where decentralization is defined as ceding a greater degree of decision-making autonomy to the lower rungs of the bureaucracy, deconcentration is defined as the provision of longer and more local 'arms' of the central bureaucracy and democratization is defined as the provision for more public knowledge, debate and influence at either local or national levels.

But, while there has been a quite deliberate policy of deconcentration in recent years – most notably in the attempt under the 1989 *Loi d'orientation* to make individual schools and headteachers assume greater responsibility for matching the delivery of education to local needs – such changes have not been enthusiastically embraced by the profession (Broadfoot *et al.* 1996). Resistance to assuming responsibility at school and classroom level for policy decisions traditionally taken by central government testifies to the fact that central control is realized as much by teachers' strong ideological commitment to it as by any formal mechanisms of external regulation (Archbald and Porter 1994).

At a deeper level, however, there is a sense in which policy initiatives in French education are always *à la marge*, for even if government can succeed in pushing through legislation 'without waiting for the necessary consensus to develop' (Weiler 1988) – which is necessarily rare given the strength, diversity and political nature of the national pressure groups which are themselves a product of centralization – they must still change the attitudes of the teaching profession. In this respect, France is very different from

England, where innovation has traditionally been based on the premise that teachers must be convinced since they cannot be coerced. Again, unlike in England, where the tradition of considerable local and institutional autonomy has, in the past, left considerable power and responsibility to senior management within the school, schools in France do not have such a well-developed structure of internal management.

Teacher accountability

Clearly the issue of central control and homogeneity of practice in French education is extremely complex, not to say confused. It is apparent that it can no longer be assumed, if it ever could, that every pupil in sixième will be studying the same page of the same text at the same hour. Indeed, in any country the classroom situation in which an individual teacher finds himself or herself will be determined by the interaction of a number of consistent factors. These are likely to include the age, ability, previous experience and expectations of the particular group of pupils concerned. Also relevant is the physical layout of the classroom, the available resources and equipment, and the size of the class. The time of day and the length of lessons are significant features, as is the extent to which the teacher is free to determine his or her own pedagogy and curriculum content. Teachers are likely to experience various forms of influence and control and impose on themselves various definitions of 'moral' accountability – from training received, from colleagues, from the management hierarchy in the school, from advisers and inspectors, from subject associations, from examination syllabuses, from national pronouncements on priorities and desirable practice and from the local community, notably school governors, where they exist, parents and employers.

This constellation of influences will not be the same for any two teachers anywhere, but clearly one of the main sources of the similarities that do exist is their common situation within a particular national education system. Thus, the way in which the provision of education is organized in France, including such things as school buildings and equipment, school curriculum provision, teacher training and community participation, influences how teachers see their role. To this long, but by no means exhaustive, list must be added the more amorphous but very powerful influence of ideology and national educational tradition, which has given rise in France, for example, to strong teacher support for centralized control as the basis for equality of opportunity, and in England, by contrast, to strong teacher support for grassroots autonomy in order for the maximum scope to be given to teachers' judgement. Thus, for French teachers, unlike their English counterparts, their civil servant status leads them to a perception of their professional accountability and their self-imposed control, as being to the national organization in the person of the inspector, rather than to the school as an institution, the head and colleagues, although in both countries a sense of moral accountability to pupils figures strongly. French teachers' criterion for such professional accountability is typically whether they have followed the centrally prescribed curriculum.

But systematic similarity in the objective conditions which surround teaching or the subjective perspectives which condition it may be swamped by variations in the personal characteristics of teachers in terms of, for example, career stage, age, sex, class background, geographical location, race or qualifications. It is quite possible to find nearly as much diversity between teachers *within* any one national education system as between teachers in different national education systems (Broadfoot and Osborn 1988).

The potential freedom available to the high-status *lycée* teacher with either Agrégation or Capès qualifications has always been potentially greater than that available to the more humble *instituteur*, whose work is closely supervised by the Inspecteurs Departementaux de L'Education Nationale (IDEN). On the other hand, since the learning of skills is gradually replaced by the learning of subject content as a pupil progresses through the school system, the *instituteur* has more pedagogic scope than her or his more senior colleagues. The recent restructuring of the teaching profession in France, which includes the redesignation of all teachers as *professeur*, seems unlikely, by itself, to lead to change in this respect (Bourdoncle 1994).

The extent to which any French teacher will seek to exploit the potential freedom, however, depends on personality and ideology. Many do not want to depart from the security of detailed prescription. Those that do so wish must bear in mind that their colleagues are also a source of professional judgement. Indeed, the continual process of review and guidance of each individual pupil's progress that the principle of *orientation* requires has made teachers more exposed to such collegial judgement. Parental pressure and the cost of frequent changes of textbook are other sources of constraint. For French teachers, as for many other national groups, it is their membership of the teaching community as a whole which constitutes one of the most significant sources of control through the perceived expectations of colleagues (Poppleton 1990).

As a profession French teachers' very considerable ability to defend themselves from all kinds of non-professional interference is rooted in the fact that it is the formalized, contemporary, secular expression of their clerical predecessors' right of immunity to canon law. Just as the church was accountable only to God, the teacher too is accountable only to the ministry. Although it has always been true in France, as elsewhere, that 'a school is judged by its exam results', individual teachers and schools who are assumed to be closely following central curriculum and pedagogic objectives are not held accountable for these results in the way that they would be in an education system where there is much greater statutory freedom for schools themselves to determine what and how to teach.

Modes of accountability

It is this context of centralized bureaucratic control and, perhaps more importantly, the ideology it reflects that supports the argument that in French education assessment control in the form of accountability has traditionally been more process-based. If in England evaluation is principally applied to learning activity and the individual pupil, in France it is applied to teaching activity and the system itself rather than indirectly through pupil assessment. If the idea of a national norm is typically alien to many countries with decentralized education systems, such as Denmark or the United States as well as England, the existence of such a national norm precludes the need for overt or formal accountability in the more romano-gallic centralized tradition of countries such as France, where it is the *manière* and the *matière* of teaching that is the principal unit of professional accountability, not the general outcomes of the school.

It is important to recognize, however, that the lack of any explicit accountability procedures is largely owing to the pervasive ideology which underpins the system rather than to any particular structural feature. 'Somehow or other, the education system has convinced the public and parents that they have not got a right to claim accountability from the system' (Le Grand 1980). Indeed, French educators would find considerable difficulty in identifying to whom they should give an account in a system preoccupied with standardizing inputs. The tradition of centralization has operated directly against even the *formulation* of this kind of grassroots or administrative pressure.

There has, in effect, long been a profound paradox within French educational provision and practice and its associated accountability procedures. A firm belief (not unaccompanied by frequent irritation with the inevitable 'red tape') in the necessity and the reality of centralization, to provide for pupils' geographical mobility, equality of provision and protection from local pressure, disguises what some at least see as 'a reality of idiosyncrasy as divergent as any in England' (Broadfoot 1981a).

This paradox is growing increasingly acute as the ideology of *la démocratisation* means that teachers with no preparation for the new demands being made on them, such as mixed-ability teaching or vocational training, find themselves increasingly torn between their theoretical belief in national equality of provision and the practical problems it brings in the classroom.

The contradictions of the teaching situation at the present time are indeed legion and centre particularly on issues of control and accountability. Teachers cling to the traditional protection of their direct relationship with the central or regional, and essentially impersonal, authority of the bureaucracy, against current moves to increase the power of the headteacher (traditionally minimal) (Holtom 1988) and parents. The demise of much of the structure of external assessment in favour of nationally imposed formative assessment (Gilles 1990) and *orientation* by teachers makes this vulnerability particularly acute at the present time. Although teachers may want to be free from the irritations of bureaucracy and to be free to respond pedagogically to the varying needs of particular groups of pupils, they do not want the responsibility for curricular decisions; nor do they want to lose that considerable freedom which was traditionally a feature of centralized control.

This is a particularly interesting paradox, since it is normally assumed in England that freedom and centralization are opposites, whereas, in both theory and practice, many French teachers see them as complementary. Centralization provides a support structure and a protection which, given the impossibility of close day-to-day supervision, leaves the individual teacher free from the sort of manifold public and professional pressures to which a teacher in a decentralized system is subject.

The particularly acute nature of the contemporary French educational crisis is more or less directly owing to the various contradictions inherent in central control. Although France is not alone in facing the educational problems caused by economic recession, falling rolls and public disillusionment, its curricular and organizational traditions have tended to inhibit attempts to make the system more responsive to changing national and individual needs. Teacher training, for example, has traditionally been and remains crucial in making a reality of centralization, since 'the subject programmes and their associated assessment determine the shape and content of the training programme' (HMI 1989: 10). 'French teachers', according to one recent critique written by a French *lycée* headmistress, 'are concerned only with academic achievement . . . they are unaware that knowledge alone is no longer enough to command the respect of a new generation of pupils' (Gentzbithel 1988). Because teachers are subjected to a common 'formation' experience, far from being prepared to adapt to change, training continues as one of the principal sources of stasis and homogeneity in French classroom practice. As one *inspecteur* put it: 'the system is involved with the reproduction of educational models which the present people in authority learned when they were kids.' It remains to be seen whether the recently initiated major reorganization of teacher training, which will give all teachers, regardless of level, a common university-based core course, will materially change this conservatism (Meirieu 1993; Judge *et al.* 1994). Teachers' reluctance or inability to change is further reinforced by equally reluctant public opinion and by the fact that, for political reasons, government can typically only depart marginally from the prevailing, tradition-based, practices (Weiler 1988).

Clearly, then, centralism remains directly and indirectly a barrier to change: directly in the inevitable inefficiencies of a huge bureaucracy which cannot easily provide the training and resources necessary to implement policy changes at the level of classroom practice; indirectly in the attitudes it encourages, in which defensiveness, passivity and traditionalism predominate over initiative and self-reliance. The foregoing analysis has suggested that recent attempts on the part of government to replace this extreme centralism with a system better geared to respond to the very significant changes currently taking place in the demands being made on the education system have so far had little real impact. Not only have they made little progress in relieving the tensions in the education system, they have at times 'fallen between two stools', arousing the hostility rather than the enthusiasm of the lower levels of the bureaucracy. The alternating and confused rhetoric of decentralization is a manifestation of the power struggles inherent in such a reform and a general lack of clarity of purpose.

At the heart of the problem in France is the reality that whereas from the time of Napoleon until recently a centralized system was able to provide the legitimating ideology of national efficiency, professionalism and democratic equality, the maintenance of these ideologies now requires practices which are divergent. The desire of central government to be able to direct educational activity towards more vocational and industrially oriented goals conflicts with the teaching profession's unpreparedness to respond to such new demands and, partly in consequence, teachers' demoralization and recourse to more traditional educational activities and the protection of their centrally based professional status. At the same time, French society as a whole has become increasingly sophisticated, diverse and politically aware and is no longer willing to tolerate the autocracy of either government or the teaching profession in deciding the nature or quality of its educational provision.

Democratization: the pressure for 'moral' accountability

Alongside the issues of decentralization and deconcentration of formal authority is another form of pressure for the devolution of a measure of educational control, which may be loosely subsumed within the term 'democratization'. This pressure reflects, on the one hand, a sense of frustration and powerlessness among parents in particular and, on the other, a desire on the part of both educational personnel and many pressure groups for a radical restructuring of educational provision to make it more accessible to the population as a whole, in terms of both availability and content.

The pressure for more lay participation in particular is associated with the more general climate of decentralization since formerly state schools could not readily have responded to parents' wishes even if they had wished to, having little autonomy of their own (Bligh 1982). In a highly centralized state, local issues and local politics have tended to be insignificant, their place being taken by national-level organizations of parents and other pressure groups (Broadfoot 1981a).[13]

By contrast, parents can make little impression at the local level. Despite their formal role in the *conseil d'etablissement*, given the control of teachers over pedagogy and the administration over finance, there is little real role for parents to play. Their part in the *conseil de classe*, which discusses the careers of individual pupils, may be overruled by the decisions of the *conseil des professeurs*.

Parents' traditional lack of interest in educational issues may be the result in part at least of their almost total powerlessness to influence teachers. Although parents are legally responsible for their children's behaviour at school (Broadfoot 1981a), teachers complain of the apathy of parents and their lack of respect. In general, a minority of parents ever consult teachers. Such involvement as there is is normally about questions of pupil progress rather than pedagogy – the jealously guarded professional preserve of teachers (Broadfoot *et al.* 1992).

The recent policy decision to encourage teachers to respond to perceived local needs in their teaching is now associated with the idea that if teachers are to have more autonomy, parents must have more choice too. Nothing could be more alien to the cherished ideal of national equality of provision in France. Pilot schemes for open enrolment are being tried in Paris and the publication of Bac results in the newspaper is seized upon by parents as a guide to school quality. Such developments towards the sort of educational 'market' of the kind currently being actively promoted in England illustrate the necessarily dynamic nature of educational control, which forces rival interests to group and re-group as central government loosens and tightens the reins of control in response to its own political situation and its need to legitimate and implement particular policies at any one time within the democratization which has been the defining rhetoric of French education in recent decades. Writing as early as 1967, Fraser was able to identify two stages in this process: first, the removal of barriers for the bright (the institution of a meritocracy); second, systemic change to provide for a mass improvement of standards. Most of the policy changes of the past decade may be interpreted as a response to this second element of the democratization agenda. However, there is currently a good deal of cynicism about whether there has been any real change in relative class differentials in educational outcomes, despite the creation of major new forms of provision and qualification.

Teachers appear to be conscious of a widening gulf between home and school, particularly with regard to working-class families, in which the reality of a school system designed for those inhabiting a very different social world can no longer be concealed beneath a traditional respect for learning and belief in equality. They argue that the reality of unemployment that has until recently been the prospect for many young school leavers, has only served to exacerbate an existing decline in family life and a rise in consumerism. This perspective, frequently voiced by teachers, is also expressed in a series of widely read books critiquing French education and French teachers, such as Hervé Hamon's *As Long as There Are Teachers* or Louis Legrand's earlier work, *Pour une politique démocratique de l'éducation* subtitled *Quinze ans d'innovations pédagogiques: le compte des illusions perdues*. As demographic, social and economic developments lead to new pupil problems, teacher morale declines.

Faced with the reality of continuing selection despite the persistent democratic rhetoric and a massive unease about how to cope with far-reaching organizational changes, teachers' unions have largely been hostile to recent reforms. As increasing demands are being made on teachers at all levels, with no real decrease in the frustrations emanating from bureaucratic control, teachers are facing an increasingly profound ideological crisis between a theoretical belief in egalitarianism and the practical problems it brings in the classroom. 'There is a gap between the political ideology of teachers and the constraints of the teaching situation which is huge in France, and they are, in a sense, contradictory' (Broadfoot 1981a).

There is, however, a more fundamental division between teachers and their political and administrative masters. What at first sight appears to be conservatism is, in the view of many teachers, their opposition to 'new industrialist' utilitarianism and their championship of traditional 'old humanist' values. As one *collège directeur* put it: 'we teachers are trying to form individuals, not technicians responding to the need to manufacture more cars, guns or whatever.' Thus teachers' traditional practice is being attacked from all sides from the ministry, which wants innovation, the parents, who want participation, and the pupils, who want relevance.

New management strategies

It is clear that at the present time there is something of a crisis in French education and that this is prompting fundamental change. At the root of the problem is the inability of the traditional basis for system control – central prescription and monitoring – to provide for a sufficient degree of flexibility and public acceptability in the rapidly changing social context in which it now operates. The knowledge explosion, the upsurge in democratic attitudes, employment protection, the power of the teacher unions and the sheer size of the operation have all in their own way helped to bring about this situation, and the need for normative rather than coercive control. Thus the place of overt control is increasingly being taken by a procedure more in keeping with the spirit of the age, namely corporate management, where this is taken to mean a technocratic, rational, problem-solving approach to planning and administration which effectively excludes explicit discussion of different policy options in terms of competing values.

The current popularity of 'administration and management' courses in many countries, including Britain, suggests that the reasons which underlie this development are not concerned solely with the idiosyncratic anachronisms of French educational administration, but reflect the common and more fundamental social changes currently affecting education. The growing scale of state activity and the availability of computer-based administrative systems are not in themselves adequate explanations for this development. More fundamental is the change in attitude it reflects, in which policy issues which are in essence political are redefined as managerial or technical problems to which the answer is simply a question of logical scientific enquiry or analysis. Given the deep crises of educational objectives which have been one of the main themes of this chapter, and the breakdown of traditional areas of consensus, a 'managerial' approach can help to disguise the strains caused by the existence of different ideologies, especially since the relationship between these different priorities and different kinds of educational practice is itself no longer clear.

The ramifications of this tendency extend into every aspect of the educational system, in that individual or group interests find it increasingly difficult to make themselves heard against the apparently impartial judgements of science. Teachers' explicitly normative stance can more easily be dismissed as sectarian, so that many professional issues can be taken out of such debate and redefined simply as technical questions.

It may be argued, then, that the effect of the deep ideological divisions between traditional and progressive elements within the education system is often, ironically enough, the provision of a major source of support for the technocrats. This is basically the problem of finding a sufficient degree of consensus over the criteria of professional accountability. As Neave (1981) suggests, the problem of accountability is at root a question of the legitimacy of the state and is thus subject to variation, as the role of the state is 'defined, confined and redefined – usually at times of conflict and legitimation'. In place of the egalitarian, centralist ideology, which has provided the legitimation for both professional accountability and ministerial activity from the earliest days of the Université until recently, have emerged the several different ideologies as separate entities – traditionalism, standards, democratization and administrative efficiency – which it once combined. As a result, policy-making and implementation become increasingly difficult and the technocratic basis for legitimation which takes issues out of the realm of values into that of mere pragmatism becomes correspondingly appealing.

It would be wrong, however, not to look for the roots of this movement in a much older tradition in French education. Ever since the *grandes écoles* were introduced during the Revolution, while the universities were closed, with the idea of providing for high-level, applied training for a specific number of specialist posts, this technocratic tradition has been identifiable. Government services have long been staffed by an elite corps of carefully selected professional administrators trained at the École Nationale d'Administration (ENA) or, within the Ministry of Education, graduates of the École Normale Supérieure. As specialists, the civil servants provide the administrative stability and continuity in contrast to the more frequent changes in political appointments. From this *culte d'administration,* this 'cleracy' of administrators comes a typically French tendency to create administrative structures even where these no longer serve any definite purpose (Smith 1980). But if 'planning and centralization are the udders of French education . . . they are dry' (Malan 1974), for, as has been suggested, traditional modes of administration are now inadequate to cope with the size and value diversity of the educational enterprise. Thus one stimulus to the institution of a more corporate management style is the need for a new legitimating ideology which can both conceal this value diversity and justify a more mechanistic approach to administration. Part of this ascendancy of a managerial approach in the Ministry is 'because education is only now becoming identified as a political phenomenon . . . there is less pedagogical and more managerial emphasis in the Ministry . . . its problems are becoming more technical' (Broadfoot 1981a).

Neave has suggested that it is significant that this more technocratic approach to educational management developed at precisely the time when education itself was becoming more problematic politically. A new, technocratic style of administration geared to producing greater efficiency began to develop in the early 1970s just at the time when education could no longer rely on the political support and hence the resources and popular support it had enjoyed in the previous decade. In this respect, the growth of technicist management strategies in France shares many points in common with similar developments taking place in England at the same time, reflecting an increasing, if still covert, concern with tightening the lines of bureaucratic accountability. In other aspects of the increasing rationalization of management, such as successive reorganizations of the Ministry of Education along more specialist lines, the tendency to reduce the amount of teacher participation in advisory bodies and the increasing number of inter-ministerial decisions, the trend may be traced back through the whole history of the Fifth Republic. Although education in both France and England has recently moved towards the centre of the policy stage again, this move has not been accompanied by a return of the public trust of previous decades. Rather a growing recognition of the key 'human capital' role of education in relation to the economy has tended to reinforce, rather than reduce, the search for more effective means of harnessing the education system in the pursuit of excellence and new areas of expertise.

Thus the activities of the Ministry of Education's division for evaluation and planning are becoming ever more high profile. Following a series of sample-based studies of national standards in a range of subjects during the 1970s, there is now mass testing of pupils on entry to each stage of schooling – junior school, lower secondary and upper secondary – which is designed to provide teachers with diagnostic information that they can use to provide more individually directed help for their pupils (Thélot 1992). The results of this testing are confidential to the school and the individual pupil's parents and, in contrast to the situation in most other countries where such mass testing takes place, there is no intention at present of using the results to provide for public, inter-school comparisons (Pluvinage 1992). More emphasis is being given to evaluating schools as a whole (Ballion *et al.* 1991). In 1992, for the first time, the Ministry published indicators of the way the system functions.

The public is provided with detailed statistical and graphic information concerning policies, costs and achievements, including international comparisons for the system as a whole and by sector. Although 'league tables' of *lycée* exam results are published annually in the national press, the search for a way of reporting school results in 'value added' terms is in stark contrast to the current English educational policy of reporting 'raw scores' on national tests. The avowed French rationale for its 'low stakes' approach is to educate public opinion better to appreciate how educational quality might properly be represented and thus to resist the growth of market forces in education. This contrast between France and England provides interesting testimony both to the common and pervasive pressures for explicit assessment information in both systems at the present time and to the very different ideological traditions, which affect the realization of such pressures in the assessment procedures to which they give rise.

Conclusion

Little has been said explicitly about assessment procedures in this second part of the chapter, which has been concerned rather with identifying some of the defining characteristics of French educational provision and how these national traditions influence the translation of changing social imperatives into educational practice. The purpose of this analysis, however, has been quite specific: namely to illuminate the part that evaluation procedures play in making the system as a whole responsive to the changing socio-economic context. It was argued in Chapter 4 that such evaluation procedures may be conceptualized in terms of accountability (i.e. control) relations, which in some countries emphasize the *post hoc* evaluation of educational *products*, and in others the *ante hoc* evaluation of educational *processes*. The foregoing analysis of the French situation provides a detailed substantiation of this argument, depicting as it does a country in which traditional modes of accountability emphasizing control of the educational *process* have become steadily more ineffective in the face of the system's increasing size and a growing diversity of social values.

In outlining some of the history of policy developments in French education, this chapter has attempted to show how such traditional modes of control are gradually being complemented by the institution of various product-based accountability procedures. Of particular significance in this respect has been the growing strength of a technicist orientation to educational provision, which both makes possible and legitimates an increasingly quantitative and impersonal, even mechanistic, approach to educational accountability based on performance indicators.

Thus France has been moving towards the traditional English reliance on the collection and dissemination of information about educational processes and outcomes to provide the criteria for the powerful normative control inherent in self-imposed professional accountability. As will be argued in Chapter 7, while England is seeking to strengthen central control of the education system by the establishment – in a number of different ways – of central norms of performance, France is translating its long-standing tradition of the central prescription of curricular objectives into similar norms of performance in which various newly instituted forms of evaluation and assessment provide for professional accountability. While it is the central identification of norms that is uncharacteristic in England, it is the emphasis on *evaluation* rather than prescription as the basis for control that is novel in France.

ASSESSMENT IN THE ENGLISH EDUCATION SYSTEM

Introduction

This chapter is concerned with the contemporary manifestations and the historical constants of the fundamental role played by various types of assessment procedure in informing the characteristic patterns of organization and practice in English educational provision. An analysis of recent policy debates and institutional practice in England provides a temporal cross-section of the changing pattern of checks and balances laid down by the constraining instrumental and expressive ideologies as they in turn reflect the dynamic social, economic and political context. Thus this chapter offers a second case study, the intention of which, like the preceding chapter, is to illuminate how assessment procedures relate to the critical characteristics of systemic functioning, rather than to attempt any comprehensive historical analysis of English educational provision *per se*.

It is part of the more general argument of this book that prevailing social pressures, both ideological and practical, may be analysed in terms of their manifestation in one of the defining characteristics of educational systems, namely assessment. The task of this chapter, as of Chapter 6, is the empirical substantiation of this general argument through an analysis of the way in which the constant requirements of educational systems are provided for in the idiosyncratic arrangements of a particular nation state at a particular time. In England this means identifying the more or less formal checks and balances which, following the model set out in Chapter 2, provide for the key functions of selection, certification and control in the context of an education system which traditionally has been at best decentralized, at worst anarchic. Pursuit of the themes of competence, competition, content and control – the last being applied to both individuals and the system as a whole – will describe the role assessment procedures played in weaving the diverse ideological and institutional developments that prompted an ever-increasing state commitment to educational provision into the coherent and remarkably uniform process it is in England today.

The first part of the chapter is concerned with the way in which assessment procedures have evolved to control competition between individuals. It considers the reasons for the rapid growth in public examinations in the late nineteenth century and the profound effect such examinations soon came to have on the provision and content of schooling. It traces the gradually changing emphasis from essentially criterion-referenced assessment procedures, which reflected a concern with the attestation of competence and, hence, with content validity, to that more characteristic concern in England with mainly norm-referenced assessment, which evolved as selection and its legitimation become the major task of public examinations. The ensuing struggle on the part of those who deplored the limiting curricular effects of such examinations, and others for whom such problems were insignificant compared to the need to open up access to such examinations to all pupils, are themes that are constant in the twentieth-century history of assessment procedures.

How such pressures were rationalized, first in the fortuitous, but quite fundamental, advent of intelligence testing and, more recently, when such tests have been to an extent discredited by the institution of more relevant, broadly based and continuous assessment, comprises a major part of the study. As such, the analysis illustrates one of the main ways in which the defining and constant characteristics of industrial societies – individualism, rational authority, bureaucracy, a division of labour, liberal democratic values and hidden forms of power – have been translated into, and hence provided for, in the provision of mass schooling within a particular society.

The second part of the chapter takes up the theme of control even more explicitly in addressing the more macro issues of systemic functioning and accountability. Drawing on the theoretical conceptualization of such control set out in Chapter 5, it looks at the way in which assessment procedures control the providers, as well as the consumers, of education and, hence, how the system as a whole is legitimated. Crucial to this case study is an explanation of how such control may be conveyed within what was, until recently, a very decentralized system. It is argued that the apparatus of public assessment procedures, which in its broadest sense provides the currency of accountability, structures the discourse of educational debate. Traditionally it was the case that self-imposed, professional values reflected the criteria of successful performance embodied in assessment procedures. More recently, that right to define such criteria has been claimed by the government, which has operationalized the currency of assessment through the imposition of an educational market. It is these informal, covert, but highly influential, relationships which provide the key to an understanding of control in the English educational system before the more explicit and controversial overt measures of central control brought in with the 1988 Education Reform Act.

The context for growth: the pre-history of educational assessment in England

Pre-nineteenth-century England was an essentially static society. Social, occupational and personal roles were bound up together and determined very largely by birth. For most people schooling was irrelevant to the process of occupational selection but was important in providing (for those who had any at all) differential socialization experiences which served as a preparation for the very different future lifestyles of the various social strata. As a result, assessment, if it existed at all, was essentially a formality.

Yet by 1772 in Cambridge University this picture had already begun to change. As Hoskins (1979) suggests, little did the Cambridge University examiner, William Farish, know the momentous significance of his suggestion in 1772 that numerical *marks* be given for *each question* in the Tripos examination, instead of, as hitherto, an overall ranking of the candidate's work as a whole. Not only was the Cambridge example soon copied by Oxford University, which in 1800 also instituted written examinations as a means of identifying the ability and rewarding the attainment of students (Lawson and Silver 1973), but from this and other apparently insignificant innovations emerged a whole new apparatus of judgement in which, as set out in Chapter 4, the relatively anonymous individual of traditional society becomes subject to a qualitatively new form of control in the modern world. This control is based on twin techniques of 'hierarchical observation', in which evaluation is a constant presence, and 'normalizing judgement', in which categorization according to a 'norm' is increasingly evident (Foucault 1977).

> Written performance and written records . . . make it possible to generate a 'history' of each student and also to classify students en masse into categories . . . This new form of power locates each of us in a place in society . . . Because it is a technique of knowledge we overlook the fact that it is simultaneously a technique of power.
>
> (Hoskins 1979: 137)

Central to this process is educational assessment, which takes a particular kind of intellectual product as the basis not only for a complex division of labour, but also for a whole range of social and political positions (Broadfoot 1981b).

Thus, soon after the beginnings of the nineteenth century, the essentially traditional picture began to change. The pressure for change in England was expressed in a rising moral and political concern among philanthropists at this time for social order and justice. There was widespread concern both to find a means of stemming the lawlessness which was widespread in the new industrial cities and to equip workers by means of education to respond to the new demands of the burgeoning industrial capitalist economy. But it was the availability of new techniques of individual judgement which led to these demands being very soon reflected in the development of assessment procedures as tools by which schooling might be made responsive to the needs of the economy.

The economic expansion of Victorian England was utilitarian and informed by an essentially pragmatic philosophy based on faith in science and individual responsibility. Such rationalism also began to inform social organizations. Many of the more cohesive professions began to feel the need to rationalize their organization and to define a specific level of competence for which visible testimony could be produced. Living in an increasingly competitive society, they were not slow to recognize the value that would accrue to individual practitioners through the creation of a monopoly over a particular profession, the entry to which was controlled according to fairly rigid standards of professional competence. Thus, from the early nineteenth century onwards, doctors, solicitors, accountants and many other similar professionals could only be registered if successful in professional examinations.[1]

This growing concern with the attestation of competence was also reflected in the provision of schooling. In 1868 the Taunton Commission advocated a system of centrally appointed inspectors to see that standards were being maintained in elementary schools and called for a central council to administer a system of examinations which would not be competitive but would rather, like the current programme of National Assessments, provide a fair test of average work (Montgomery 1965).

Although the first HMI inspectors were appointed in 1840, the recommendation for a central council to control school examinations was not fulfilled until 1917, with the establishment of the Secondary School Examinations Council (SSEC), but even then it was the universities that continued to exercise the principal control in practice.[2] It was in keeping with the *ad hoc*, pragmatic spirit of English educational provision that examinations to control the flood of new aspirants (Roach 1971) were initially the spontaneous creation of the universities. The first stage of this provision involved a system of 'locals' in which a respected outsider – often a fellow of an Oxford or Cambridge college or a local clergyman – was commissioned to evaluate the education being provided by a school and the level of standards being attained. But as Mortimore and Mortimore (1984) suggest, such 'moderation' was expensive and somewhat haphazard, since many schools, including those most needing inspection, chose not to invite external assessment.[3]

Before long, yet another significant innovation took place, which moved the assessment focus away from the quality of school provision and towards assessing the achievement of individual pupils. The 1857 'Exeter Experiment', in which *competitive* examinations were organized for pupils from local schools in the South West, heralded a whole new dimension in the nature of schooling. Thus, following the 1850 Oxford and Cambridge Royal Commission, in 1857 and 1858 respectively these universities also set up school examination boards to organize a new form of 'locals', which would provide the necessary link with the increasing number of middle-class schools and hence with the new industrial and professional sections of society. The slightly later advent of the issue of certificates in 1877 represented yet another stage in this process, in further depersonalizing and hence apparently rationalizing the process of selection.[4]

The fact that the universities were so quick to follow the example set by the professions in instituting formal entrance examinations meant that very soon schools could not resist the backwash effect. Thus the mid-nineteenth century saw a gradual change not only in the mechanisms of assessment, but also in the content of schooling itself as it reflected changing educational aims: 'the age of school examinations controlled by university boards had begun' (Lawton 1980).

The institutionalization of mass assessment: the effect on curriculum content

In England the elite public schools of the nineteenth century continued to emphasize social training as much as academic prowess for the future leaders of the Empire, whose elite status was so firmly ascribed that they could continue for a time to hold themselves aloof from the growing competition for educational qualifications.[5] It was the rapidly expanding grammar school sector in which were to be found the aspirants to the newly created clerical, scientific and managerial jobs, which were increasingly oriented to the burgeoning industry of competitive examinations. The rapid growth of examinations at this time may be indicated by the massive increase in the numbers of those taking the Department of Science and Art examinations, which grew from a modest 5,466 in 1865 to 202,868 in 1895, and included as many candidates from mechanics' institutes and other similar institutions as from schools. Indeed, many Victorians saw success in examinations as a guarantee not only of knowledge, but also of those qualities so necessary in middle-rank occupations: common sense and diligence (Roach 1971).

But very quickly after the institution of university-regulated school examinations in the 1850s, the development of 18-plus and girls' examinations by Cambridge University in 1869 and the City and Guild's examinations in practical subjects in 1880,[6] a practice which had initially been adopted as essentially a means of quality control began to exercise an undesirable effect on the curriculum.[7]

Concern about the effects this proliferation of examinations was having even at the higher elementary school level led the Board of Education, which had been set up in 1899 and included among its functions the running of non-elementary schools, to publish a report of its consultative committee in 1911, which urged instead of examinations for school-leavers the use of a more appropriate school record and closer liaison with employers. This attempt was unsuccessful, as have been most other attempts to encourage a more relevant and vocational emphasis in assessment since that time in England and in other countries. The status of formal academic examinations was already firmly established.

Thus, 1917 saw the formal legitimation of academic school examinations in what was to prove the momentous move of establishing a national qualification – the School Certificate. The new examination was a grouped certificate requiring passes in five or more academic subjects drawn from each of four groups of English, languages, science and mathematics, with music and manual subjects a fifth optional group. Thus the new certificate established incontrovertibly the primacy of academic subjects and formal written assessments, relegating the aesthetic, practical and non-cognitive aspects of schooling to the relatively low status which still endures today. It is significant that, although the Secondary Schools Examination Council was set up at this time to advise the Board about maintaining standards, thereby ensuring some degree of state control over the content of education, even at this relatively early stage of 'secondary' education the universities were recognized as the appropriate bodies to conduct secondary school examinations. It was nearly a century later, in the 1990s, that this assumption came to be seriously challenged by much tighter government control of syllabuses and examining procedures. University responsibility for school examinations constituted implicit support for the emphasis in such examinations to be on intellectual attainment and academic subjects.[8] It is hardly surprising that the traditional pinnacles of the education system should be given the task of determining the structure of the newly emerging school curricula and hence the evolving new mechanisms of social selection. Nor is it surprising that these were determined in a way that mirrored the culture of what had long been the preserve of the upper classes, such that the education system, though it was changing, still strongly supported those traditional interests.

For the population as a whole, especially the aspiring middle classes, the route to success now lay almost exclusively via examinations, either in winning one of the increasing number of free-place scholarships to the grammar school or, once there, in doing well in Lower and Higher School Certificate. As a result, argues Dore (1976: 15), 'the social definition of the purpose of schooling changed and with it the motivation of students and the quality of learning.'

One aspect of this change in the 'quality of learning' concerns the kinds of competency rewarded by examinations. The consultative committee report of 1911, in discussing the effects of examinations upon pupils, pointed out that examinations place a premium on the reproduction of knowledge, passivity of mind and a competitive or even mercenary spirit and, by contrast, do not encourage independent judgement, creative thinking, true learning and criticism. Such criticisms of examinations have been consistently made ever since, reaching a new stridency at the present time as it becomes increasingly apparent that it is these very skills which industry in its current state of development most needs.

There are links here with the importance of assessment as a means of social control, because the encouragement of passivity and acceptance of prevailing knowledge, values and standards, and the restriction of entry to elite positions to those willing to conform to such definitions, are vital aspects of the process of social reproduction. Arguably it was not an accident that this kind of learning came to be emphasized in schools, given the Victorian belief that education should not encourage people to question their station in life or the standards laid down by their betters, but should rather serve to induce a greater degree of orderliness, morality and diligence. This straitjacket was very conveniently provided by the form and content that came to characterize school examinations and to this day restricts the acquisition of school qualifications to those willing and able to accept the values of the school and to reproduce existing forms of knowledge.

The rapidly expanding economy of early nineteenth-century England not only depended on the discovery of new techniques and the creation of new markets; it also required a new type of worker who was prepared to sell his or her labour in return for money. The decline of the family as an economic unit of production and the concomitant rise of individualism, which the process of industrialization had brought about, coincided with the need in the economy for a new class of more scientifically educated managers. Thus schools were increasingly looked to as providers of individuals with the requisite knowledge and skills (Musgrave 1968).

So rapidly did the emphasis on educational qualifications for entry to occupations grow, at the expense of the more traditional methods, that it was not very long before the pressure on entry to many of the professions made selection imperative and gave schools a new role in preparing and adjudicating between candidates for an increasing variety of occupational roles. The result was that schools at all levels – elementary, grammar and public – began to place a growing emphasis on competition.

The institutionalization of educational competition

A significant example of the trend towards a merit and achievement ethos at this time was the Northcote–Trevelyan reform of the Civil Service, which led to the institution in 1855 of examinations for entry into the Home and Indian Civil Service after the model of those of ancient China (Broadfoot 1995), a model which was soon emulated in the entry for training in the armed services at Sandhurst and Woolwich. These examinations were significant not only as *qualifying* examinations but particularly for their emphasis on *selection*. In many ways they marked the translation of the very explicit capitalist belief, current then as now, in raising standards of production by competition to a similar philosophy for education (Lawson and Silver 1973). The increasing use of examinations to determine the awarding of scholarships and the allocation of vocational opportunity represents not only the origins of 'criterion-referenced' assessment – the measurement of specific competencies – but also the origins of 'norm-referenced' assessment – the comparison of the performances of candidates to produce a rank order. It was not long before the use of examinations to determine competence paled into comparative insignificance beside their use in selection.

During the nineteenth century, the almost total gulf between elementary and other forms of schooling and the perpetuation of the traditional attitude of accepting as given one's social level were enough to prevent a significant pressure for more open access to educational opportunity. The creation of the School Boards in 1902, and with it the significant expansion of the scholarship system, was both a reflection of and a contribution to the widespread emergence of a concern for greater opportunity to compete – a pressure which, as in France, the social upheavals of the First World War greatly increased.

This development is well illustrated in the use of examinations to determine the allocation of scholarships in the late nineteenth and early twentieth centuries.

Scholarship examinations

After the Education Act of 1870, the Endowed Schools Commission was responsible for selecting children from public elementary schools for secondary school scholarships. The scholarship route was greatly expanded after the 1902 creation of local authority secondary schools and the Free Place Regulations of 1907, which required grant-aided secondary schools to offer a quarter of their places to elementary school pupils (Sutherland, G. 1977). But what had initially been intended as a device for the attestation of competence – a qualifying test – was almost immediately translated into an intensely competitive examination.[9] Thus the qualifying examination instituted in 1907 to ensure that the introduction of free places 'shall not have the effect of lowering the standard of education provided by the school',[10] by 1936 had become formally recognized as a selection device, in which 'The purpose of the examination is the selection . . . of children fit to profit by secondary education . . . The main business is to get the right children.'[11]

Concern with quality control was thus relatively unimportant when compared with the need to identify and foster talent from all levels of society (i.e. selection) and the associated, if unarticulated, need to legitimate the status quo by providing a measure of

opportunity for all. It was particularly important that such opportunities should be allocated by apparently objective, scientific
means, so that those not chosen accepted their own unworthiness as
the reason.

This change in emphasis from the use of assessment procedures in
the attestation of competence to their use in the regulation and
control of popular aspiration may be traced through both the major
educational selection devices that were widely used in the early
twentieth century: intelligence testing and school certificate examinations.

Intelligence testing

Intelligence testing became of enormous significance in providing an
acceptable means of rationing grammar school scholarships and,
after 1944, grammar school places. The work of Galton, and
Spearman, Burt and Thompson (Sharp 1984) could not have been
more timely. The interrelation of cause and effect in the growth of
intelligence testing will probably never be known, or whether it was
just its timeliness that led so quickly to such testing being fundamentally incorporated into educational thinking. The power of
intelligence testing as a potential policy tool is underlined by a
number of historical studies of the advent of intelligence testing on a
large scale in England (Simon 1953; Sutherland and Thom 1983;
Sharp 1984), lending support to the work of American revisionist
historians (e.g. Karier 1973; Kamin 1974), which suggests that
psychologists were powerless to influence the way in which their
work was used to inform policy. Although a combination of local
and national pressures determined when, and in what way, each
local authority resorted to the use of intelligence and other kinds of
standardized tests, 'It was the conviction that children can and
should be classified at an early age, according to inborn intellectual
differences that underlay the entire remodelling of the school system
at this time' (Rubenstein and Simon 1969). From the Hadow Report
(1926) onwards, when the setting up of a system of separate schools
to provide post-elementary 'secondary' education for all was first
mooted, the use of tests for the necessary 'differentiation' was never
in doubt.

During the next decade the 'intelligence' testing movement grew rapidly. Thus by 1938 the Spens Report, in recommending a tripartite secondary school system, could say with conviction that, 'with few exceptions', it is possible at a very early age to predict with some degree of accuracy 'the ultimate level of a child's intellectual powers'. As a result, the few dissident voices, which included the Trades Union Congress (TUC) and the teachers' unions, as well as academic psychologists such as Godfrey Thompson, who argued for a common (if internally divided) multilateral secondary school, were drowned by the prevailing consensus in favour of separate schools designed to cater for children with different types of ability and inclination. This consensus informed the Norwood Report of 1943 and the Butler Education Act of 1944, which enshrined the principle of education according to age, aptitude and ability and led in England, in common with many other European countries, to the establishment of the 'equal but different' secondary 'grammar', 'technical' and 'modern' schools that between them would provide for the new commitment to mass secondary education. Although some argue that this Act did not create the 11-plus as such, since in many cases it merely rationalized existing practice (Sutherland and Thom 1983), Sharp questions this. He suggests that the development of intelligence testing was itself central to the way in which mass secondary provision came to be provided for in the 1944 and 1945 Acts, in that, without it, the idea of selection according to innate ability, which could be seen to be growing steadily in earlier government reports, such as those of Hadow and Spens, could not have been justified or even conceived. Intelligence testing was critical as a legitimating ideology. (See also Torrance (1981), which identifies Cyril Butt's contributions to these influential reports.)

Thus it is now largely taken for granted by both experts and the general public that it is both necessary and desirable for teachers and external examiners (but seldom the pupils themselves) to grade pupils according to certain kinds of performance (usually academic) in particular groupings of knowledge (some of higher status than others), usually in some kind of rank order, and on that basis to select some for opportunities leading to prestigious positions and usually high material rewards, and to reject others (i.e. the majority) for occupational roles of little reward and influence.

Certainly the idea of innate, measurable intelligence played a central role in the development of educational policy concerned with expanding provision in the early twentieth century, the notion of pupils' different attributes not only justifying, but apparently making desirable for all concerned, a situation in which 'selection by differentiation takes the place of selection by elimination' (Hadow 1926, quoted by Rubenstein and Simon 1969), although the result has continued to be in practice largely the same, given the differential status of the schools in question.

It was not the test themselves that were critical, *but the ideas on which they were based* and their scientific quality, which together provided for the administrative and pedagogic rationalizations necessary for mass educational provision, notably the hierarchical authority and normalizing judgement discussed in more detail in earlier chapters.[12]

Nor was the influence of the concept of differentiated and fixed innate ability confined to the provision of three distinct types of secondary education. The 11-plus examination, which included tests of English and maths as well as of intelligence, just as formerly the scholarship examinations for entry into grammar school had done, was in fact only an arbitrary cut-off point in a much longer process of categorization and channelling, which became increasingly the norm in both primary and secondary schools. Many of those who rejected the idea of differentiated secondary schools on the grounds of their being socially divisive accepted the need for differentiation within them – and still do. This view was supported by the continuing influence of the child-centred movement, which was informing both a philosophy and a psychology of education emphasizing the importance of responding to the differing needs and interests of individual children.

As early as 1926, after the publication of the Hadow Report, a great deal of effort was put into providing both senior and junior schools in which there could be three or more parallel classes to provide suitable learning environments for children of differing 'ability'. After 1944, 'streaming' in the primary school was common from the age of seven onwards, to give 'bright' children the maximum chance of developing their abilities and passing the 11-plus. The constraining effects of the 11-plus examination on the work of the primary school were to figure prominently in the movement for its abolition during the next decades. This movement eventually achieved success with the widespread introduction of comprehensive secondary schools during the 1960s and 1970s, which freed most primary schools from the constraints of the

11-plus. Arguably it is this same freedom from the constraints of external assessment that lies behind a good deal of recent popular concern about 'falling standards' and the pressure that has led towards the institution of new mechanisms to monitor and control standards in the National Curriculum and Assessment provision of the 1988 Education Reform Act.

Even the new secondary modern schools, which after 1944 were catering for perhaps 75 per cent of each year group, soon took to streaming, so that the more highly achieving pupils might have some chance of transferring to the grammar school or, later, of GCE success. The result, especially when compounded by the effects of the competition for external examination certificates, was effectively to preclude any independent ethos of curriculum and evaluation developing in the secondary modern school. However, the provision for even a very small number of secondary modern pupils to transfer to grammar schools to sit for external certificates (still only one in eight were sitting for GCE by 1960) allowed the belief in the system's capacity to identify and respond to ability at evey level to persist. It encouraged confidence that the educational system was genuinely meritocratic, in that, for those few pupils who as late developers or for some other idiosyncratic reason had not demonstrated their ability early on in their school careers, the door to opportunity was never shut.[13]

During the 1950s the concept of 'intelligence' as fixed and inherited gradually became untenable, as a result of a series of research studies (e.g. Halsey and Gardner 1953; Simon 1953; Yates and Pidgeon 1957) which showed among other things the social class and environmental influences on 'intelligence', and that the IQ of pupils selected for grammar schools improved, while that of their counterparts in secondary modern schools deteriorated.

Such studies did little to attack the idea that it was possible to measure 'intelligence' objectively, however, but rather fuelled the fires of those who believed that 'intelligence' was determined by environment rather than heredity and that some pupils were being prevented from developing their full potential by various kinds of disadvantages in their home background, such as coming from a large family or having parents with low aspirations (Douglas 1964).

The result was, on the one hand, pressure towards 'compensatory' education which found its major expression in the Plowden Report's (1967) recommendations for the establishment of Educational

Priority Areas. Schools in these 'deprived' areas would receive additional funding to help them overcome their pupils' background disadvantages. On the other hand, there was a parallel pressure against selection for secondary schools, which could no longer be justified on the assumption of fixed and differing levels of intelligence. An NFER study in 1957 (Vernon 1957), for example, showed that 122 pupils out of every thousand had been wrongly assessed in the 11-plus. Thus the pressure for a common non-selective secondary school that would allow much more flexible provision for different abilities and interests – a pressure which had been eclipsed by the rival ideology of selection in the 1940s – became increasingly intense until it was finally incorporated as government policy, in the commitment to comprehensive schools expressed in Government Circular 10/65 of 1965.

It seems probable that even without the specific development of intelligence tests to justify different kinds of secondary provision, the deeply entrenched class divisions of English society would have ensured a longer struggle to introduce comprehensive secondary schools than in some other countries, such as the United States, Japan and Sweden, or even the closely related Scottish system. However, the progressive 'cooling out' and 'guidance' process (see Chapter 6 for a description of France in this respect), which has tended to replace the 'one-off' selection hurdle, is arguably a reflection of the delicate balance between the need for the powerful legitimation of impersonal, carefully controlled assessment procedures at key points of selection – which was formerly in England at 11-plus but is now arguably at 18-plus – and the replacement of such formal assessment mechanisms by the subtle, pervasive surveillance of continuous assessment at those stages of education which no longer involve critical points of competition. This is because in this latter case the assessment priority shifts from that of legitimation – rendering the assessment judgement acceptable – to that of sustaining motivation for those lower achievers who are now obliged to stay in education for longer and longer periods of time, while still providing for a more covert form of selection via different orientations.

The demise of formal 11-plus selection in favour of comprehensive secondary schooling must thus be seen as a change prompted by the need for more publicly acceptable selection procedures in keeping with the growing strength of egalitarian and democratic educational ideologies. The balance at any one time between selection based on traditional examinations, selection based on standardized tests and guidance based on teacher assessment may thus be interpreted as a reflection of prevailing expressive ideologies rather than as any real change in the basis of that selection.

School Certificate examinations

Meanwhile, higher up the school system, the increasingly important role of educational selection was being reflected in, and in turn reinforced by, a growing pressure for educational qualifications. Such was the emphasis on competition rather than competence that the content of assessment often came to have little to do with the nature of the activity for which it was acting as a filter. School examinations, in particular, were prone to this lack of content validity, especially after the institution in 1917 by the Board of Education of the School Certificate, which put an end to school examinations linked to particular professions and replaced them with a standard school-leaving and university entrance qualification. School Certificate examinations and those that replaced them have continued to be used as a selection mechanism for employment, even though much of their content bears little relation to the competencies needed for the job in question. Research has shown in some cases a low or even negative correlation between school examinations and subsequent vocational training or job performance (for example, Williams and Boreham 1972; SCRE 1976).

Despite these limitations, the convenience and communality of school examinations meant that by 1922 and the establishment of the Higher School Certificate, a rationalized system of competitive, norm-referenced school examinations was firmly established. It must be pointed out, however, that these examinations still combined a large measure of attestation with competition, in that with the huge gulfs between the elementary, grammar and public schools, the crucial determining point for career chances was still gaining entry to the grammar school or, even better, via the largely nominal Common Entrance examination, to a public school. (The institution of this latter examination is another telling example of how prevalent the emphasis on overtly *educational* competition had become, even if much more important selection devices, such as family connections or wealth, were still decisive covertly.)

However, after 1944 and the provision of 'secondary education for all', public examinations became much more accessible. Despite a series of research studies building on Hartog and Rhodes's famous 1935 study of the unreliability of examinations and despite a series of attempts to introduce more school-based reporting of achievement in place of examinations – notably by the 1943 Norwood Committee, the 1947 Report of the Secondary Schools Examination Council and Circular 205 in 1949 – the demand for public examinations appeared insatiable, leading to the introduction of the General Certificate of Education, Ordinary and Advanced levels, in 1951.

This new, non-grouped certificate had the apparent advantages not only of allowing more flexibility in the curriculum, but also of giving a greater proportion of pupils some hope of success in at least one subject. It also had the advantage of allowing secondary modern pupils to compete and still, because of its higher standard than the old School Certificate, effectively preventing open competition. Thus on the one hand it created ostensibly greater opportunity, in allowing more pupils to achieve external certification, and, in so doing, kept motivation and conformity to the system high – as demonstrated by the ever-increasing number of entries. But it also allowed a more finely divisive ranking of achievement, in terms of the number and status of subjects passed as well as the grades achieved in each.

It is arguable that the finer differentiation and greater specialization provided for by the new examinations, while apparently better serving the economy in its increasing need for different kinds of expertise, created a 'division of labour' among pupils which had important repercussions for social reproduction. In particular it allowed a situation of 'divide and rule' – a fragmentation which prevented the formation of united, self-conscious disaffected groups in the education system[14] and it allowed the elite to reproduce itself by identifying the more abstract and esoteric subjects which formed part of their traditional culture as 'hardest' and thus of the highest status academically.[15] This central role of external examinations in determining career opportunities made it impossible for the secondary modern schools to remain uninvolved in the competition, so that their organization and curriculum reflected ever more closely those of the grammar school. As a result, the secondary modern school could scarcely avoid regarding itself as second best, with the pupils regarding themselves as failures for not having passed the 11-plus, even though the policy of giving the maximum number of pupils at least the chance to compete in the system was strongly endorsed by most liberal educational reformists at the time.

The grip of the liberal ideal of opportunity of the education system had become so strong that, despite these problems, demand for the *extension*, rather than the *abolition*, of the public examination system multiplied during the 1950s. The Beloe Committee, set up in 1958 to investigate the possibility of such an extension, reported in 1960 in favour of a new Certificate of Secondary Education (CSE), once it saw that the extension of the public examination system was inevitable. The CSE instituted in 1965 was designed to provide the goal of a pass in at least one subject for about 60 per cent of the year group, the top grade of the CSE being equivalent to an O level pass.

Thus, once again, the public examination system was redesigned to prevent too great a build-up of frustration, which might threaten the meritocratic system. The provision of an educational goal designed – as in the case of the O level – to be achieved by only some 20 per cent of a year group was already an anachronism in 1944. The creation of the CSE allowed far more, if not all, pupils to participate in the race without any serious threat to the reproduction mechanisms of the system.[16]

Changes in assessment procedures since 1965

While it remains generally true that industrial societies still look at the education system to provide the basis for occupational selection, England has clung more tenaciously than many other countries to more traditional institutional forms for such selection, notably public examinations, as the basis for certification. Indeed, the recent history of assessment practices in England testifies to the tensions the increasingly incompatible demands being made on public examinations are producing (Broadfoot 1986). While public examinations are still a key part of the apparatus of systemic control and the maintenance of standards, many people feel they do not emphasize the needs of industry and the economy for a suitably skilled and socialized workforce. Nor do they provide adequate motivation, and hence control, for the significant numbers of pupils who cannot look forward to success. Because of the role examinations have tradition-ally played in providing public evidence of curriculum control in England, standardized, so-called objective, tests, such as the Scholas-tic Aptitude Test (SAT) in the United States, have made little impact beyond the level of selection for secondary schooling.

After the creation of the CSE in 1965, the search for reform was based upon the need for a rationalization of the existing system – the provision of more relevant information for employers and the search for an assessment goal which would be within the grasp of, and thus motivating for, all pupils. The two decades that followed the institution of the CSE in 1965 saw four significant policy develop-ments as part of this search: the pursuit of a common system of examining at 16-plus; the rise of teacher assessment; a series of attempts at broadening and vocationalizing post-16 qualifications; and, perhaps most important of all, the 'profiles' movement. Each of these trends echoes a more general international trend, as discussed in Chapter 3. Together they reflect new expressions of the use of assessment procedures to influence content, regulate competition, attest to competence and control frustration.

While the recommendations of the Beloe Committee, which resulted in the institution of the CSE, disappointed many education-ists in neither abolishing public examinations nor including the whole population in their scope, the CSE was radically different from the traditional GCE in at least two important respects. First, unlike the mainly university-run GCE boards, the CSE boards were regionally based and explicity designed to be teacher-dominated, so that they were sensitive to, and able to respond to, local needs. One result of this regional autonomy was enormous divergence between the different boards in examination procedure. The potential for such divergence had been considerably increased by the provision in the Beloe Committee's recommendation of three different modes of CSE examination: Mode I, an external examination based on a syllabus drawn up by a regional board; Mode II, an external examination based on the school's own syllabus; and Mode III, a school-based syllabus internally assessed.

While the CSE boards varied in their support for Mode III examining, the CSE was highly significant in allowing teachers a much greater role than hitherto in external certification. At the same time, however, it was a reactionary step, for in appeasing the pressing demands for public certification among the hitherto disenfranchised 'middle 40 per cent' – the top secondary modern pupils – it postponed the necessity to face up to the provision of a truly comprehensive certification procedure for at least twenty years. The CSE also presented an administrative and curricular problem for schools in deciding which pupils to enter for GCE O level and which for CSE, given that the latter was an explicitly inferior qualification and also lacked the credibility of tradition. Not surprisingly, therefore, the CSE examinations had hardly begun before attempts were being made to devise a common system of examining at 16-plus.

A common system of examining at 16-plus

The Schools Council presented its proposals for a new 16-plus in 1971 (Schools Council 1971), and in 1974 trial examinations were taken by nearly 70,000 candidates, with a target date for introduction of 1980. It was recognised that a common examination *per se* was unlikely to be able to discriminate adequately across the ability range concerned, so that a common *system* of examining rather than a single exam might be more appropriate (Tattersall 1982). Although reaction to the feasibility studies was mixed (Schools Council 1973), by 1976 the Schools Council nevertheless felt able to recommend 'a joint 16-plus' to the Secretary of State for Education. However the reaction of the Secretary of State, Shirley Williams, was to initiate still further study by setting up yet another committee. In 1978 the Waddell Committee reported that a single system of examining at 16-plus based on a seven-point grading scale and tied in to existing GCE and CSE grades was feasible. Notable in the proposals was the recommendation that the new examination be run by three or four regional consortia combining both GCE and CSE boards and the proposal for national criteria on subject titles and syllabuses.

It is these two aspects of the Waddell Committee proposals, rather than the 16-plus examination itself, which have proved of major significance, since they have allowed the Department of Education and Science (DES; later the Department for Education or DFE and now the DFEE) to legitimate a much greater involvement on the part of central government in the whole public examination process in recent years. Given the key role such examinations play in curriculum control, this represented a significant increase in central government's ability to influence the educational system more generally.

Despite the endorsement of many of the Waddell Committee's proposals by the 1978 White Paper, *A Single System of Examining at 16+*, even provisional commitment to a new 16-plus examination was not forthcoming until February 1980, and the advent of a Conservative Secretary of State. It was Sir Keith Joseph who, in 1984, finally gave the go-ahead for the new GCSE examination to be launched, with the first candidates to be examined in 1988. Unlike the GCE examinations, for which the DES laid down only a framework, the GCSE was tightly controlled from the centre. In most subjects there was a detailed and restrictive framework, setting out a common core for each subject, detailed assessment objectives and methods, specified weighting in the marking schemes and compulsory assessment by teachers of coursework. The CSE also tried to prepare grade-related criteria for each of the main examination subjects. So, as the prospectus for the new examination sets out, the new common system of examining at 16-plus was not just a unification of the old GCE and CSE. Rather, it reflected the new priorities in public examinations, which were set out by the secretary of state in a much publicized speech in Sheffield at the North of England Conference in January 1984. In this speech, Sir Keith Joseph identified the need for a more criterion-referenced approach to certification in order both to provide information on what candidates could actually do and to raise overall standards by improving motivation.

The history of attempts to reform public examinations since the early 1960s is revealing of many characteristic features of English educational provision. The apparently widespread desire for a more relevant and broadly based curriculum was in practice never strong enough to defeat the vested interests of tradition and the market. The Schools Council, nominally charged with the responsibility for such development, proved largely impotent to influence policy-making in practice, and ironically its ultimate demise in 1982 was largely legitimated by this very failure to influence the course of events. Clear demonstration of the increasingly arbitrary exercise of power by successive Secretaries of State for Education, which was reflected in their riding roughshod over the combined weight of professional opinion, was provided when Sir Keith Joseph rejected the proposed criteria for the GCSE physics exam, although these had the support of teachers' unions, the Association for Science Education, the Institute of Physics, the CBI and HMI (Mortimore and Mortimore 1984). The drastic reduction of the course-work element for many GCSE courses which was announced in 1992 on the government's instructions, against the combined opposition of teachers, parents and employers, provides another, more recent illustration.

Perhaps most important of all in the history of recent attempts at exam reform in England is the amazing intensity of debate over the details of a procedure which most equivalent countries have already abandoned (see Chapter 3). Indeed, Nuttall (1984: 143) argues that the GCSE, even when it was first introduced, was already 'divisive, bureaucratic, retrogressive and obsolescent'. It is divisive, he suggests, because in many subjects there are different papers for children of different attainments. It is bureaucratic because all syllabuses must comply with detailed national criteria. It is retrogressive because it has led to the curriculum becoming more 'monolithic, more subject-based and more traditional in its specification under GCSE than it was capable of being under O-level and CSE' (Nuttall 1984: 147). It is obsolescent because it is 'increasingly irrelevant given the changing structure of education and training and the fact that few young people now enter the labour market directly at 16+' (Nuttall 1984: 147).

Thus it would appear that it is changes in the procedures and content of the GCSE, rather than its organization, which have been of critical policy significance. As Nuttall suggests, 'It is the first time . . . in the history of English education since the war that such detail has been specified by government of the objectives of learning, the content and the types of assessment device that had to be used for all courses of study in twenty of the major subjects of the curriculum' (Nuttall 1984: 144).

Examinations post-16

The recent history of other attempts at public examination reform in England tells a similar story. Another major strand of examination reform since the 1960s has been the search for a means of broadening the sixth-form curriculum by the provision of some kind of two-stage examination in place of GCE A level. Thus in its Working

Papers 5 and 13, the Schools Council set out proposals for a new 'modular' sixth-form course based on a typical pattern of two 'major' and four 'minor' subjects. The far-sighted proposal for a modular sixth-form course based on 'Q' (qualifying) and 'F' (further) examinations[17] was defeated by the Governing Council of the Schools Council in July 1970. The vested interests of the GCE boards, who feared the demise of A level, of the universities, who feared a dilution of standards, and of the teachers' unions, many of whose members feared the constraining effect on the curriculum of an extra level of examinations, combined to defeat the proposal.

The 'Q' and 'F' proposals re-emerged in a modified form in 1973[18] as 'N' and 'F' levels, in which 'F' would be further study in two of the five subjects taken at 'N' level. But, after four years of feasibility studies, this proposal was also defeated, again largely because the universities were unwilling to countenance any lessening in sixth-form specialization. What this opposition in effect amounted to was an unwillingness on the part of the intellectual elite to accept any erosion of the 'collection code' (Bernstein 1982), which underpins the existing university structure and thus their own status. In this they were, not surprisingly, supported by the GCE boards. The result, reinforced by the advent of the 1979 Conservative Government, was to exacerbate the division between the 'old' and the 'new' sixth, with the former continuing to take A levels and the existence of the latter leading to the continuing search for an alternative qualification.

In 1976 the Schools Council recommended the establishment of the Certificate of Extended Education (CEE) – a new one-year, five-subject course for those who had obtained CSE grades 2–4. In 1977, the Schools Council put forward proposals for yet another examination – the Intermediate or 'I' level – designed to broaden the traditional sixth-form curriculum by being equivalent to about half an A level course. While in its 1980 Green Paper *Examinations 16–18: a Consultative Paper* the government expressed some limited support for this proposal as a complement to the traditional two or three A level course, later introducing in 1984 the 'AS' level with this intention, it rejected a CEE modelled on such traditional lines. It has also steadfastly resisted any attempt to change the character of A level despite strong support for a more broadly-based course more in line with continental practice which was advocated by the Higginson Committee in 1989.

In 1982 the government published its proposals for a Certificate of Pre-Vocational Education (CPVE), to be run by a consortium of further education, GCE and CSE boards and local authority associations, who would between them provide comprehensive assessment of a wide range of courses and so provide a means of linking the bewildering array of different courses available in further education and schools.[19] As many people had predicted, this examination became more and more the preserve of the further education Business and Technical Educational Council and the City and Guilds Examining Boards.

From its inception, the CPVE was characterized by several novel features which distinguished it from conventional school examinations and marked it out as more explicitly vocational in orientation. For example, it was a unitary qualification that could not be taken as a series of individual courses; it contained a strong emphasis on profile assessment in relation to specified targets; and work experience constituted an important element. CPVE courses were often characterized by collaborative pedagogies and negotiated curricula, in which students were regarded much more as responsible, active learners than would typically be the case in more conventional courses. Many of these characteristics are also to be found in the new General National Vocational Qualification (GNVQ) courses, which replaced the CPVE.

Records of achievement

Another strand in recent assessment policy in England that is also associated with the 'new vocationalism' is the move to institute records of achievement for all pupils.

A common system for examination at 16-plus and a new, more vocationally oriented 17-plus examination reflect deep contradictions in educational priorities and are, therefore, highly controversial policy initiatives. However, records of achievement and profiles have enjoyed almost universal support. The reasons for this are quite clear cut. On the one hand, they have the support of those who advocate justice for pupils who are disenfranchised by the examination system. On the other hand, they are seen as a means of meeting the needs of employers for more relevant information on what school-leavers can and cannot do, and thus of helping young people to get jobs. Despite the heterogeneity of the large number of independent developments and initiatives which took place in the late 1970s and 1980s (Broadfoot 1986), most records include detailed information on a pupil's progress over several years in all areas of school or college life, compiled by both pupil and teachers. Normally, these formative records culminate in some type of summative report. Typically, they include information on basic skills, subject achievement and personal qualities, and a statement of other activities in which the pupil has participated. However, the scope of records varies enormously.

The degree of variation in profiling practice reflects the traditionally decentralized approach to policy-making in England, in which each school or local authority has been encouraged to pursue its own initiatives. Lacking even the degree of communality that central legitimation and wide geographic spread gave to the activities of the GCE and CSE examination boards, in the early years profile development proceeded in a similar way to curriculum development in the 1960s; that is, through dissemination based on a small number of highly influential models. So powerful had the movement become by the late 1970s, however, that in the early 1980s the Schools Council, many local authorities and the examination boards established their own research and development groups. Both the education and the employment arms of the government – were active in this respect. Initiatives such as the Youth Training Scheme (YTS), the Technical and Vocational Education Initiative (TVEI) and the DES Low Achievers Project (LAP) used profiling, as did several of the further education examination boards, notably the City and Guilds of London Institute (CGLI) and the Royal Society of Arts (RSA) in their pre-vocational foundation systems. In 1984 the DES committed £10 million, under the rate support grant, to development work on local authority pilot schemes that might provide the basis for a national proforma. After the 1984 policy statement on records of achievement, it was explicit DES policy for all school-leavers to receive such a record. The government also commissioned a national evaluation, the results of which were available to the government in 1988. This provided much of the evidential basis for the Records of Achievement National Steering Committee (RANSC) policy recommendations, most of which were not implemented.

Apart from the momentous impact of the provisions of the 1988 Education Act, we may also trace other reasons for a growing government coolness towards records of achievement. Partly as a result of the increasing institutionalization of records of achievement and profiling within formal assessment, the hitherto relatively uncontroversial status of such records began to change. Not only was there deep concern about teachers having the necessary skills and time to undertake this additional commitment, but, as the main source of development initiatives shifted to the larger-scale activities of examination boards and local authorities, such records began to be seen as an *alternative* to traditional examinations. Certainly, many records of achievement incorporate results of traditional examinations, graded tests and a profile assessment in one certificate, thus giving the latter two components a status nominally equal to that of the GCSE.

Potentially even more significant is the shift in the focus of concern from the provision of a *summative* record of achievement, with which the movement started, towards the *formative* process of recording, in which students reflect on their own academic and personal development. However, many problems were attached to the introduction of records of achievement. Some teachers found difficulty in allowing pupils to set their own criteria of development. This is, after all, quite contradictory to the traditional rhetoric of schooling. Furthermore, in exposing a much greater part of their personality to a continuous, pervasive and, above all, benign assessment process, students themselves, as well as the content of their curriculum, may become subject to much greater control in the future.

Thus, although a National Record of Achievement was finally launched in 1991 as a joint initiative on the part of the Department for Education and the Department of Employment the emphasis in this record is once again summative, as a mechanism for recording and communicating achievements through both school and working life. Significant as this is as an innovation which promotes the notion of life-long learning and a continuous process of target-setting and achievement, the introduction of a radically new assessment culture, which the advent of records of achievement promised, has now been considerably hindered by the imposition of a national assessment framework, based on a very different, and much more traditional, approach to assessment. The novel assessment language that the thinking behind records of achievement helped to develop emphasizes the use of assessment as a way of helping students to become more effective, confident and motivated learners, through involving them in every stage of the planning, execution, assessment and reporting of the learning process. The introduction of 'high-stakes' national testing based on formal, timed, impersonal assessments represents a direct attack on the use of assessment to *promote* learning.

Graded tests

An important parallel development was of 'graded tests' based on the attainment of specified levels of skill, as, for example, in the Associated Board of the Royal Schools of Music examinations. Pursuing the typical emphasis in profiles upon positive, personal assessment, graded tests were designed to increase motivation and attainment by the provision of short-term mastery objectives. Despite many practical problems, the initiative had considerable success (Pennycuick and Murphy 1988), not least in providing one of the key informing principles of the National Curriculum which followed.

The concerns originally voiced about the implications of graded tests for the organization of schooling (e.g. Mortimore 1983) now have much greater pertinence in relation to the National Curriculum. If curriculum organization is truly to reflect the individual needs of each pupil (Mortimore 1983), does this mean replacing age-based classes with mixed age teaching groups? While this idea has considerable theoretical appeal and appears to work well in hierarchical subjects such as maths and modern languages, it also results in much tighter curriculum control at every level of schooling in which such levels operate and a much greater emphasis on formal testing than at the present time. While there may be advantages to such staged assessments in terms of pupil motivation, the idea of pupils learning along a narrow path defined by a whole series of assessment hurdles once again evokes the Foucaultian concept of the norm. In a very real sense, despite their apparent psychological advantages, such curriculum and assessment packages are fundamentally a *source of control*, legitimating even narrower bounds to the content of schooling than exist at present. We shall return to an analysis of National Assessment in this respect later in the chapter.

English institutional tradition largely restricts such innovation to 'the back door', since the need for radically new forms of assessment as a basis for the attestation of competence and the regulation of competition conflicts with the key role *external examinations* have traditionally played in providing for *system* control. The comparison with France is particularly helpful here, since, in France, the traditional dependence on a rather different basis for *system* control has meant that competence, competition and individual control requirements have received priority in recent educational policy-making. In the place of a plethora of local initiatives has been a centrally designed and nationally imposed 'orientation' procedure, the spirit of which – as is apparent from Chapter 6 – is in some ways similar to the English profiles movement.

Thus under the continuing and pronounced national differences in assessment practice, it is possible to identify in both France and England at the present time a common pressure towards a quite different set of assessment procedures, in which the overt and explicit sorting of examination-based selection, like the overt categorization of subjects under the 'collection code', is being replaced by the covert 'channelling' of continuous, detailed and pervasive assessment. As Bernstein (1977) has suggested, this form of evaluation, along with other aspects of 'invisible pedagogy' such as integrated curricula and progressive pedagogy, provides for an altogether new form of social control based on 'mechanical soli-darity' (see Chapter 4). The replacement of 'sudden death' assess-ment by benign and positive guidance is producing a form of control that is very much more difficult for the individual to resist and of which he or she may not even be aware. Although important in providing a goal for all pupils – thereby reducing frustration and promoting social control – such procedures also allow a much wider application of norms than hitherto, in which it is not just the individual's intellectual activity that is subject to 'hierarchical authority and normalizing judgement' but, as in the elementary schools of the nineteenth century, the whole person (Broadfoot 1990).

Ranson (1984) has extended this argument to suggest that a 'new tertiary tripartism' is operating at 16-plus, constituting almost an exact replica of the old secondary tripartism and the control that provided. The combined effect of this trend towards educational utilitarianism combined with on-going 'orientation' is likely to be, Ranson suggests, earlier, rather than later, selection for different curriculum paths, a selection every bit as divisive as that provided for under the 1944 Act, but now endowed with the new legitimating rhetoric of guidance and personal choice necessary to a much more aspiring society. This idea has recently been resurrected by the Dearing Review of the National Curriculum (Department for Education 1994).

Towards a national qualifications framework

Other more recent developments in English assessment policy arguably reinforce this analysis. Despite the strong and continuing support for traditional public examinations at 16-plus and 18-plus by government, there has also been an equally strong policy thrust to develop an alternative national structure of vocational and vocationally related qualifications. The newly established National Council for Vocational Qualifications (NCVQ) was charged with devising a comprehensive framework to accredit all forms of vocational competence in a series of clearly defined and common levels ranging from one as the most basic to five, corresponding to the level of competence of a professional. Each competence is defined in detail and can be assessed in a variety of different ways in appropriate vocational contexts.

Linked to this initiative is the move to accredit 'core skills'. Government interest in core skills became explicit in 1989 with the launch of a national programme to identify what these might be. The publication of *Towards a Skills Revolution* by the Confederation of British Industry in 1989 underlined employers' support for the initiative. Following an analysis of existing syllabuses in vocational and academic courses in the post-compulsory stage, theoretical approaches and previous core-skills frameworks, agreement was reached on the specification of what the core skills should be – and the NCVQ formulated them into their existing model of elements and units based on five levels of increasing difficulty.

In May 1991, the British government published *Education and Training in the 21st Century*. This document stressed the need for parity of esteem between academic and vocational routes and initiated General National Vocational Qualifications, which would be the vehicle for more general qualifications linking vocational and academic courses and in which the recording of so-called 'core skills' would be a central feature. This so-called 'third route to excellence' (GNVQs) was launched on a pilot basis in Autumn 1992 with level 3 GNVQs ('advanced') intended to be on a par with two A levels and GNVQ level 2 ('intermediate') equal to four GCSEs. Part 1 GNVQs are also now being offered at pre-GCSE standard. Each is an inclusive course with a core of compulsory content and some option models, like the earlier CPVE.

The government's intention seems to be to move towards a framework of qualifications based on outcome statements according to a common and universally recognized unit format for both education and training at all levels. This common language of competencies and attainments (i.e. outcomes) is intended to provide for progression in learning either vertically to more complex and demanding activities or laterally to new and different areas of learning. It is intended to make vocational qualifications of equal status with academic ones such as A level.

Although it cannot yet be said with certainty whether this will happen, the common deep structure of the contemporary assessment policy initiatives in England would suggest that this is unlikely. Given the continued unwillingness on the part of central government to dismantle any of the more traditional aspects of secondary schooling – indeed its commitment to strengthening them through increasing parental choice, scholarships and new examinations – the new assessment procedures are likely to reinforce, rather than redress, existing educational divisions and their associated inequalities. Research indicating that the uptake of GNVQ courses is typically by lower-achieving GCSE candidates would appear to give weight to this prediction (Further Education Unit, Nuffield Foundation 1994).

Part of this reinforcement is likely to be associated with the differential status of the various qualifications in the eyes of consumers. But, perhaps even more importantly, little will have been done to break down teachers' stereotypes of 'able' and 'less able' pupils, which are still strongly related to the latters' anticipated ability to achieve particular public examination targets. While considerable government concern with improving the level and quality, and hence status, of vocational preparation is expressed, this coexists with the frequently articulated ideology of traditional standards, the benefits of *competition* and tighter central control of both curriculum and assessment.

This contradication is also evident in the level of institutional ideology. The *comprehensivization* of assessment could lead to wider opportunity, more meaningful goals and social justice. Alternatively, its very pervasiveness could allow it to be an instrument of greater social control. Criteria referencing too can provide more positive, motivating and meaningful certification. Equally, it has led to greatly increased scope for central curriculum control and with it the potential deskilling of teachers, to the extent that pedagogy becomes centred on mechanistically teaching to the test in a way reminiscent of the English nineteenth-century Revised Code.

Last but not least is the notion of *differentiation*, which is based on the idea of replacing vertical distinctions in *levels* of achievement by horizontal, more egalitarian distinctions in terms of *types* of achievement. The introduction of novel assessment procedures, such as credit accumulation and records of achievement, without any significant dismantling of the hierarchy of existing accreditation procedures suggests that genuine change in the status quo is unlikely to happen.

The current tension between what appears to be an increasing emphasis within the National Curriculum-associated GCSE examinations and A level on traditional, academic learning and developments in other parts of the education system, which emphasize modes of curriculum, pedagogy and assessment more in line with the needs of industry, would seem to be contradictory. The presence of such a contradition in curriculum and assessment policy, however, can be explained by the need, on the one hand, for government to maximize political advantage through recourse to the traditional legitimating ideology expressed in words such as 'standards' and 'rigour' and in practices such as the learning of esoteric, specialized subject matter and highly discriminatory assessment procedures. On the other hand, there is an equally pressing need to bring educational priorities into line with the needs of the economy at the level of instrumental legitimation (see Chapter 5) and this is resulting in the rather paradoxical attempts to introduce more relevant, vocationally oriented yet high-status qualifications, which are subject to a very different, and hence potentially divisive, kind of assessment procedure.

System control: the English approach

This tension between the powerful legitimating ideology embodied in traditional, formal modes of assessment and the almost equally powerful pressure for radical change in all aspects of the education system if it is to meet, and, perhaps even more importantly, to be seen to be meeting, the needs of consumers, needs to be understood as part of the broader and complementary role assessment procedures play in system control.

The concept of system control, and hence of accountability, had little meaning before the advent of mass, state-provided educational provision. As it became necessary that the state should provide at least an elementary education for all in order for the population as a whole to acquire both relevant skills and appropriate work and social disciplines, so it became necessary for the state to be able to control the amount and content of schooling according to the needs of the economy and the funds available.

But when a form of education system eventually emerged, in the latter half of the nineteenth century, its character was quintessentially English. In no sense could it be an explicit attempt to impose a cultural norm through the education system, as in the French *mission civilisatrice* or the German *Kulturstaat* (Neave 1981). The power of local interests (Simon 1965) and an ideology of grassroots autonomy which was already deeply rooted in English institutional history meant that control of the English education system was likely to be largely indirect and covert.

It will be argued, following the theoretical model set out in Chapter 3, that in England *assessment* procedures have had a crucial role to play in this respect, as the currency on which accountability is *based*. In Chapter 3 it was suggested that whereas in the centralized system the emphasis is on the evaluation of education provision and processes to see if central directives are being carried out, the emphasis in a decentralized system is much more on the evaluation of educational products. The market economy of qualification trading is able to ensure a very high level of institutional conformity despite the ideology of professional autonomy.

The remainder of this chapter is devoted to a detailed consideration of the foregoing argument through an analysis of the evolving framework of accountability procedures in the English educational system. It considers the different forms of control provided by the three major dimensions of accountability – the professional, the moral and the bureaucratic – with the last being inevitably weak in a traditionally decentralized system, and essentially the backdrop against which the struggle between central, local and professional interests for control of the 'currency' of moral, professional and, more recently, market accountability is waged.

This 'currency' is conceptualized in terms of educational assessment procedures, notably public examinations and other forms of testing and monitoring on the basis of which individual, institutional and systemic performance can be judged. A central element in the argument is that the very effective control so provided is control by colonization rather than coercion, though 'normative re-educative' rather than 'power coercive' strategies (Chin and Benne 1978), since the education goals represented in these various assessment procedures became the currency of the *self-imposed* moral and professional accountability of teachers and other actors in the educational system. To put it another way, in the decentralized system where bureaucratic prescription and coercion cannot be legitimated, it has been the ability to influence professional values that has been of critical importance in determining which educational goals are pursued. How this can be brought about is explored in the pages that follow.

The beginnings of control

In the past the English education system has been decentralized to an extent that has at times bordered on anarchy. It was born of a very different feudal legacy from the French (Veulard 1970; Archer 1980), political and ecclesiastical interests having combined to support the development of strong local government from medieval times. The establishment of a legal basis for a system of education in 1870 was more an act of recognition than the result of any very deliberate attempt to create such a system. The necessarily rapid development of other public services, such as transport and welfare, at this time required a state infrastructure which only served to reinforce the independent power of local government (Burgess and Travers 1980).

It would be quite wrong, however, to deduce from the formal allocation of responsibilities between central and local government that central government has not had a powerful role to play. In the case of education the DES exerted a strong normative influence despite, and perhaps to a degree even because of, its weak bureaucratic powers. Other arms of central government have exerted strong financial control, notably the Treasury. Just as HMI was by far the most formally independent government inspectorate, yet was subject to considerable hidden 'channelling', so the 'guidance' which Whitehall exerts has had a powerful role to play. But the earliest and most enduring control devices were particularly concerned with 'assessment': gathering information in a variety of different ways – testing, inspection, examinations – in order to monitor, and hence influence, the standards being achieved by schools and the workings of the system as a whole.

One of the earliest manifestations of the desire to use assessment to monitor and hence influence the standards achieved by schools was the setting up in 1839 of the Committee of the Privy Council on Education, whose role was to monitor the expenditure of grants-in-aid to the national and British societies for school building. This was to be done through the first national machinery for evaluating and influencing schools, Her Majesty's Inspectorate, which was set up in 1840 (Silver 1979). The function of HMI, however, was to disseminate good practice and to provide information for government on the state of the nation's schools; they were a 'communication system between government and its main educational agency on the one hand and the schools for which they provided support on the other hand' (Silver 1979: 5). Characteristically, control was explicitly excluded from the terms of reference.

But the widening gulf between the elementary and 'secondary' provision (Higginson 1981) in the second half of the century and the rapid increase in state financial involvement in the provision and management of mass education (Simon 1965) soon produced a need for more explicit control procedures for elementary education. The result was the Revised Code recommended by the 1861 Newcastle Commission to provide for formal control of the elementary school curriculum, which soon became known as the 'payment by results' system. Morris (1970) suggests that one of the principal reasons for instituting the payment by results system in 1862 was that it enabled the volume of central government activity to be reduced, given that the trebling in the number of schools between 1831 and 1861 had made the Kay–Shuttleworth system of *ad hoc* grants for each school unmanageable – an explanation which may have some bearing on current French reforms.

The Revised Code offered each school a block grant based on a common formula. 'If indeed its immediate aim was to curb expenditure then it was successful' (Simon 1965). By contrast, Silver (1979) has put forward the view of some historians (e.g. Hurt 1971) that one of the principal if covert motives for the Revised Code was to reinforce the secular nature of the curriculum and the centrality of the three Rs against the traditional power of the church. By successfully introducing the Revised Code, Lowe had vindicated the state's right to make the 'content of elementary education meet the wider needs of contemporary society' (Hurt 1971).

The precise balance of motives in the institution of the Revised Code is less important than its palpable effects, which provide clear testimony to the significance of assessment procedures in the emerging system of education in terms of the themes identified, namely competence, content, competition and, through it all, control. The principles of the Revised Code corresponded exactly to the cost-effectiveness principles characteristic of business at that time. In Robert Lowe's famous words, this means a system which 'if it is not cheap, it shall be efficient, and if it is not efficient, it shall be cheap.'

The system required the overall level of school grants – from which teachers were paid – to be dependent on the proficiency of individual children in meeting the standards laid down for the various grades. The effect of such 'high-stakes' assessment, predictably enough, was to encourage drilling, rote learning and frequent testing in the three Rs. The overt emphasis on character training that had characterized elementary schooling in the early part of the century became progressively incorporated into the 'hidden curriculum', where it has largely remained, leaving the formal curriculum to emphasize the diligent application of pupils to the learning of a range of basic skills according to precisely defined standards. Echoes of the principles behind the Revised Code may be clearly traced in the twentieth-century version of National Assessment. These include the use of assessment procedures to control the content and to monitor the quality of the curriculum, and to value those learning outcomes that can be readily measured; and, perhaps most important of all, the concept that accountability for the use of public funds could and should be reckoned in terms of the academic performance of pupils.

In 1867 it became possible under the Code of Regulations governing elementary schools to add other subjects to the original standard subjects so that by the 1890s the number of subjects had greatly increased (Simon 1965). Teachers were given 'guides' rather than set books, so that by the turn of the century there was considerable local flexibility in curriculum provision. Musgrave (1980) explains the 'rise and fall' of the Revised Code in terms of the newly established education system's development through the three stages of 'formalism', 'transition' and 'meaning', identified by Beeby (1966). All education systems, Beeby suggests, develop through to a point where teachers are assumed to have sufficiently internalized the systemic priorities as to pursue them without the need for formal supervision.

While marked differences in the evolution of the two systems which form the subject of this study highlight the disadvantages of any deterministic theory, Beeby's model points up the importance of certain administrative and professional developments in the education system at this time, which allowed, and before long required, a more flexible system of control to be found, and hence tolled the knell of the Revised Code.

There is a certain irony in the history of teachers' attitudes to assessment and especially to the use of standardized achievement tests. In the very early days of mass educational provision, the payment by results system reflected an assumption that it was the teacher, rather than the child, who was responsible for learning having taken place. The rise of intelligence testing and its associated assumptions about fixed learning capacity should arguably have been welcome to teachers as a means of absolving them from taking the responsibility for pupils' learning. Instead, their attitude has tended to be ambivalent, reflecting a tension which was already apparent in the earliest days of standardized testing. In the early days of the century, teachers campaigned vigorously for the formal inclusion in scholarship examinations of some kind of teacher record based on observations and class tests. Their motives may be deduced as a mixture of 'public educator' concern over the anti-educational effects of examinations and concern over their own professional status, both bound up in the recent professional folk memory of the Revised Code. While standardized tests in one way boosted teachers' professional status in giving the learning process and the assessment thereof an esoteric status based on specialist knowledge, they were also a serious threat, implying as they did that the teacher could make little difference to the child's development. Thus, where such tests contradict their estimation of a child's ability of achievement, teachers have always tended to trust their own judgement (Gipps and Goldstein 1983; Croll *et al.* 1984), partly at least because not to do so would be to devalue their own claim to professional expertise and indirectly their bargaining position.

The rapidly growing structure of public exminations in the late nineteenth century provided another 'quality control' device. Since, as has already been suggested, these examinations were increasingly important in restricting access to various points in the occupational hierarchy to those with proven competence, the pressure to gain such qualifications was highly instrumental in ensuring the efficient functioning of schools. It very soon became apparent that a system of external examinations would have the power to bring about curriculum unity, common organization and a raising of standards in the teaching profession, while at the same time safeguarding the schools from state control as such (Roach 1971). Thus examinations were already being regarded as the alternative to a centralized system of teaching and inspection and, in this sense, they were a political device.

The fact that public examinations were so early enshrined into English educational provision, with the explicit intention of protecting local autonomy, significantly affected the organizational development of the educational system thereafter.

It is no accident that educational provision in England has been traditionally characterized by one of the highest degrees of school autonomy and, at the same time, one of the greatest preoccupations with public examinations of any country. In recognizing public examinations as an alternative to a centrally directed education system, many people also recognized the potential power of such examinations to impose their own form of control and, as was suggested in the first part of this chapter, many feared and deplored their effects, for although the precise emphasis on different control procedures varies according to the prevailing economic and social climate, the importance of assessment procedures in this process does not.

Control in the post-1944 era

A thumbnail sketch of the essential aspects of English educational provision in the early twentieth century reveals a system still dominated by the nineteenth-century legacy of the struggles of different interest groups for control over the emerging educational system – a struggle which gave rise to a strong belief in the need for teacher autonomy and in governmental interference as a monstrous entity to be resisted at all costs. By charging the local authority with the statutory responsibility for the running, staffing and teaching of its schools, the 1944 Act posed no threat to the traditional alliance between teachers and local authorities, and made it possible for schools and headteachers to enjoy considerable autonomy. When the grouped School Certificate Examination was replaced in 1951 by the single-subject O and A levels, this gave yet more freedom to individual schools (Brooksbank 1980). The growing willingness to trust teachers' 'professionalism', which was evident in the 1950s and 1960s and which made possible this autonomy at the level of practice, was also the basis for a consensus between the providers and the practitioners that enabled teachers to have a strong voice in policy-making at both local and national levels.

The establishment of the, nominally at least, teacher-dominated Schools Council in 1964 reflected more than any other single event the prevailing trust in teachers and the general enthusiasm for reform and development, particularly with regard to the curriculum. The Plowden Report of 1967 also emphasized the conviction that schools could help to overcome social problems if teachers were allowed to exercise their professional judgement in relation to the needs and interests of the individual child (Becher and McLure 1978).

But the apparent movement away from traditional curricula, pedagogy, discipline and internal grading practices in schools, in favour of teacher autonomy and the development of examinations designed to give maximum freedom to individual schools and teachers in curriculum and assessment, where before, through the Secondary Schools Examination Council, the DES itself had had close control over public assessment and thus educational standards, began to prompt misgivings in certain quarters. The fact that the three different modes of CSE greatly increased the number of syllabuses – thus preventing any close scrutiny of courses by the Schools Council of either CSE or O level syllabuses, unlike in pre-1964 practice – was typical of the source of such misgivings. The relatively minor change of uniting GCE and CSE into a common system of examining at 16-plus – the GCSE – provoked much criticism from traditionalists. At the same time, education policy began to be influenced by industry's demand for a vocationally skilled labour force rather than the less utilitarian professional ideology of teachers.

As confidence in the power of education to bring about social reform waned, central government was more or less consciously abrogating to itself more and more responsibility for the direction of the education system. Given the economic climate and the associated rise of the New Right *laissez-faire* monetarism, such a move for a government committed to individual initiative was at first sight contradictory. In this respect it is important to consider the precise nature of this increasing control. The two principal goals of central government in this respect may be identified as the control of expenditure on education and the control of educational standards through a combination of curriculum and assessment strategies.

The first overt step in this direction was Mr Callaghan's famous Ruskin College speech in 1976, which echoed prevailing public concern over supposedly falling standards and launched the 'Great Debate', in which the call for a 'core' curriculum and more vocationally oriented skill training were prominent. Nevertheless, the apparent failure of teachers to prepare young people for work adequately provided an ideal excuse for central government to take out of the hands of teachers the responsibility for defining educational goals. If previously the education system had been a rather indeterminate process in professional hands, it was now to come under public control. This signalled a quite specific change: the deliberate intention to intervene centrally in the shape and content of the curriculum. Much more significant, however, was the strengthening of product-based accountability through the introduction of provision for national assessment.

National assessment

The changing balance of power over public examinations between the Schools Council, the examinations boards and the DES might seem to have been the most influential effect of changes in DES policy, but in the early 1970s it was the Assessment of Performance Unit (APU) that embodied the prevailing concerns over standards. Although the APU has not played the overtly coercive role that many feared when it was first instituted (see, for example, Dennison 1978), it has played an increasingly important part in defining education standards, and so has had an increasingly powerful influence on the major means of control in English education. More significantly still, it has paved the way for a very different kind of national assessment.

Given the tradition of quality control by examination, dating from the earliest days of mass education in England and Wales, and with the nineteenth-century Revised Code of payment by results system as a model, it was not hard for central government to revive the idea of centralized monitoring. Indeed, the post-1881 expression of the Revised Code contained many similar elements to the APU, in providing for the monitoring of a one-third sample of pupils in key subject areas. However, the APU differed fundamentally in that it did not focus on individual schools and teachers. Rather, its establishment transferred the responsibility for accountability from individual pupils, teachers, schools and local education authorities (LEAs) to the teaching profession as a whole. Thus, the APU may be seen as yet another manifestation of government distrust of the professional values of teachers that had prevailed for the previous two decades, and as a part of the move towards greater control of the profession.

As expected, the APU spawned a testing explosion, not least among local authorities. In 1980 a survey by Gipps and Goldstein (1983) revealed very few local authorities that did not have testing schemes. Three-quarters engaged in blanket testing for reading and a considerable number did so for maths. The year 1980 saw the debut of the related and even more controversial practice of publishing examination results on a comparative, authority-wide basis. Thus, as is often the case with policy initiatives, although the APU did not have the effect that was intended or expected, it was not ineffectual. In keeping with the style of control in English and Welsh education, the APU may be seen as having a major role in influencing discussion and legitimating particular educational priorities. Although the APU itself stopped well short of providing machinery for judging individual teachers' performance, it did introduce the notion of testing in key curriculum subjects at different age points as a basis for the national monitoring of standards. It only required the advent of the powerful New Right political movement to translate a general belief in the benefits of competition into the concept of market accountability and for APU technology to be transformed into the basis of a national assessment programme.

The scheme for carrying this out was proposed by the Task Group on Assessment and Testing (TGAT). Set up by the government in 1987 it embodied many of the current trends in assessment thinking and policy. The report emphasized formative and diagnostic assessment as well as summative, criterion-referenced assessment and reporting in terms of 'profile components'. Assessment was intended to be positive and cumulative, an aid to teachers in helping them to chart their children's progress. But it was also explicitly *evaluative* in that it was designed to provide generally available comparative data about teachers', schools' and LEAs' levels of attainment as an explicit focus for market accountability. The clear assumption behind the policy is that the pervasive influence of comparison and competition and the provision for systematic appraisal and accountability would lead to increased efficiency and, hence, increased productivity in education. It was a *market* model.

The core of the government's intentions in this respect and the thinking behind them were embodied in the following paragraphs of the *National Curriculum 5–16* consultation document:

Attainment targets will be set for all three core subjects of maths, English and science. These will establish what children should normally be expected to know, understand and be able to do at around the ages of 7, 11, 14 and 16, and will enable the progress of each child to be measured against established national standards. They will reflect what pupils must achieve to progress in their education and to become thinking and informed people. The range of attainment targets should cater for the full ability range and be sufficiently challenging *at all levels* to raise expectations, particularly of pupils of middling achievement who frequently are not challenged enough, as well as stretching and stimulating the most able. This is a proven and essential way towards raising standards of achievement. Targets must be sufficiently specific for pupils, teachers, parents and others to have a clear idea of what is expected, and to provide a sound basis for assessment.

There will also be attainment targets for other foundation subjects where appropriate, in Wales for the study of Welsh, and for other themes and skills taught through each of the foundation subjects. For art, music and physical education there will be guidelines rather than specific attainment targets.

The attainment targets will provide standards against which pupils' progress and performance can be assessed. The main purpose of such assessment will be to show what a pupil has learnt and mastered and to enable teachers and parents to ensure that he or she is making adequate progress. Where such progress is not made, it will be up to schools to make suitable arrangements to help the pupil.

The Secretaries of State envisage that much of the assessments at ages 7 (or thereabouts), 11 and 14, and at 16 in non-examined subjects, will be done by teachers as an integral part of normal classroom work. But at the heart of the assessment process there will be nationally prescribed tests done by all the pupils to supplement the individual teachers' assessments. Teachers will administer and mark these, but their marking – and their assessment overall will be externally moderated.

(DES 1987: 9–11)

The discourse that informs such policies is that of psychometrics, an approach to assessment that has almost completely dominated the conceptualization of both policy and practice in education for nearly a century. The long-standing pre-eminence of psychometric concerns about accurate comparative measurement of both student potential and student achievement has only been matched by the associated concern about selection, prediction and accountability.

There is now a growing body of literature that seeks to account for and assess the implications of the increasingly interventionist stance towards education on the part of central government in recent years (e.g. Salter and Tapper 1981; Crispin 1983). Although recently there have been quite explicit manifestations of this trend – notably in the 1988 Education Reform Act – formerly this evidence was extremely difficult to unravel from a confusion of other developments in which changing ideologies, economic recession, local government reorganization and institutional reform have been prominent. Consequently there is less agreement about why the DES actually set out to pursue such a policy. Overall, a consideration of such developments supports the argument that growing central government influence in education must be seen as both the overt exercising of hitherto covert powers and the enactment of fundamentally new powers of control in response to apparent public concern over standards, economic imperatives and an increasingly corporate management approach to government.

The move towards more central control of the education system during the past decade might have been planned like a series of complex moves towards checkmate in a game of chess. The careful articulation of ideological and practical developments, the complementary effects of covert and overt steps towards greater central control, the careful manipulation of curriculum, assessment and budgetary pieces in the overall strategy designed first to demoralize and then to subdue – all these might have been planned as part of a deliberate intention. But they were not. Rather they must all be seen as flotsam on the tide of rationalization and stringency of which the shift towards greater control in education is but one manifestation. What is now taking place arguably is a quite fundamental change in the mode of policy legitimation through the growing dominance of a technocratic rationality informed by mechanistic evaluation as the basis for decision-making. Changes in centre–local relations must therefore be interpreted as part of a much larger restructuring of the relationship between education, work and society and, most notably, in the forms of social control.

The nature of this restructuring is apparently contradictory since it revolves around attempts to impose a greater measure of *consistency* on to the educational system on the one hand and attempts to justify and encourage (centrally approved) *diversity* on the other. The various recent attempts to strengthen central government control over such key areas as curriculum, assessment procedures, finance and teacher supply to ensure more uniformity in the system have been matched by a climate of parental choice and local participation in school governance. Both trends are justified by central government on the basis of increasing democracy in the system – the centralist notion of democracy inherent in *equality* of provision versus the traditionally English liberal notion of democracy as *participation and freedom of choice*. Thus it is now explicit government policy to enhance parental choice in education and, of necessity, the schools' ability to respond to market forces. But as early as 1981, Donald was speculating that: 'The fascination of a Conservative education policy [would] therefore be tosee how long the incompatible threads of international corporatism, decimated public expenditure, "parental choice" and "standards" could be held toegther before the whole garment came apart at the seams' (Donald 1981: 112).

At the same time it is the concept of accountability which has given form to the increasing dominance of industrial values in the education system. This has taken a variety of forms, ranging from an acceptance on the part of some teachers of a vocational 'new industrialist' rather than liberal 'old humanist' bias in curricular priorities on the one hand, evidenced, for example, by the success of the very substantial Technical and Vocational Education Initiative (TVEI) of the 1980s, to a growing imposition on the teaching profession of an input/output model in which educational quality is judged by an evaluation of its products. This latter development is evidenced in the provision for reporting levels of pupil attainment by class and by school under the 1988 Education Reform Act and the growing interest in the identification of suitable 'performance indicators'. In recent years, the market forces of falling roles, strained resources and unemployment have provided powerful support for those industrial and bureaucratic values of efficiency and utilitarianism that a strong government majority in Parliament was been able to impose through a whole series of policy measures.

The developments of recent years have been associated with a very rapid rise in the prominence of assessment as a policy issue. Indeed, the success of much current policy-making is heavily dependent on associated assessment initiatives. The GCSE national criteria, the National Assessments provided for in the Education Reform Act and the institution of National Vocational Qualifications are just three among many other possible examples that could be cited in this respect. Thus the final part of this case study of assessment-based system control in England is devoted to a more specific exploration of the characteristic way in which assessment procedures have provided for control in English education and how the nature of this control has changed in recent years, from an almost complete reliance on the powerful influence assessment procedures exert on the identification of professional values and hence the criteria for *self-imposed* accountability to a more overt and explicit manipulation of assessment-based *control*.

The language of assessment

Part of the explanation for teachers' acceptance of *examination* constraints was because it provided *an acceptable basis of accountability* to the two audiences teachers in England identify as paramount: 'clients' (i.e. parents and pupils) and the headteacher (Broadfoot *et al.* 1989). There was certainly a significant reaction on the part of teachers in England against accountability based on product evaluation criteria emanating from central or local government alone, which was expressed partly in the form of a quite novel concern among teachers and schools to develop their own criteria of accountability through institutional and personal self-review.

While an analysis of policy changes undoubtedly points to increased limitations on teachers' professionalism throughout the past decade, teachers themselves seem to have been, until 1988, remarkably unaware of these new controls. Instead they seemed to feel that in their professional role they were still insulated by the norms and institutions of educational governance from both top-down and bottom-up pressure. In another empirical study, Nias (1981) found that 'between their practice and every aspect of accountability, teachers erect the barrier of professionalism', so setting limits to their *legal* accountability to govenors and to LEAs by reference to their professionalism. Similarly, in their self-confessed *moral* accountability to clients and consumers, 'when the crowd begins to cry "the emperor has no clothes", teachers have nothing but their own protestations of professionalism with which to disguise their nakedness' (Nias 1981: 224).

That they exercised this influence effectively is revealed in a study by Munn (ed.) (1993), in which the authors were surprised to find most parents unwilling to challenge teachers' professionality. Thus greater regulation in practice could only come through voluntary compliance on the part of teachers to external influence or enforced conformity backed up by power coercive sanctions. As Hargreaves (1989) argued, the failure of the teaching profession to respond to more than a decade of such normative re-educative exhortation by central government to put their house in order was the main cause of the largely power coercive provisions of the 1988 Act and its almost unprecedented provision for direct control of teachers, schools and local authorities. Although 'management' remains in its traditional place as a professional *responsibility* for leadership, this is now accompanied by the responsibility to impose bureaucratic directives.

If, hitherto, the English teacher could go a long way before the sanctions inherent in his or her *formal* accountability began to apply, teachers are now experiencing clear directives about the organization, content and, above all, communication of their work. Thus at both school and departmental level, teachers now have to justify their curriculum framework in relation to the National Curriculum as part of explicit school policies, as expressed, for example, in the institutional development plan (IDP) or the school assessment policy. Whereas before it was sufficient simply to *claim* professional status as the basis of autonomy, now it is necessary to *demonstrate* professional competence as well.

Clearly, the idea of communication is central to the concept of 'accountability' and the growing importance of this idea of 'giving an account' can be traced through all levels of the system: from schools to parents, governors and local authorities; from local authorities to local government and the DFE; from the DFE to Parliament and the people. But although it is possible to trace growing formal requirements in this respect, such as the requirement on schools to publish their curriculum policy and that on governors to report annually to parents, it still remains to be seen how far the traditional view often expressed by teachers that 'once you are in the classroom you can do very much what you want' will be fundamentally affected. Since for English teachers it has always been their informal accountability which has been the real constraint, with the formal accountability associated with such bureaucratic concerns as the provision and use of resources being viewed as a necessary, but far from critical, determinant of the real business of education, namely teaching, it is hard to predict how they will react to such overt controls. The power of informal accountability, because of the (professional) expectation that teachers will care about pupils, has always been a very effective source of teacher motivation.

There is now increasing evidence that the new continuous assessment procedures under the National Curriculum are most significant in this respect, since teachers' concern about fostering pupils' progress and the publication of league tables is sufficient to ensure widespread consensus about what standards and goals are to be pursued (Pollard *et al.* 1994). Along with the new emphasis on formal accountability, where criteria are spelt out bureaucratically and backed up with the threat of sanctions, there is the more traditional emphasis on informal accountability based on a large measure of agreement over the standards to be pursued, which can then be translated into more or less explicit professional norms that guide teachers' practice. The key to the whole apparatus is the fact that it is on these norms, and the results of teachers' practice based on them, that judgements will be made of individual teachers, schools, local education authorities and, ultimately, the system as a whole.

Thus the common value framework represented by the National Curriculum and the formulation of national assessment criteria are an attempt to impose a measure of more formal accountability within the system, based on bureaucratic and consumer, rather than professional, criteria. Such attempts have included reforms to provide for tighter 'top-down' constraints via increased financial control of local authorities, and tighter 'bottom-up' constraints through formal provision for greater parental choice in school selection and community representation through very much more powerful governing bodies.

Equally, government policy initiatives in the field of assessment since the 1970s – the institution of the Assessment of Performance Unit, the encouragement of local authority testing, the requirement of national criteria for the GCSE examination, the establishment of a series of increasingly powerful national bodies for curriculum and assessment control (currently the Schools' Curriculum and Assessment Authority or SCAA) and, above all, the institution of comprehensive testing according to nationally agreed 'level descriptors' (Dearing 1994) – are initiatives that should not be seen simply as an attempt to gain greater formal control within the system by the institution of new formal accountability criteria. Instead they must be seen also as an attempt to influence the criteria teachers themselves adopt as the basis for their own, self-imposed, professional accountability. This latter form of influence has the dual advantage of being both more effective and less likely to provoke opposition.

The implications for education provision of this style of government and the associated forms of professionalism are considerable, because they mean, following Bernstein's argument as set out in Chapter 4, that the power of any one group within the education system to exercise effective control depends upon the ability of that group to establish efficient ways of gathering knowledge and, just as

important, of being able to influence the content of such communication.

Once more it is *assessment* that would appear to be central to the
formulation and imposition of systemic values as embodied in
particular criteria of performance – not least by keeping certain
items off the policy agenda and even preventing some potential issues
being recognized as concerns. As Hextall (1984: 249) suggests,
educational policies and practices 'may be expressed and presented
as issues to be formulated and resolved in objective, technically
neutral ways, but to delimit their discussion in such a way loses sight
of their social resonance.' Although Hextall was referring explicitly
to the APU, his argument is extremely pertinent to the much more
powerful National Assessment programme because there is, as
Wood and Gipps (1981) suggest, 'a strong tendency for quantitative
data to overwhelm other sources of information, whatever the
protestations to the contrary', because of the legitimatory power of
apparently objective science.

As educational administration becomes 'depersonalized' it must
become increasingly dependent on the provision of some apparently
objective information about the quality of the service being provided. The onus put on schools in recent years to provide information about themselves, and notably the requirement to publish
public examination results enjoined in the 1980 Education Act, and
considerably extended under the 1988 and 1992 Acts, underlines the
potential importance of assessment procedures in this respect. The
results of public examinations and other kinds of standardized tests
are often interpreted uncritically and out of context, their use
involving the application of simple bureaucratic criteria rather than
the application of the expert professional analysis which would be
necessary to draw any true meaning from them (Gipps and Goldstein
1983). Indeed, the government's insistence on publishing 'raw
scores', despite a substantial lobby arguing for more contextualized
'value added' measures suggests that the motive behind using
assessment results as the currency of the educational market is not
simply the desire to compare the true quality of schools – as far as
this is possible. The inevitable widening of the gulf between high and
low scoring schools can only be interpreted as being rooted in a
desire to reinstate a more explicitly divided system in which 'elite'
schools are once more clearly identified. If this is so it takes the
debate beyond issues of assessment as a mechanism for system

control as such, to include new dimensions for understanding the way in which competition is to be provided for in the context of a changing social and political context. These issues are explored in more detail in Chapter 8. At the present time it is the unproblematic acceptance of the content of such testing by lay people, who are not versed in the language of professional concerns but who have been taught, through recent policy initiatives in the field of assessment, how to address the issue of standards, that is encouraging the technicist interpretation of educational problems and, in particular, the symbolic value of testing (Airasian 1988).

It seems likely that the new assessment initiatives will have an increasingly significant normative re-educative influence within the teaching profession. To the extent that they do they will have succeeded in imposing an unprecedented degree of control on the education system. The DFE's concern with establishing national criteria for the 16-plus examination, its increasingly overt role, through SCAA, in the instigation of qualifications,[20] as in the direct powers under the 1988 Act to monitor all public exam syllabuses and to decide which courses may be accredited for use in schools, and its formal control of the National Assessment programme means that central government's role has been progressively strengthened in this respect. Thus Dale predicted in 1981a: 'both the definition of quality and what counts as its achievement are to be taken out of the hands of teachers. Teachers are to be made accountable for the achievement of externally set targets at an externally set level.' Educational priorities are now increasingly being defined at the greatest possible distance from the chalkface – among the professional administrators of the DES, the professional test-constructors in their consortia, the exam boards and, above all, politicians.

Most of the debate about such assessment initiatives has centred on the technical issues of implementation. In practice, its most controversial aspect should be the assumption of a value consensus about educational goals. In effect it is yet another example of the way in which apparently benign, rational techniques of assessment are currently being used to impose norms by reducing value debates to technical questions. A more extended exploration of this theme is the subject of Chapter 8.

8

OVERVIEW, PROSPECTS AND COMMON TRENDS

Towards convergence

One of the principal themes of this book has been the need to maintain a perspective which can encompass both the common trends and pressures of advanced societies and the specific outworking of these pressures in the educational policy and practice of any particular nation state. It is necessary in this final chapter to make some attempt to bring these two levels of analysis together, partly for the sake of completeness and partly because the economic, political and social problems facing advanced capitalist societies at the present time are sufficiently fundamental to render problematic the kind of traditional, analytic distinction in the organization and control of education systems, such as centralized and decentralized, that have been used up to this point. In particular, it will be argued that these common problems are likely to be met by a move away from overtly political judgements about educational policy in favour of a technocratic ideology which legitimates policy decisions in terms of an objective, rational process of decision-making. Such a move postpones the potential legitimation crisis of state institutions implicit in the erosion of traditional values and in the growing powerlessness of the individual to resist the effects of an increasingly intrusive state machinery.

Thus, while two countries starting from radically different administrative traditions must of necessity be very different in their approach to policy innovations brought about by such pressures, it is increasingly possible to pick out similar trends in the two countries. Particularly notable in this respect is the basis for educational control, which in both England and France finds at the present time a common legitimating ideology in the language of information science and technological efficiency. In curriculum, management and finance, but above all in the nature and application of educational assessment procedures, the power of the norm is increasingly characteristic. Although these general observations leave unresolved more specific policy issues of power relations and innovation strategies, the purpose and character of such innovations in both countries, despite superficial differences, are increasingly similar.

It has been suggested that educational activity in both England and France is closely controlled by prevailing assessment procedures, although these have traditionally taken and continue to take different forms in the two countries. In England there has been something of an oscillation between a more 'free market', decentralized approach to assessment control mediated by the semi-autonomous exam boards and the links they in turn have with the universities at times of plenty, and more directive, centralized strategies based on the tighter control of public examining and institutional accountability when economic and social problems dictate, as at present, a more utilitarian direction for educational activity.

In France, by contrast, the development has been from what was in fact the relative freedom of a highly centralized system in which assessment control was vested in national, government-run selective examinations and personal teacher inspection. This has been replaced by a nominally more decentralized, positive control based on a reflexive relationship between teacher-conducted continuous assessment according to nationally prescribed norms and an increasingly technicist management approach to educational administration, provision and control. The information thereby generated provides an increasingly powerful means of directing both the careers of individual pupils and the education system as a whole. By the same token, the institution of continuous assessment based on national norms now not only exhorts teachers – as the system has always done – but arguably makes that exhortation effective, as these norms relate directly to the assessment of pupil progress and simultaneously provide for the national statistical monitoring of educational standards within the system.

Typically, the trends in England are less clear cut. The activities of the English Assessment of Performance Unit during the 1970s and 1980s were very similar to the programme of national monitoring launched by Minister Fontanet in 1974 in France. The imposition of national norms as assessment criteria at the present time in England is also to an extent comparable with French national curriculum and assessment provision.[1] Both countries are developing ideas of assessment based on student-centred learning and idiosyncratic records of achievement. While these initiatives have much to recommend them educationally, they also have the potential to provide for the very effective imposition of both curricular and social norms, since they require the extension of formal assessment into much wider areas of development than hitherto. If in some ways such developments can be seen as a step towards greater equality of educational provision, they are also paradoxically a potential step towards the kind of invisible control Bernstein describes (see Chapter 4).

In the past, English teachers' autonomy was safeguarded by the lack of central curricular prescriptions, which meant that, despite the very powerful control exerted by the emphasis on 'product evaluation', there was considerable room for individual teachers, pressure groups and semi-autonomous bodies such as the exam boards to influence the content of that control. In the same way, in the past, French teachers' autonomy was safeguarded by the relatively minor role of 'product evaluation', despite their location within a highly centralized, bureaucratic education system in which every aspect of pedagogic activity, and especially curricular objectives, was tightly controlled. The increasing similarity at the present time between the two systems reflects the fact that each is tending to institute now, in addition, the aspects of control hitherto characteristic of the other, so providing in both cases a novel, and very powerful, basis for the central direction of education.

Perhaps even more important than these attempts to make control more effective, however, is the growing association of educational administration in both countries with a quality management approach based on various forms of 'account' and information generation. Such an approach is likely to disguise the essentially political nature of educational goals, in an ideology of scientific rationality. In this event, value judgements appear as merely administrative decisions dictated by rationality and the goal of maximizing efficiency. This development underlines the argument set out in Chapter 5 that assessment procedures have an important role to play, at the level of the expressive ideology of education, in helping to determine the very ways in which educational discourse is structured, as well as having a more obvious role in legitimating the directly instrumental role of assessment procedures in allocating opportunity.

It is arguable that it is the way in which assessment procedures help to bring about a social order which finds itself concurring in a particular *definition* of educational goals and, in so doing, makes a major contribution to social control that is ultimately more significant than the role of such procedures in *enforcing* such goals. It has been one of the principal arguments of this book that it is the ideological work done by assessment procedures which has been of fundamental significance in shaping the provision and organization – that is, the very *conceptualization* – of mass education, although the associated role of such procedures in implementing that organization has clearly also been critical (Freedman 1995). This last chapter represents an attempt to balance these two levels of analysis in a theoretical discussion of the implications of some of the contemporary trends in assessment procedures identified in Chapters 6 and 7.

It is already clear from this summary of some of the more significant contemporary initiatives in assessment procedures in the two countries that there is no simple, derived relationship between broader social pressures and national institutional responses. The precise configuration of these will depend on the constraints on policy-making provided by existing forms of structuration, together with the ongoing struggle between a variety of vested interests within that society. Nevertheless, it is clear from the case study material of Chapters 6 and 7 that there are some common features in the contemporary role of evaluation procedures in the two countries under study. Thus it is appropriate to conclude this book with an analysis of such general trends couched at the same level of theoretical generality as that of Part I.

Developments in capitalism and associated forms of accountability

The far-reaching changes currently visible in both English and French education can at one level be taken as oscillations of policy caused by changes in the legitimating context. The changes in England from the Plowden era to a climate of utilitarianism and overt accountability and, most recently, to a market ideology, may be seen in this light as equivalent to the shift of emphasis from expressive to instrumental goals, from an egalitarian, integrative ideology to an elitist competitive ideology, which took place in French education between the French Revolution and Napoleon's advent. There are, however, good grounds for believing that current changes in educational provision are responses to a more profound change in the nature of the state demands being made upon education in response to the broader but equally fundamental pressures being experienced at the present time in the social order as a whole.

The cultural basis of education policy – like other areas of social life – is increasingly unstable. Affluence, rising expectations, the media, technical innovation and modern forms of communication, the decline of religion and the success of modern science have all broken up the traditional life-world of more strictly constrained life choices. As the horizons of self-identity are pushed out in the 'postmodern' world to embrace a broadening range of alternative forms of life and a myriad of possible futures, traditions are robbed of their authority. They lose their normative force. As culturally rooted world views have increasingly been thrown into juxtaposition, 'relativized and manipulatively manipulated', there has been a corresponding weakening of normative consensus and of what Rieff (1973) called the 'controlling symbolic' of Western society. This is both a political and a psychological phenomenon – the psychological dimension concerned with the erosion of the culturally grounded 'interpretive systems' (Habermas 1976) which produced the 'controlling symbolics' and were the basis of 'creedally authoritative institutions' (Rieff 1973), such as schools. The result, as Offe (1975) suggests, is that the state has lost the ability to legitimate itself on normative grounds. It must have recourse to alternative legitimating strategies, such as material gratification or coercive repression, each of which tends only to further exacerbate the real legitimacy problem.

The erosion of the traditional normative order also erodes the credibility of the state apparatus as a benign machine acting in the interests of the majority. As Habermas (1976: 96) argues, 'because the reproduction of class societies is based on the privileged appropriation of socially produced wealth, all such societies must resolve the problem of distributing the surplus product inequitably and yet legitimately. In educational terms, this 'Tocquevillean dilemma', this tension between liberalism and democracy, between the democratic demand for levelling and the continuing existence of inequalities (Aron 1980: 285; Bocock *et al.* 1980), tends to generate expectations and needs which the education system is necessarily unable to meet. The instrumental order of education is based on hierarchical control while the legitimating ideology, the expressive order, is that of the liberal discourse of the state, according to which rights are vested equally in all members of the community. This contradictory position of education explains its dual progressive/ reproductive role: promoting equality, democracy, toleration, rationality and inalienable rights on the one hand, while legitimizing inequality, authoritarianism, fragmentation, prejudice and sub-mission on the other (Gintis 1980: 3).

Bacon (1981) suggests that 'welfare bureaucracies' such as the education system are forced to adopt a 'quasi-political' role in which they are vigilant over their relations with competing groups and forces in society, and especially over their need to maintain their authority, to maintain the stability and security of the organization and the need to justify their continued claim on the wider resources of society. Thus very often legitimation is achieved by the appear-ance of democratic participation and choice, which conceals a 'discrete manipulative co-option' in which a semblance of freedom conceals the limitation of the agenda and potential decisions which are necessary to support the existing power structure.

It follows that education systems, along with other state bu-reaucracies, are increasingly faced with the problem of carrying out and, to that extent, legitimating the politics and practices of an ever more expensive and intrusive state machinery which must continue to perpetuate inequality at a time when the traditional normative order is being deeply eroded. Weiler's empirical analyses suggest that three modes of 'compensatory' legitimation are currently being employed: legitimation by participation, legitimation by legalization and legitimation by expertise (Weiler 1981). These three modes of legitimation are readily matched to the three forms of accountability identified in Chapter 2: 'moral' accountability, the responsiveness of the system to clients; 'bureaucratic' accountability, the responsiveness of the system to the formal bureaucratic hierarchy; and 'professional' accountability to self and colleagues for maintaining self-imposed standards. The continued functioning of the education system in the interest of the state requires the creation of a common language of accountability, which will provide for the consensual expression of public, bureaucratic and professional goals within the education system.

In recent years there have been moves in England to increase both the bureaucratic accountability and the 'moral' accountability to which schools and teachers are subject. On the one hand measures such as the imposition of a National Curriculum and a whole host of detailed national regulations concerning the conduct of schools mean that there has been a movement, in Dale's terms, from a situation of licensed (i.e. professional) autonomy to a more 'regulated' autonomy (Dale 1980). At the same time, a host of related policy initiatives designed to create a market in education through increasing parental choice and obliging schools to give an account of their performance is explicitly based on the notion of making the system more responsive to its clients.

In France, where 'regulated autonomy' has traditionally been the norm, movement has principally been towards increasing the amount of 'moral' accountability through increased 'participation'. But although the changing balance between different forms of legitimation or accountability is one indication that there are these strains in both countries, it is arguably the *content* rather than the *form* of accountability which is critical. That is to say, it is in the ideological assumptions which provide the basis for a common language of accountability that there is the greatest potential for legitimation, and thus for control. Thus notions of accountability reflect a hegemony that refers both to the *ultimate goals and values* pursued by groups or individuals and to the *processes* of attaining them.

As the sheer size of the state machine makes it increasingly difficult for coercive or traditional bureaucratic modes of control to be effective on their own, it becomes more than ever necessary that some way be found of ensuring a system of normative order, of self-regulating professionals who will nevertheless pursue goals identified by the state. Implicit in the idea of accountability – performance measured against goals and subsequent response – is the identification of criteria: what constitutes adequate curriculum provision, for example, or when does a particular teacher's or school's score on public examination passes cease to be acceptable?

Changing modes of control: England

Recent events in England are revealing in this respect. As demands for accountability have become more explicit in the past few years, these criteria have become more apparent, though initially they did not substantially change. If anything, the school self-evaluation movement of the early 1970s allowed teachers a greater say in the identification of such criteria. Despite the fact that HMI began to publish their reports, schools began to publish their exam results and national and local monitoring of standards was increasingly widespread, the criteria for such evaluations continued to be largely defined by educational professionals, whether these were inspectors, teachers or testers. While this was the case, it was still the professionals who were the major source of influence on the 'normative climate' perpetrated through professional discourse. However, the passing of the 1988 Education Reform Act, which provides for the imposition of a National Curriculum and Assessment framework that is subject to the direct authority of the Secretary of State for Education, represents a fundamental change in this respect by substantially increasing the formal power of central government to impose particular educational priorities and associated criteria of quality as the basis of assessment.

It is important to recognize, however, that there have long been other, more bureaucratic, channels of accountability pertaining to education, which are associated with financial and legal sanctions. While the existence of such accountability was always a source of formal authority within the system, in the past it was hard to exercise in practice, as the William Tyndale School case of the 1970s well demonstrated. Explicit challenges to the status quo that required the mobilization of such formal sanctions were relatively rare. This was because more often than not the informal, normative influence of professional accountability was broadly in agreement with the policy goals of central government. Indeed, traditionally the translation of general political objectives into explicitly educational policy has been recognized as being, typically, the taking up of 'ideas in good currency', the legitimation of a 'bandwagon' whose origin is obscure and probably irrelevant once it is supported by a sufficiently broad consensus of support.

But with the progressive breakdown of consensus over educational goals that economic recession and unemployment began to bring about in the 1970s, and Thatcherism deliberately exacerbated, has come what is arguably an unprecedented move by central government to strengthen its framework of formal control and accountability. Although the former DES lacked the legal and financial means to ensure immediate and unreserved compliance even with clearly established national policies (Dale 1983), there is now plenty of evidence in recent policy initiatives by the DFE in the field of finance, curriculum and assessment to support the view that this is no longer the case.

The reality of implementation, however, is likely to be considerably more complex than the imposition of national legislation *per se.* Different sorts of interests and different levels of concern combine to produce a pattern of power relations which is still strongly influenced by the informal processes of personal negotiation and the *puissance* of certain individuals at any one time. Rather it is the normative assumptions on which such interaction is based that are the real source of power, albeit unremarked and unopposed, since they carry the power to determine selectively the way in which issues are discussed and solutions proposed. Thus, in the 1960s, policy initiatives took place against a largely implicit range of normative assumptions, which included the need for a measure of professional autonomy alongside human capital investment, national growth and egalitarianism. In the 1980s and 1990s prevailing modes of discourse reflect a normative climate based on quite different assumptions, notably *laissez-faire* elitism and utilitarianism. It was not the DES that created this climate; the DES was the body charged with translating this change of political climate into a redirection of educational policies and practice. But, while always formally accountable for this role, the DES hitherto largely lacked the bureaucratic apparatus to provide for such overt steering. Caught between the upper and nether millstones, the DES tended to depend on its informal channels of influence to affect policy debates. It has been argued that this situation is now radically changed as central government in particular has steadily strengthened both its power to influence evaluative criteria through, for example, the national prescription of GCSE criteria and the National Assessment framework, and its direct control of curriculum content.

The new status of the DES, embodied perhaps in its change of name to the Department for Education, with the addition in 1995 of 'and Employment', centres on its substantially increased powers to command, to impose obligations and to receive accounts. These accounts detail both the compliance of schools to central commands and the schools' effectiveness as measured by a range of nationally determined criteria. However, the informing principles of these commands and associated criteria of accountability, in the shape of performance indicators, emanate from the government itself. They are political creations and, as such, reinforce the important distinction between changing modes of control on the one hand and the principles which inform that control on the other. If the current English *mode* of control centres on bureaucratic and democratic forms of accountability at the expense of the professional, the current *substance* of control is embodied in the legitimating ideology of a New Right political perspective, with its emphasis on competition, *laissez-faire* individualism and elitism as the way to economic growth and, ultimately, as the informing vision of 'the good life'.

Thus recent years have seen repeated direct political interventions by ministers in the formulation of educational policy (Simon 1992), often in the face of widespread disagreement from a whole range of interested bodies, including those the system is purporting to serve, namely industry and parents, as well as the much maligned community of professional educationists. The GCSE examination continues to provide pointed examples in this respect. Given that the exam represents one of the most powerful and highly visible mechanisms of system control, it is not surprising that, since its inception, decisions concerning both curriculum content and the mode of assessment should have been characterized by struggles between the 'old humanists', the public educators and the 'new industrialists' (Bowe and Whitty 1984).

Recently, however, such struggles have been replaced by apparently arbitrary, political dictats which have only a combination of ideological prejudice and power coercive implementation strategies to sustain them. Thus, for example, in the face of considerable evidence of the positive impact of GCSE course-work on student motivation and achievement, as embodied in steadily rising levels of success, in 1992 the Prime Minister imposed a substantially reduced course-work limit, arguing against an overwhelming body of research evidence that 'paper and pencil tests' and 'unseen exams' are more rigorous. Such direct ministerial interventions in education in the face of concerted opposition are almost unprecedented in England.

Thus, while one effect of recent disquiet about educational standards has been the move by the government to exert more formal control, arguably more important have been the orchestrated and sustained efforts of government to redefine teachers' professional expertise as mere left-wing ideology and instead to impose its own market-oriented, populist ideologies through their incorporation as the normative criteria of the underlying structure of educational discourse. In both these initiatives, accountability and the evaluation on which it is based have a central role to play.

Changing modes of control: France

In France, such an increase in control is more difficult to envisage. Such a capacity would depend on the creation of a network of reciprocal evaluation and communication systems, systems which can loosely be subsumed under the rubric of professional 'accountability' procedures and which alone could ensure, given the prevailing power structure within education, effective control of teachers.

The development of such systems requires a shift from bureaucracy, which is characteristic of central education systems, to a more 'managerial technology', which emphasizes *outcomes* as much as, if not more than, *processes* (Therborn 1978, quoted in Dale 1980). The extent to which this transition to a *post hoc* control has taken place will determine both the policy questions and the policy answers that can be posited in any particular education system. Thus, it may be argued that France's traditional reliance on, and commitment to, an almost classically bureaucratic form of educational provision and control, in comparison with England's traditional emphasis on control through outcomes, may account for the fact that stresses in the capitalist mode of production and in the bases of social integration, currently a feature of both countries, have not brought about in England the same kind of profound educational crises evident in recent years in France.

Certainly, both countries are experiencing the effects of the contemporary crisis of the state. In both countries the normative certainties underpinning curricular, administrative and all other decisions about educational content, processes and organization are being questioned. Similar structural and economic tensions in each society confront schools with quite incompatible demands: to integrate and to select; to teach creativity and conformity; to be vocationally oriented in an era of mass youth unemployment. Both French and English teachers are presented with something of an identity crisis about the scope of their professional responsibility and their educational objectives.

But this is not only a legitimation crisis. It is just as fundamentally a crisis of control. Senior administrators and the government are still held formally accountable for activities – teaching in the classrooms – which value pluralism and which the sheer size of the enterprise leaves them impotent to control. To avoid collapse, the French system has had to move towards the mode of control traditional in English education; from one based on direct instructions to one based on indirect ideological messages and a combination of bureaucratic and democratic accountability. Central to the efficacy of these changes is a very substantially increased role for assessment of students, of schools, of the system as a whole.

> The imposition of standardized curricula, the external examinations, and the inspector's report are no longer effective or acceptable means of governing the work of teachers . . . control is reaffirmed indirectly through outside agencies ie the teacher training institutions, research organisations and specialists in the fields of curriculum development, educational administration and educational evaluation.
>
> (Pusey 1980: 47)

Thus, for example, under the new 'national assessment' arrangements in France, information about their child's performance is given to parents, and many schools are setting aside time for discussion of results with parents (Le Guen 1994). The unprecedentedly high level of parent interest and response provoked by the evaluation is regarded as one of the main outcomes of the initiative, providing, as it does, both for the kind of active collaborative dialogue between schools and families which has not hitherto been a feature of French education and for a measure of direct account-ability to parents concerning standards (Thélot 1992).

If the aim of improving student learning through nationally initiated, formative assessment also embraces training teachers in assessment and helping them to devise ways of responding to student need in a 'regular and rigorous manner', an associated aim is to encourage a school-wide response to this need. Although the main role of these assessments is, officially at least, to provide formative information for teachers and to encourage and equip them to be better formative assessors themselves, the programme also has an important summative dimension in that aggregated results are published nationally so that parents, teachers and headteachers can compare their 'results' against national norms.

Although the availability of such information has provoked considerable media interest nationally, the ministry has so far resisted pressure for results to be made public and thus to provide for inter-school or inter-region comparisons. The still strongly held French belief in the notion of equality and commonality in edu-cational provision militates against the adoption of the notion of using competition and market forces to stimulate efforts by individ-ual schools to improve standards. But, given the experiments with open enrolment currently taking place in Paris and the intense interest that the annual publication of Baccalauréat results in *Le Monde de l'Education* provokes, it may not be long before the pressure for aggregated results to be published becomes irresistible – at least on a regional basis.

As the process of decentralization proceeded, the laws of 1983 and 1986 promoted the idea of the school as a local public establishment, which must now develop, with the support in each academy of teams of trained teachers or consultants, a written and public plan against which the whole community can judge the institution's degree of success in meeting its own goals. An assumption, now enshrined in law, that individual schools might vary in their policies and that teachers should be accountable through their institutions, rather than as individuals subject to personal inspection, represents a major change in French education. This change is reflected in the fact that the national inspectorate is also now responsible for evaluating institutions rather than, as they were before, nominally at least, charged with inspecting individual teachers.

In 1989 the *Loi d'Orientation* laid down the procedures for evaluating schools. The school has to carry out a detailed self-evaluation as a preparatory study to an external inspection using a range of indicators, and the results of both studies form the basis of subsequent discussion between school staff and inspector (CERI 1990). Currently schools are not using student results gathered for the *orientation* process as part of their public accountability profile, although there is pressure on them to do so (Coqblin 1991).

Common themes

Despite some continuing important differences of emphasis, developments in both England and France testify to the advent of what Weber referred to as 'a new order of domination', in which more covert, technologically inspired forms of power, meaning and rationality are changing the basis for social order and control. It is arguably the growth of 'scientism' that more than anything explains the increasing similarities in the educational arrangements of advanced industrial societies, which have hitherto been characterized by major differences in the organization of their educational systems.

Thus, as was suggested in Chapter 4, the language of bureaucracy, with its vocabulary of rational judgement, objectivity, fairness and efficiency, has characterized post-Enlightenment social organizations. The preoccupation with rules and normality, which is the basis for bureaucratic rationality, necessarily involves the making of judgements on others in relation to prevailing norms. Evaluation of individual performance is legitimated in the language of scientific rationality, so that the criteria against which that evaluation is made, criteria which in practice embody the goals of the organization or system, are implicitly taken to be neutral or self-evident while in reality they are arbitrary, reflecting existing power relations.

Typically the most fundamental power relations inherent in educational judgements are also the most effectively hidden. They are an example of Lukes's (1974) 'third order' power. While challenges may be aimed at relatively superficial manifestations of the dominant instrumental order – curriculum content or school organization – the systems of national prescription and local quality assurance that are increasingly characterizing modern education systems largely conceal their value assumptions and thus protect them from fundamental opposition. A central value assumption is that of efficiency: the rational and optimum ordering of means to meet defined needs. Equally central is evaluation: the means by which needs are identified and the success of particular strategies or personnel in meeting those needs. This is, of course to use the term evaluation in the broadest sense as a means of appraisal. Nevertheless, the value commitment to rational judgement on the part of both administrators and practitioners is crucial. If such a commitment has always been a defining characteristic of mass schooling systems, it is the argument of this chapter that both the rhetoric and the reality of evaluation are becoming much more prominent at the present time, with highly significant effects.

While the analyses of this book underline the central role of various types of assessment procedure in educational systems, they also help to explain the growth of scientific rationality, from being a means to an end into apparently being the end itself, from being the instrumental ideology to being the expressive ideology. It is important to stress, however, that the control provided by the new language of scientific rationality is a control which emanates from the multiplicity of interacting micro-powers. It is not *per se* the ideological expression of an increasingly centralized state or a particular social class. Nevertheless, it is not neutral but must be seen, as Foucault suggests, as part of that ongoing power struggle between individuals and groups which accumulates into structuration and the particular versions of truth that underpin political power. The pseudo-neutrality of technology disguises the significant power relations behind who buys, who uses and who develops the new technology. The significance of these questions in relation to contemporary assessment arrangements in education has been the theme of this book. The ideology of scientific rationality which increasingly provides the common language for accountability is not the 'cultural arbitrary' (to use Bourdieu and Passeron's term) of any identifiable group. Its current pre-eminence as a mode of control, however, is the result of a protracted struggle between different interest groups, and its growth as an ideology embodied in notions such as standards, quality, indicators and targets is reflexively related to the need and ability of dominant groups to retain that dominance.

The increasing association of the rendering of various kinds of 'accounts' with technicist notions of control is linked by the French sociologist, Berger to changes in the approach to assessment. Hitherto, Berger (1981) suggests, the dominant form of the evaluation was a *visible* form of social power in which the teacher or the examiner was vested with the personal right to pass judgement on a pupil's performance. Although open to all the vagaries of arbitrary personal preference, this system did at least allow some comeback by the individual pupil if he or she disagreed with the assessment, because the judgement was clearly, in the last resort, the inevitably personal judgement of an individual. It was a system clearly based on values. This system also allowed a good deal of diversity, given the equally inevitable differences in the personal predilections of examiners within the broad limits laid down by the examination, often much to the candidate's chagrin.

The trend in recent years, however, has been to deplore the various injustices inherent in such an approach and to seek a more 'objective', scientific and thus fairer approach to assessment. This has led to the increasingly sophisticated identification of behavioural norms upon which to base both teaching, as in the pre-specification of learning targets, and assessment, as in the recent fashion for criterion-referenced approaches.

In their call for a new 'science' of educational assessment, Berlak *et al.* (1992) mount a major critique of such developments, arguing that performance is inevitably heavily context-bound and influenced by various affective dimensions, such as learners' values and their confidence and motivation in a given situation. Recent empirical work (Shavelson *et al.* 1992) also appears to bear out the argument that, whether the assessment is tightly focused and 'objective' or an 'authentic' judgement rooted in real performance situations, results are likely to be affected by such factors. These studies and many similar (Black 1993; Wolf 1993) suggest that assessment of students' achievements ought to be seen as an art, rather than a science – interpretive, idiosyncratic, interpersonal and, thus, essentially relative. Why this is not so and why, instead, the development of individual procedures over the past two centuries or so has been characterized by systematic efforts to emphasize their *scientific* character has been explored in some detail in this book. It has been argued that in the post-Enlightenment age of rationality, judgements endowed with a scientific origin have achieved the advantage of apparent irrefutability. Perhaps even more importantly, the presentation of such judgements as scientific has disguised the particular values and hence the power relations embodied within them.

The rise of 'the new Evaluative State' (Neave 1989) in recent decades arguably represents a further stage in the process both of using formal assessment procedures as a mode of control and of disguising the value relativity of such assessments by means of an apparently neutral, technicist discourse of objectives and indicators. Linked as this movement is, both practically and ideologically, with the growth of quality assurance strategies at every level of the educational system, it is a short step from the use of regular and overt 'monitoring' and reporting as a pedagogic strategy, to their use as an administrative strategy – a means of individual and, indeed, system control. As the assessment is increasingly oriented to explicit norms of performance, to centrally, or perhaps regionally, generated criteria rather than, as hitherto, to the largely implicit criteria of the individual assessor, the social power which the imposition of those norms represents becomes increasingly invisible, hidden in the disguise of a bland and neutral technology in just the same way that 'corporate planning' disguises value judgements as scientific, rational, objective solutions to problems.

This is not to suggest, however, that different interest groups in the education system – central government, local education authorities, inspectors, teachers and consumers – will not continue to dispute the policy priorities implicit in the more general goals they define for education. Their different location within the education system will continue to ensure that short-term resource disputes informed by a variety of professional and political concerns are still characteristic of systemic functioning. But increasingly, it is suggested, in the underlying ideological context for such debate, the criteria of what constitutes the nature of 'the good life' – the expressive ideology of society as a whole – become synonymous with what was hitherto merely one form of instrumental ideology, that of scientific rationalism. The language for discussing educational goals becomes, like that for discussing the more general goals of social life, progressively subsumed within the language for discussing educational and social government. In no sense can this be a uniform development, nor is it unresisted, since the currency of power struggle makes it of differential utility to different groups. But it is arguably the most pervasive feature of contemporary educational discourse. If the implications are currently more visible at the more explicitly scientific end of the assessment scale, such as the psychological labelling of children with learning or behavioural difficulties, examples of this trend, which will affect all teachers and pupils and which are likely to become increasingly significant, are not hard to find.

In England, for example, the imposition of standardized criteria for each subject in the GCSE public examination was a clear step in this direction, as was the rapid growth of the 'graded tests' movement. The government's Assessment of Performance Unit and similar moves towards monitoring school and system performance on the part of local authorities were equally manifestations of the same trend. In 1984, Black *et al.* argued that the assessment procedures of the APU might come to define standards without the assumptions on which they were based being examined. The APU, they suggested, emerged as a powerful 'middle agent' in the public formulation of standards:

> The extreme possibility is that knowledge of *what is* will anaesthetise our power to distinguish from *what ought to be* or *could be*. Whilst it is true in practice that criteria are always linked to knowledge of norms, it is also true that they cannot be derived from norms alone, and that where they appear to do so, some assumptions have slipped by without being required to identify and justify themselves.
>
> (Black *et al.* 1984: 10)

The truth of this prediction has been demonstrated by the incorporation of much of the APU apparatus and expertise in the development of the National Assessment framework for the measurement of pupils' progress in relation to the National Curriculum.

In France, as Chapter 6 described, there have also been significant and similar developments in the field of national monitoring of standards. In addition, the increasing responsibility being given to teachers at all levels of the school system to assess pupils' progress in relation to nationally agreed objectives is also significant. The system of *orientation* informed by national standardized tests, in which a panel of teachers *collectively* decides on the recommended future courses for each pupil, has the dual effect of being very much harder for the pupil to dispute and of encouraging conformity of standards. There is less and less place for the vagaries of the individual teacher or for the pupil to resist the label in a way she or he might have done in the one-off attempt of a formal examination. Because standards and recommendations are collective, they are impersonal and 'objective', their arbitrary nature so well hidden as to be removed from the agenda of discussion.

The growing involvement of teachers in assessing pupils at *lycée* level in France represents an extension of this trend hardly evident as yet in England. Its significance will depend on the extent to which the *criteria* for such assessments are influenced by the state or, to put it another way, how far the professional language of French teachers is influenced by the prevailing utilitarian, rationalist, technicist ideology at the expense of their 'traditional', 'humanist' orientation. The upheavals in French universities over government attempts to make courses more vocational suggest that the necessarily overt nature of such moves is likely to result in a more stormy and explicit process of capitulation than in England, where the overt strategies employed have, arguably, been relatively insignificant compared to the covert influences at work.

In both England and France, however, the legitimating rhetoric of such developments is their apparently benign purpose, the assumption that increased rationality and openness and more widely available information is as much in the interest of the individual as it is in that of the organization or the state. Thus, as the school becomes increasingly dominated by techno-scientific knowledge as the knowledge of most worth, the ideological structuring of the school's activity as a whole, notably organization and management, also becomes centred on the pursuit of efficiency and the 'scientific' canons of objectivity, impartiality, formality and standardization. The logic is further extended in the increasingly explicit role of parents as 'consumers' of education who, on the basis of apparently rational judgements about relative institutional quality, will exercise their right of choice. In the competition so engendered it is assumed that institutional efficiency will be further encouraged.

Weber suggests that, with the advent of capitalism, the rational bureaucratic allocation of authority progressively replaced the authority of tradition and charisma and other more coercive, illegitimate forms of power (Spencer 1970). Now in the late capitalist era it is possible to trace the beginnings at least of a further stage in this development, a stage in which the rationality of bureaucratic organizations combines with the rationality of scientific logic into a single legitimating ideology of technological rationality.

The growth of this ideology in schools reflects and reinforces changes in the legitimating ideology more generally, in which

> the imperatives of scientific, technical progress . . . alone can guarantee economic growth and stability. Society must be run on rational lines by technical experts. The only problems are technical problems and the development of the social system must obey the logic of scientific progress.
>
> (Wilby 1979)

At the level of the system as well as of the school, the need for increased 'steering capacity' brought about by the growing scale, complexity and uncertainty in the context of state activities results in the extension of such activity into new areas of social life, a phenomenon which in turn requires the emergence of new modes of rationality and new techniques of management. In particular, it has been suggested that there is a tendency for these new forms of ideological control typically to be reflected in the more traditional reliance on overt, bureaucratic structures being reinforced by the more indirect pressure of quality assurance and control devices combined with market forces. Such an approach to control operates on a currency of assessment information generated against centrally imposed criteria of performance. These are both practical and ideological changes, for since administrative systems cannot themselves produce the meanings which motivate individuals to act within specific social situations (Habermas 1976) – those being generated only through socio-cultural interaction (*Praktisch*) – the technical efficiency argument itself becomes the goal as well as the means, thereby effectively disguising the fact that what is 'worth' knowing, and hence every aspect of educational policy, is essentially a value question.

Thus, as was suggested in Chapter 4, under the cloak of scientism, value decisions and the power relations they reflect continue to be taken, albeit unconsciously. The concern with what was *humanly* possible in the eighteenth and nineteenth centuries has become, in the twentieth century, a concern with the *technically* possible: 'the culture of positivism in which truth is taken to be neutral, thereby robs history of its critical possibilities and provides uncritical support of the status quo' (Husserl, quoted in Giroux 1981: 56). As Giroux (1981: 56) further suggests, 'critical thought has lost its contemplative character and has been debased to the level of technical intelligence, subordinate to meeting operational problems.' Or, in the words of the social historian G. M. Trevelyan, 'Education . . . has produced a vast population able to read but unable to distinguish what is worth reading.'

Conclusion

The search for an explanation of contemporary developments in the educational assessment practices of England and France involves the identification of evolving frames of reference of the most fundamental kind. Overt assessment policies and practices are only one manifestation among others in education, and indeed outside it, of a changing basis for social control in which the lack of a shared set of cultural values and the rapid erosion of the apparatus through which such values and common interpretations are generated is compensated for by the elevation of social and economic efficiency – as expressed in notions of 'quality' – to being taken to be the *meaning* as well as the *means* of social life. Although evaluation as expressed in a variety of more or less formal assessment procedures plays a largely determined, rather than a determining, part in this process, it plays this part at many different levels, for the notion of judgement and responsibility and hence of accountability is inherent in the concept of rationality itself.

In this book it has been argued that, with the advent of industrialization, the evaluation which is central to all interpersonal communication became progressively formalized to provide the rationale on which to base the organization of mass educational provision. In Chapter 2 it was suggested that assessment procedures were critical in providing for the formal organization of curricula and in the identification of appropriate standards, functions which endured but became increasingly overshadowed by the ever more intense pressure on the school system to assume the responsibility for legitimating and, to some extent, performing the process of social selection.

Why assessment procedures were, and still are, able to perform such a critical role in the perpetuation of educational control, and hence, ultimately, social control, can only be explained by reference to the commitment to the ideology of the responsible individual, which, more than anything, separates modern from pre-industrial societies, as discussed in Chapter 4. On this ideology rest the social forms which characterize contemporary society, such as democracy, wage-labour employment and bureaucracy, in which it is both the right and the responsibility of the individual to judge and be judged. The commitment to scientific and technical progress that is the other face of rationality not only identifies technology as the chief instrument of progress, but also led to the proliferation of various kinds of administrative bureaucracy through which the burgeoning infrastructure of the state could be provided and controlled. One element of this was state provision for mass education.

However, while the institution of such provision is common to all industrial societies, there is clearly a good deal of variation between societies in the way in which elements of different national education systems have emerged. If elements of Weber's 'ideal type' of bureaucracy are necessarily manifest in every national education system, there are equally significant variations in bureaucratic style, so that notions of hierarchy, general rules, continuous and impersonal offices and the separation between official and private life must be interrelated with historically specific social situations (Gouldner 1952).

Just as there are differences in the 'bureaucratic cultures of the Western world' (Bendix 1952), so there are significant differences in all the other social institutions in countries which nevertheless share a common capitalist and industrial character. This was the argument of Chapter 5, which set out the theoretical justification for the inclusion of the two separate case studies that form the empirical basis of this analysis. Any explanation of the way in which educational practices vary between societies which share a common capitalist order must be grounded in historical analysis. Any one point in time witnesses the interaction between objectively changing social, political and economic conditions and the purposes and perceptions of individual and, hence, groups of actors, which are structured by, and in turn serve to structure, the changing social reality. This book has sought to illustrate how the precise form of national educational problems, the way in which they are perceived and the range of potential solutions that may be considered must be understood as the general problems of education within capitalist societies, mediated by the constraints of existing social forms – geographical, cultural, legal, economic, socio-political and religious – which together build up the patterns of meaning and perception at national, institutional and individual levels.

To understand sociologically the differences in assessment practice of two countries such as England and France it is necessary to consider the whole fabric of their respective social orders. Clearly this is an enormous task and the empirical case studies of Chapters 6 and 7 are necessarily selective. They are designed to extend the theoretical arguments of Part I by exploring both the common and the idiosyncratic features of the assessment procedures in each society as these provide for the attestation of competence, the formalization of content, the regulation of competition and the control of individuals and the system as a whole.

The necessarily dynamic nature of such an analysis reveals the quite fundamental developments currently affecting advanced capitalist societies such as England and France. In these, as in other such countries, there are the various social, political and administrative ingredients of a legitimation crises: the breakdown of traditional norms and values, a state locked into a vicious circle of justification through ever greater expenditure, the political dilemma of democratic equality and the need to perpetuate elitism, and the increasing impossibility of adequately running an edifice of such enormous size. That these developments have not yet had the destabilizing effect on the social order which might have been expected is due not least to the extension of a technicist ideology into all areas of social life. Not only does a benign scientism increasingly underpin the processes of individual selection, so that the attestation of competence, curriculum organization and the processes of competition and control become redefined on the basis of new, positive, impersonal and, by the same token, uncontestable norms, the educational bureaucracy itself is increasingly dominated by the impersonal procedures of scientific management and information generation, of product- rather than process-based control, in place of the old, informal, personal and often irrational modes of organization.

Because the commitment to technical efficiency is increasingly being incorporated at the level of meaning and volition, as well as that of practice, this provides pressure for the non-bureaucratic, potentially contradictory languages of professionalism and democratic participation to define their own criteria of value and, hence, personal accountability in the same terms. Thus, from the evaluation of systemic performance to the evaluation of individual schools, teachers and pupils there is a common pressure on both producers (teachers and pupils) and consumers (parents and employers) to assume that value can be quantified and expressed in terms of a variety of 'performance indicators' (OECD 1992). The revolution in thinking which led to the institution of the first quantitatively marked degree examinations in the eighteenth century and the mass institution of school assessment that followed it in the nineteenth century has had a fundamental influence on the development of mass schooling over the past hundred years. It is the argument of Chapter 8 that the significance of that innovation may well in the end be matched by an equally significant 'quality revolution': the extension of the concept of scientific, quantitative evaluation into the structuring of the educational system itself.

On the other hand, there are small but nevertheless detectable signs that, in true classical tradition, even at the very height of its domination, this assessment ideology already contains the seeds of its own destruction and the apotheosis of a new order. It may be that, as Habermas suggests, the assessment which was so instrumental to the formation of contemporary society proves in the long run also to be its undoing, in a growing

> lack of understanding why despite the advanced stage of technological development the life of the individual is still determined by the dictates of professional careers, the ethics of status competition, and by values of possessive individualism and available substitute gratifications: why the institutionalised struggle for existence, the discipline of alienated labour, and the eradication of sensuality and aesthetic gratification are perpetuated. To this sensibility the structural elimination of practical problems from a depoliticised public realm must become unbearable. However, it will give rise to a political force only if this sensibility comes into contact with a problem that the system cannot solve. For the future I see one such problem. The amount of social wealth produced by industrially advanced capitalism and the technical and organisational conditions under which this wealth is produced make it ever more difficult to link status assignment in an even subjectively convincing

manner to the mechanism for the evaluation of individual achievement.

(Habermas 1971)

The need for a sociological understanding of the role of assessment in industrial societies is increasingly pressing, as the tentacles of rational evaluation intrude ever further into the provision and process of education as well as all other areas of economic and social life. Equally, such an understanding may soon prove necessary to explain the progressive breaking down of the traditional methods of legitimation and social control within the institution of mass education which has been largely provided by assessment procedures. If it has helped at all to further such an understanding, this book will have fulfilled its intention.

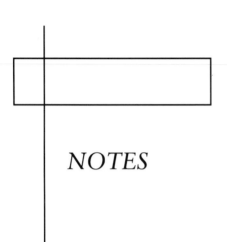

NOTES

Chapter 1

1 The vulnerability of even tightly controlled public examinations to criticisms because of problems of this kind is well demonstrated by the furore surrounding 1992 GCSE examination results in England, following the submission of a report by Her Majesty's Inspectorate detailing some problems of comparability.

Chapter 2

1 See, for example, the evaluation of the impact of the Enterprise in Higher Education Initiative, which traces its relative lack of impact to the continuing domination of traditional assessment procedures (Department of Employment 1994).

Chapter 3

1 It is recognized that such non-selective 'elementary' education has a much longer history in some other countries, notably the United States. In 1946 the Report of a Royal Commission in Sweden proposed a new comprehensive *grundeschule* for all pupils, thereby pioneering in Europe the

model of non-selective schooling throughout the period of compulsory education – a model which was already established in the Soviet Union and the United States. This was perhaps owing to a more long-standing preoccupation in these countries with education as a means of creating equality of opportunity and national unity, in contrast to the more single-minded European association of secondary schooling with academic excellence.

2 In the Netherlands, for example, the selective examination for secondary schools has been replaced by an admissions committee composed of the school's governing authority, the school's principal and some teachers, who make a decision based on the report of the head of the primary school. In Germany, examinations have been replaced by selection based on teacher assessment, followed by a common orientation stage in the fifth and sixth classes, which decides, again on the basis of class tests, whether the pupil has truly been allocated to the appropriate secondary school. This spirit of positive guidance continues in Germany, as it does in France, with continuous monitoring of the pupil's progress. In Italy, the traditionally elaborate system of teacher grades and annual promotion in the elementary and intermediate (11–14) schools has been abolished and replaced by an assessment card providing an 'analytical and rounded assessment for each pupil', which is also the basis for school reports.

3 The United States is a good example, in this respect, where the inclusion of information about extra-curricular activities such as debating or sport, and personal qualities such as leadership and sociability, has always made the school record an important complement in the largely ungraded High School Certificate. King (1981) argues that schooling in the United States has always of necessity given highest priority to the need to socialize and weld into a social unit all the diverse cultures represented in its immigrants. Arguably such an emphasis continued to be possible in the USA because it has never had a system which puts a strong emphasis on overt selection. The stress on democracy and patriotism in American schools, as evidenced by, for example, the morning flag-raising ceremony, may indeed be at considerable cost given that one in five American adults have been claimed to be functionally illiterate (Binyon 1976). At the other end of the political spectrum, the former communist countries of the Eastern bloc and China clearly recognized the political and ideological conformity that could be reinforced by taking into account a very much wider range of information about pupils than simply academic attainment (Price 1976, 1977).

4 Throughout Europe, the traditional policy of open admission to higher education for those with matriculation in, for example, Austria, Switzerland, Belgium, Italy, West Germany and France is now being modified in many countries to restrict entry within the most popular faculties. In

Germany, for example, the grouped subject *Abitur* is carefully graded to allow university admission on a strict *numerus clausus* basis.

5 England's preoccupation with public examinations is an interesting manifestation of the important and close relationship between certification mechanisms and mechanisms of system control and accountability. The hitherto very informal methods of system control characteristic of all the education systems of the British Isles to a greater or lesser extent have resulted in their being much slower to respond to the pressures for change in assessment procedures that have led to the international trends under discussion, which is an important constraint on changes in certification procedures. Thus Britain is currently the only country in Europe still setting formal external examinations on a mass basis at 16-plus. The tensions surrounding the GCSE are some evidence of the effect of 'comprehensivization', in allowing a much larger number of pupils than before to gain a qualification at least nominally equivalent in status to GCE O level. The effect of this is to prompt worries about 'standards' – as manifested by the then Secretary of State for Education, John Patten, calling for a national enquiry into the conduct of GCSE when better than expected results were achieved in the summer of 1992.

6 Such trends are not yet typical of Third World countries because, as has been suggested, the particular assessment policies of individual countries will be a reflection of the stage of development reached, combined with the particular institutional traditions, policy priorities and resources characteristic of that particular country. But, despite their very different stage of development, Third World countries are still identifiably on the same continuum of examination practice as the developed world, albeit at an earlier stage. As King (1976) suggests, 'as long as selection remains more important than socialisation at all levels of the educational system, it is probably unrealistic to expect any significant retreat from formalism . . . The parents seem not at all anxious that they adapt the formal government curriculum to the solution of local community issues . . . The main community issue still seems to be securing through education a few more jobs outside the local community.' This phenomenon remains typical of developing countries despite vigorous attempts to overcome it. See also Little (1992).

Chapter 4

1 'Rationality' is taken here to refer to both forms of logic and ideology.

2 These terms embody a Marxist conceptualization of the relationship between economic and social relations (see, for example, Williams 1961).

3 Although some industrialized societies, such as Japan, retain a 'collectiv-

ist' rather than an 'individualist' orientation in general, underneath there is intense individualist competition in what is now regarded as an excessively competitive educational system (Takeuchi 1991). As Weber points out in his book *The Protestant Ethic and the Spirit of Capitalism*, there are major national differences in the impact of capitalism. The Japanese case usefully emphasizes the point that while the provision of a rational means of allocating individuals to differential social roles, and hence educational assessment, is a necessary feature of an expanding division of labour, the precise way in which this process is organized will be specific to the societal context. Japan arguably still represents an extreme case of 'sponsored' mobility (Turner 1960), in that, once selected for elite educational institutions, individuals no longer need to compete for status. After entry, such status comes from seniority.

4 For an analysis of Japanese society in these terms, see Shimahara (1979) – see note 3 above.

5 See Max Weber (1947). Also H. Gerth and C. Wright-Mills (1946).

6 Marshall (1982: 33) cites the examples of Italy, France, Spain and Portugal which had capitalism long before the Reformation and conversely, where ascetic Protestantism seems to have given no impetus to capitalist development in Switzerland, Scotland, Hungary and parts of the Netherlands.

7 Matthews (1980) argues that pre-capitalist society was also essentially pre-ideological society, the term 'ideology' being coined by Antoine Destutt de Tracy in 1795.

8 Hence the conservatism of the teaching profession – at least in some countries – identified by Durkheim and Bourdieu.

9 The three levels of the medieval French university – the Baccalauréat, the License and the Aggregation – are still essentially the same today nearly eighty years after Durkheim remarked upon this.

10 The links with the ideas of another French writer, Foucault, are explicit here. Foucault's analysis of the increasing tendency of society to remove into institutions the criminal and the insane so that they might be subject to hierarchical authority and normalizing judgement strangely echoes Durkheim's analysis of changing social attitudes towards another only semi-socialized group, the young, who were at this time also increasingly subject to surveillance and enclosure.

11 For a description of the Jesuit system see Durkheim (1947: 260).

12 The title of Derek Rowntree's book, *Assessing Students: How Shall We Know Them?*, is particularly revealing in this respect, but the tone is essentially similar in any of the standard works on classroom assessment techniques. See, for example, Dunn (1967), Schofield (1972), Jackson (1974), MacIntosh and Hale (1976) and Sumner (1982).

13 It is important to note that it was the prevailing rhetoric, far more than

the practices themselves, that changed – more traditional pedagogy now being supported by a legitimating ideology that is the product of recent years of recession and disquiet.

14 Quoted by Habermas (1970: 84). See also Schostak (1983).
15 An interesting parallel with the context for Durkheim's work.
16 See also Giddens (1982: Chapter 15).
17 See Durkheim's (1947) description of the advent of the monastic ideal of schooling in the seventeenth century.
18 Bell and Lancaster's monitorial system is described by Foucault (1977).
19 In some Victorian school buildings elements of this panopticism are still visibly represented and in current use in the architectural design of a large central hall and an encircling gallery to allow for supervision.
20 The significance of such 'self-control' is discussed in Chapter 2 in relation to accountability, where it is argued that the exposure of teachers to both public and bureaucratic 'surveillance' is a great deal more effective in influencing how teachers set their own canons of moral and professional accountability than the more formal authority of a central bureaucracy.

Chapter 5

1 A debate that ultimately cannot be resolved – at least with the current array of conceptual tools – for, as Marshall (1982: 150) suggests, 'discussion of which changed first – the world (Marx), or people's understanding of it (Weber) – is likely to be interminable because what is at issue is not the status of this or that body of empirical material but is rather the validity of competing frameworks for the interpretation of social reality.'
2 It is interesting to note that Antoine Destutt de Tracy, who, as mentioned earlier, coined the term 'ideology', was a member of the newly founded Institut de France (1795), whose members were known as ideologues – progressive, radical, liberal-scientific scholars – during the French Revolution (see Matthews 1980; see also Larrain 1979).
3 See also Ranson (1983).
4 The example Ranson *et al.* cite of when the increasing size of an organization constrains it to become more bureaucratic and, at the same time, it is located in a turbulent environment and therefore constrained to become more flexible and adaptable in its structural arrangements, is very clearly the situation facing the education of advanced industrial societies.
5 See also Ranson (1983).
6 A point made by a senior HMI inspector in interview.
7 A point made by IDEN in interview.
8 See Broadfoot (1980) for an enlargement of this argument.
9 It would be misleading, however, to regard the trends depicted in Figure 5.2

as anything more than general tendencies and to ignore the many examples of resistance on the part of educational practitioners and consumers to such changes that can be identified, and the associated pattern of negotiation between politicians, administrators, teachers and the public that this has made necessary.

Chapter 6

1 Non-elite, elementary education, which had a very different purpose and was almost totally separate in its provision, was only tenuously included (see Archer 1979: 201–3).
2 Thus, for example, Bourdieu and Passeron found that working-class students were the highest achievers in the Latin sub-group of the *lycée* because, they suggest, these students have had to exhibit exceptional qualities in order to be selected for and to persist in a channel so unlikely for students of their background. Such students compare badly, however, against the most talented middle-class students, who 'invest' their cultural capital in those high-status subjects on which there is most return. The continuing significance of such cultural capital among, for example, the highly selected academic elite of the *grandes écoles* is still readily acknowledged by the students themselves.
3 It is important to stress, however, that these are largely policy changes, with the degree of real change in the ethos and institutional organization of schooling varying from school to school, since the common school and the common course could not, of themselves, democratize a system in which none of the fundamental controls or ideologies were changed.
4 Notably the Compagnons de la Nouvelle Université (1917–24).
5 The Prost Report (see note 7) gives a mean national rate of appeal against *orientation* decisions in 1982 of 6.6 per cent and a successful appeal rate of 17.8 per cent.
6 Christian Beullac, interviewed in *Le Monde de l'Education*, March 1981.
7 A. Prost, *Les lycées et leurs études au seuil de XXIème siècle*. Rapport au Directeur des lycées presenté par le Groupe de Travail National sur les seconds cycles, Service d'Information, November 1983.
8 This attitude is well paralleled in the more recent opposition by teachers to the Le Grand Report on *collège* reform. As an article in *Le Monde* (25 January 1983) expressed it, 'It was crying "No to the Le Grand Report: or Reform the Collèges, yes; on the backs of the teachers, no" that the participants afterwards demonstrated in Paris.'
9 See, for example, *Ecole et Socialisme*, no. 26, May 1983. For other views, see *Le Quotidien de Paris*, 24 January 1983; *Le Matin*, 15 June

1982; *Pourquoi*, no. 192, February 1984; *Le Monde de l'Education*, February 1983.

10 Between 1962 and 1966 Baccalauréat entries doubled, and totalled 223,384 in 1967. In 1967, 59.8 per cent of candidates were successful (Rothera 1968). In 1979, 65.8 per cent of candidates passed the general Baccalauréat. In 1980 the figure was 66.1 per cent. The Baccalauréat de Technicien was passed by 58.6 per cent in 1979 and 59.4 per cent in 1980 (these figures break down into percentages of: Bac E 72.0, Bac C 67.9, Bac B 64.5, Bac A 65.0 and Bac D 63.4). The number of entrants to *grandes écoles* is difficult to specify exactly since there are ambiguities of definition involved. The largest estimate is about 240 such institutions if *écoles nationales* are included, housing about 100,000 students in 1982 (Neave 1984).

11 After the Second World War there were several attempts to raise the number and status of technical qualifications – such as the Bac Technique in 1946 – but these came to nothing with the continuing domination of the 'old humanist' influence of university professors (Archer 1979).

12 Among school-leavers going on to higher education in 1978, for example, 85.4 per cent of Bac C holders went on to long course higher education as against 54.3 per cent of Bac E holders.

13 The legal requirement for parents to be consulted about educational policy is facilitated by the existence of these organizations, which are frequently allied with a teachers' federation of similar complexion. The four major federations are: Fédération Nationale des Associations de Parents d'Eléves de l'Enseignement Public (FNA); Union Nationale des Associations Autonomes des Parents d'Eléves (UNAAPE); Fédération des Parents d'Eléves de l'Enseignement Public (PEEP); Fédération des Conseils de Parents d'Eléves des Ecoles Publiques (FCPE).

Chapter 7

1 In 1815 the first professional qualifying examinations were instituted by the Society of Apothecaries to ensure that doctors were adequately trained. The institution of written examinations for solicitors followed in 1835, for the Civil Service after the Northcote–Trevelyan Report of 1853 and for accountants in 1880. Gradually, 'the lazy doctrine that men are much of a muchness gave way to a higher respect for merit and for more effectual standards of competence' (Morley, quoted in the Beloe Report 1960).

2 The contrast between England and other European countries, such as Germany and France, where it was the state that controlled examinations which gave entry to university, is a significant one in informing

the subsequent significance of central control within the education system.

3 Again there are strong parallels with the move by the Conservative Government in 1991 to insist on all schools being regularly inspected by an 'appropriate' local body – not necessarily professionally involved in education.

4 The institution of Matriculation entrance examinations by London and Durham Universities at the same time was yet another manifestation of this trend.

5 It should be noted that these examinations were directed almost entirely at boys, the object of girls' education still being almost exclusively domestic, rather than intellectual (Delamont 1983).

6 No certificates were given until 1905.

7 Edmond Holmes's famous work *What Is and What Might Be*, published in 1911, expresses a view of the undesirable effects of examinations increasingly recognized by people at this time. 'A school that is ridden by the examination incubus is charged with deceit . . . all who become acclimatised to the influence of the system – pupils, teachers, examiners, employers of labour, parents, MPs and the rest, fall victims and are content to cheat themselves with outward and visible signs – class lists, orders of merit – as being of quasi-divine authority' (quoted in Broadfoot 1979a).

8 Until the institution of the School Certificate in 1917 the universities actually inspected schools where they had 'local' candidates because schools were able to mark their own examinations (M. Kingdom, in interview, 1980). Thus it is not without relevance that pupils had to have attended an inspected school continuously for two to three years before they could enter for such examinations.

9 Sharp (1980) describes a similar pattern for Scotland, where in 1923 'local examinations' administered by county education authorities were set up to regulate access to the different types of secondary provision. Against the intentions of the authorities, these, inevitably, operated as competitive examinations.

10 Annual Report of the Board of Education, 1906, p. 7, quoted by G. Sutherland (1977: 144).

11 *Special Place Examinations*, Board of Education pamphlet, 1936, p. 4, quoted by Sutherland (1977: 147).

12 Hamilton (1981) puts forward a parallel argument about the origin of schooling itself, which at about the end of the twelfth century replaced older, more informal forms of education when the administrative demands of a changing social order required the inculcation of particular skills and attitudes and thus a greater formalization of educational provision.

13 The existence of such possibilities has encouraged many 11-plus failures,

including some notable educationists such as Sir Rhodes Boyson, to support the continued existence of the tripartite system.

14   The success of such strategies is perhaps best illustrated by the Jesuit educational practice of institutionalized individual and group competition (see Durkheim 1977).

15   The comparability of different subjects' results is a vexed question in public examining, but the fact that certain subjects are *perceived* to be harder – whether this is true or not – is sufficient to bring about the effect being described.

16   The CSE was designed so that a Grade 1 pass in it was equivalent to a Grade C pass at O level. It was thus aimed at pupils from the 40th to the 80th percentiles. Almost all pupils were entered for at least one CSE. The value of them, however, is shown by the fact that many candidates did not bother to collect their certificates when the grade they achieved was lower than 3.

17   Schools Council Standing Conference on University Entrance, Joint Working Party on Sixth Form Curriculum and Examinations (the Schools Council's Second Sixth Form Working Party), *Proposals for the Curriculum and Examinations in the Sixth Form* (Butler–Briault Report), 1969.

18   Schools Council, Working Paper 46 (1973) *16–19 Growth and Response 2* and Working Paper 47 (1973) *Preparation for Degree Courses*. See also Schools Council Examinations Bulletin 38 (1978) and Working Paper 66 (1980) for further discussion of these proposals. The similarity with the pre-GCE School Certificate is striking. It is interesting to note the very different Scottish tradition in this respect, in which a less specialized 'highers course', sometimes but not necessarily complemented by a sixth year studies qualification, is still the normal entrance qualification for university (see, for example, Gray *et al.* 1983). Part of the explanation for this difference was the development of Scottish universities within the more liberal European tradition, shared by France, in which specialization and selection takes place within, as well as before, university entrance.

19   Again the comparison with the more centralized Scottish education system is instructive: there is a much greater degree of coordination between assessment and curriculum initiatives and a much greater rationalization of post-16 provision, as set out in the Scottish Education Department's 1984 *Action Plan for 16 to 18s in Scotland*.

20   A recent example is the initiative to reduce the amount of choice in the public examination syllabuses that the examination boards are able to make available to schools (*Times Educational Supplement* 7 January 1995).

Chapter 8

1 Circular 74-204 (24 May 1974) *Sur les missions et attributions du service d'informations economiques et statistiques*, Ministre de l'Education, Paris.

REFERENCES

Airasian, P. W. (1987) State mandated testing and educational reform: context and consequences, *American Journal of Education* 95: 393–412.

Airasian, P. W. (1988) Symbolic validation: the case of state-mandated High States Testing, *Educational Evaluation and Policy Analysis* 10 (4): 301–15.

Anderson, R. D. (1975) *Education in France 1848–70*. Oxford: Oxford University Press.

Apple, M. (1976) Commonsense categories and curriculum thought. In R. Dale, G. Esland and M. MacDonald (eds) *Schooling and Capitalism*. London: Routledge and Kegan Paul.

Archer, M. S. (1979) *Social Origins of Educational Systems*. London: Sage.

Archer, M. S. (1980) Education. In J. E. Flower (ed.) *France Today*. London: Methuen.

Archer, M. S. (1981a) Fields of specialisation: educational systems, *International Social Science Journal* XXXIII (2): 261–84.

Archer, M. S. (1981b) On predicting the behaviour of the educational system. Extended review, *British Journal of Sociology of Education* 2 (2): 211–19.

Archer, M. S. (1982) Educational politics: a model for their analysis. In P. Broadfoot, C. Brock and W. Tulasiewicz (eds) *Politics and Educational Change*. London: Croom Helm.

Archibald, D. A. and Porter, A. C. (1994) Curriculum control and teachers' perceptions of autonomy and satisfaction, *Educational Evaluation and Policy Analysis* 16 (1): 21–39.

Aron, R. (1969) *The Elusive Revolution*. New York: Praeger.

Aron, R. (1980) La Lutte des Classes. In R. Bocock, P. Hamilton, K. Thompson and A. Waters (eds) *An Introduction to Sociology*. Glasgow: Fontana.

Atkins, M. J. and Brown, G. A. (1984) *Testing for Learning*. York: Longman for FEU.

Bacon, W. (1981) Professional control and the engineering of client consent. In R. Dale, G. Esland, R. Fergusson and M. MacDonald (eds) *Politics, Patriarchy and Practice*. Lewes: The Falmer Press.

Ball, C. (1992) *Ladders and Links: Prerequisites for the Discussion of an International Framework of Qualifications*, keynote address at Qualifications for the 21st Century, International Conference, Victoria University of Wellington. Wellington: New Zealand Qualifications Authority.

Ball, S. (1990) *Politics and Policy-making in Education*. London: Routledge.

Ballion, R., Bayait, D. and Mayer, P. (1991) *Indicateurs de compte rendu au conseil d'administration des lycées, etablissements du second degre, colleges, lycées professionnels*. Paris: Ministere de l'Education.

Banks, O. (1955) *Parity and Prestige in English Secondary Education*. London: Routledge and Kegan Paul.

Banks, O. (1978) Macro and micro perspectives in the sociology of education. In L. Barton and R. Meighan (eds) *Sociological Interpretations of Schooling and Classrooms*. Driffield: Nafferton.

Bates, R. (1980a) Educational administration, the sociology of science and the management of knowledge, *Educational Administration Quarterly* 16 (2): 1–20.

Bates, R. (1980b) The function of educational administration in the process of cultural transmission. Paper presented at conference on the origins and operations of educational systems, International Sociological Association, Paris.

Bates, R. (1980c) Bureaucracy, professionalisation and the control of knowledge. Paper presented to the National Conference of Professors of Education Administration. Norfolk, Virginia.

Bates, R. (1984) Educational versus managerial evaluation in schools. In P. Broadfoot (ed.) *Selection, Certification and Control*. London: The Falmer Press.

Becher, R. and McLure, S. (eds) (1978) *Accountability in Education*. Slough: NFER.

Becker, H. (1952) Social class variations in the teacher–pupils relationship, *Journal of Educational Sociology* 25: 451–65.

Beeby, C. E. (1966) *The Quality of Education in Developing Countries*. Oxford: Oxford University Press.

Bendix, R. (1952) Bureaucracy and the problem of power. In Merton, R. K., Gray, A. P., Hockey, B. and Selvin, H. C. (eds) *Bureaucracy*. New York: The Free Press.

Berger, P. (1966) *Invitation to Sociology: a Humanistic Perspective.* Harmondsworth: Penguin.

Berlak, H., Newmann, F. M., Adams, E., Archibald, D. A., Burgess, T., Rowen, J. and Romberg, T. A. (1992) *Towards a New Science of Educational Testing and Assessment.* New York: State University of New York Press.

Bernbaum, G. (1977) *Knowledge and Ideology in the Sociology of Education.* London: Macmillan.

Bernstein, B. (1977) *Class Codes and Control*, vol. iii. London: Routledge and Kegan Paul.

Bernstein, B. (1982) Codes, modalities and the process of cultural reproduction: a model. In M. Apple (ed.) *Cultural and Economic Reproduction in Education.* London: Routledge and Kegan Paul.

Bernstein, B. (1988) 'On Pedagogic Discourse', mimeo. University of London, Institute of Education.

Binyon, M. (1976) Equality or quality, *Times Educational Supplement*, 19 March.

Black, P. (1993) Conference paper given to Association of Assessment Inspectors and Advisers. Reported in *Times Educational Supplement*, 1 October.

Black, P., Harlen, W. and Orgee, T. (1984) Standards of performance – expectations and reality. Assessment Performance Unit Occasional Paper 3.

Blau, P. M. (1964) *Exchange and Power in Social Life.* New York: Basic Books.

Bligh, D. (ed.) (1982) *Accountability or Freedom for Teachers.* Research into Higher Education Monographs. London: The Society for Research into Higher Education.

Bloom, B. S., Hastings, J. T. and Madaus, G. F. (1971) *Handbook of Formative and Summative Evaluation of Student Learning.* Chicago, IL: McGraw-Hill.

Bocock, R., Hamilton, P., Thompson, K. and Waters, A. (1980) *An Introduction to Sociology.* Glasgow: Fontana.

Bottin, J. (1991) Etudes des pratiques d'evaluation des professeurs en classes de troisieme et de seconde. Rapport sur IGEN (Ministère de l'Education, Paris).

Bourdieu, P. (1974) The school as a conservative force: scholastic and cultural inequalities. In J. Eggleston (ed.) *Contemporary Research in the Sociology of Education.* London: Methuen.

Bourdieu, P. and Passeron, J. P. (1977) *Reproduction.* London: Sage.

Bourdieu, P., Passeron, J.-C. and de Saint Martin, M. with Baudelot, C. and

Vincent, G. (1994) *Academic Discourse, Linguistic Misunderstanding and Professional Power*. Cambridge: Polity Press.

Bourdoncle, R. (1994) La Professionnalisation des enseignents, *European Journal of Teacher Education* 17(1–2): 13–25.

Bowe, R. and Whitty, G. (1984) Teachers, boards and standards: the attack on school-based assessment in English public examinations at 16+. In P. Broadfoot (ed.) *Selection, Certification and Control*. Lewes: The Falmer Press.

Bowles, S. and Gintis, H. (1976) *Schooling in Capitalist America*. London: Routledge and Kegan Paul.

Boydell, D. (1974) Teacher–pupil contact in junior classrooms, *British Journal of Educational Psychology* 44: 313–18.

Branthwaite, A., Trueman, M. and Berrisford, T. (1981) Unreliability of marking: further evidence and a possible explanation, *Educational Review* 33 (1): 41–6.

Braudel, F. (1973) *The Mediterranean and the Mediterranean world in the age of Phillip II*. London: Collins.

Broadfoot, P. (1979a) *Assessment, Schools and Society*. London: Methuen.

Broadfoot, P. (1979b) Communication in the classroom: a study of the role of assessment in motivation, *Educational Review* 31 (1): 3–10.

Broadfoot, P. (1980) Assessment, curriculum and control in the changing pattern of centre-local relations, *Local Government Studies*, November: 57–68.

Broadfoot, P. (1981a) Accountability in England and France: the centralist alternative?, *Educational Policy Bulletin* 10 (1): 55–68.

Broadfoot, P. (1981b) Towards a sociology of assessment. In L. Barton and S. Walker (eds) *Schools, Teachers and Teaching*. London: The Falmer Press.

Broadfoot, P. (1981c) Constants and Contexts in Educational Accountability: a Comparative Study. Final Report to Social Science Research Council.

Broadfoot, P. (ed.) (1984) *Selection Certification and Control. Social Issues in Educational Assessment*. Lewes: The Falmer Press.

Broadfoot, P. (ed.) (1986) *Profiles and records of achievement: a review of issues and practice*. London: Holt Saunders.

Broadfoot, P. (1989) Towards Curssessment: the symbiotic relationship between curriculum and assessment. In N. Entwistle (ed.) *Handbook of Educational Ideas and Practices*. London: Croom Helm.

Broadfoot, P. (1990) Cinderella and the ugly sisters: an assessment policy pantomime in two acts, *The Curriculum Journal* 1 (2): 199–215.

Broadfoot, P. (1991) The significance of contemporary contradiction in educational assessment policies in England and Wales. In R. Stake (ed.) *Advances in Program Evaluation: Volume 1 (Part A)*. London: JAI Press.

Broadfoot, P. (1992) Assessment developments in French education, *Education Review* 44 (3): 309–16.

Broadfoot, P. (1993) Assessment procedures in French education. In J. Nisbet (ed.) *Curriculum and Assessment*. Paris: Organization for Economic Cooperation and Development.

Broadfoot, P. (1994a) Assessing quality in education: some international examples. In W. Harlen (ed.) *Towards Quality Assessment*. London: Paul Chapman.

Broadfoot, P. (1994b) Performance assessment in perspective. In H. Torrance (ed.) *Evaluating Authentic Assessment*. Buckingham: Open University Press.

Broadfoot, P. (1996) But do I have to write it all down? In P. Croll (ed.) *Teachers, Pupils and Primary Schooling*. London: Cassell.

Broadfoot, P. and Dockrell, B. (1977) *Pupils in Profile*. London: Hodder and Stoughton for Scottish Council for Research in Education.

Broadfoot, P. and Osborn, M. (1987) Teachers' conceptions of their professional responsibilities: some international comparisons, *Comparative Education* 23 (3): 287–301.

Broadfoot, P. and Osborn, M. (1988) What professional responsibility means to teachers: national contexts and classroom constants, *British Journal of Sociology of Education* 9(3), special issue.

Broadfoot, P., Gilly, M., Osborn, M. and Paillet, A. (1989) Teachers' Conceptions of their Professional Responsibility in England and France, final report to Economic and Social Science Research Council.

Broadfoot, P., Abbott, D., Croll, P., Osborn, M., Pollard, A. and Towler, L. (1991) Implementing national assessment: issues for primary teachers, *Cambridge Journal of Education* 21 (2): 153–68.

Broadfoot, P., Harlen, W., Gipps, C. and Nuttall, D. (1992) Assessment and the Improvement of Education, *The Curriculum Journal* 3 (3): 215–30.

Broadfoot, P., Pollard, A., Croll, P., Osborn, M. and Abbott, D. (1994) *Changing English Primary Schools*. London: Cassell.

Broadfoot, P., Osborn, M., Planel, C. and Pollard, A. (1996a) Primary Teachers and Policy Change 1993–4, Final Report to Economic and Social Science Research Council.

Broadfoot, P., Osborn, M., Planel, C. and Pollard, A. (1996) Teachers and change: a study of primary school teachers' reactions to policy changes in England and France. In Winther-Jensen Thyge (ed.) *Education in Europe: A Comparative Approach*. Copenhagen: Comparative Education Society of Europe.

Brooksbank, K. (1980) *Educational Administration*. London: Councils and Education Press.

Brown, S. and MacIntyre, D. (1977) Differences among pupils in science classes: the contrast between teachers' perceptions and pupils' performance. Department of Education, University of Stirling. Paper given to the annual conference of the Scottish Educational Research Association, 7 September.

Burgess, T. and Travers, T. (1980) *Ten Billion Pounds*. Bury St Edmunds: Grant McIntyre.

Burke, J. W. (ed.) (1989) *Competency Based Education and Training*. Lewes: The Falmer Press.

Burstall, C. and Kay, B. (1978) *Assessment: The American Experience*. London: Assessment Performance Unit.

Burt, Sir Cyril (1912) The inheritance of mental characteristics, *Eugenics Review* 4(2): 168–200.

Burt, Sir Cyril (1933) *How the Mind Works*. London: George Allen and Unwin.

Burt, Sir Cyril (1945) The reliability of teachers' assessments of their pupils, *British Journal of Educational Psychology*, June, xv(11): 80–92.

Buswell, C. (1984) Sponsoring and stereotyping in a working-class English secondary school. In S. Acker, J. Megarry, S. Nisbet and E. Hoyle (eds) the *World Yearbook of Education*. London: Kogan Page.

Caroff, A. (1991) Evaluation et validation des acquis: le diplome national du brevet, in: Ministère de l'Education. *Rapport sur l'Evaluation des Acquis des Elèves à la fin des cycles d'Apprentissage*. Paris: Ministry of Education.

Caspard, P. (ed.) (1990) Travaux d'éleves, *Histoire de l'Education*, Numéro Spécial. Paris: Institut Nationale de Rescherche Pédagogique.

Cassels, J. (1990) *Britain's Real Skill Shortage*. London: Policy Studies Institute.

CERI (1990) The Role of Central Inspectorates in the Assessment of Schools: Report on France. Paper presented at Organization for Economic Cooperation and Development Conference, Strasbourg.

Chervel, A. (1874) *Dictionnaire Historique des Institutions moeurs et coûtunes de la France*. Paris: Librairie Hachette.

Cherkaoui, M. (1977) Bernstein and Durkheim: two theories of change in educational systems, *Harvard Education Review* 47 (4): 156–66.

Chin, R. and Benne, K. (1978) General strategies for effecting changes in human systems. In W. G. Bennis, K. D. Benne, R. Chin and K. E. Corey (eds) *The Planning of Change*, 3rd edn. London: Holt, Rinehart and Winston.

Clark, B. (1962) *Educating the Expert Society*. San Francisco, CA: Chandler Publishing Corporation.

Clark, B. (1982) *The 'Cooling Out' Function Revisited*, working paper no. 3. Los Angeles, CA: Comparative Higher Education Research Group, Graduate School of Education, University of California.

Claxton, G. (1994) *Noises From the Darkroom: the Science and Mystery of the Mind*. London: Aquarian.

Cockcroft, W. H. (1982) *Mathematics Counts*, report of the Committee of Inquiry into the teaching of mathematics in schools. London: HMSO.

Coleman, J. (1968) The concept of equality of educational opportunity, *Harvard Educational Review*, Special Issue, 38 (1): 7–22.

Collins, R. (1979) *The Credential Society*. New York: Academic Press.

Compère, M. M. and Pralon-Julia, D. (1990) Les Exercices latins au collège de Louise-le-Grand vers 1720. In P. Caspard (ed.) *Histoire de l'Education, numéro spécial*. Paris: Institut Nationale de Rescherche Pédagogique.

Cookson, C. (1978) Testing, testing, testing, *Times Educational Supplement*, 10 February p. 73.

Coqblin, A. (1991) *La Politique d'Orientation des colleges in Rapport sur l'evaluation des acquis des eleves a la fin des cycles d'apprentissage*. Paris: Ministere de l'Education Nationale de la Jeunesse et des Sports.

Corbett, R. and Wilson, B. (1988) Raising the stakes in state-wide mandatory minimum competency testing, *The Politics of Education Association Yearbook* (special issue of *Journal of Education Policy*) 3 (5).

Crispin, A. (1983) Finance as a means of control in English education: recent trends towards centralisation. Paper given to annual comparative education workshop, London Institute of Education.

Croll, P., Moses, D. and Wright, J. (1984) Children with learning difficulties and assessment in the junior classroom. In P. Broadfoot (ed.) *Selection, Certification and Control*. Lewes: The Falmer Press.

Crooks, T. (1988) The impact of classroom evaluation practices on students, *Review of Educational Research* 58 (4): 438–81.

Crooks, T. (1989) *Assessing Student Performance (Green Guide No. 8)* Kensington, NSW: Higher Education Research and Development Society of Australasia: University of New South Wales.

Crozier, M. (1970) *The Stalled Society*. New York: Viking.

Cumming, D. (1982) or (1983) *School leavers, Qualifications and Employment*. Desford: Bosworth Community College.

Curtain, R. and Hayton, G. (1995) The use and abuse of a competency standards framework in Australia: a comparative perspective, *Assessment in Education: Principles, Policy and Practice* 2 (2): 205–24.

Dale, R. (1980) *The State and Education Policy*. Milton Keynes: Open University Press.

Dale, R. (1981a) The state and education: some theoretical approaches Unit 3, E353. *Society, Education and the State Course*. Milton Keynes: The Open University.

Dale, R. (1981b) *From Expectations to Outcomes in Educational Systems*. Milton Keynes: The Open University.

Dale, R. (1983) The political sociology of education: review essay, *British Journal of Sociology of Education* 4 (2): 185–202.

Dallmayr, F. (1982) The theory of structuration: a critique. In A. Giddens (ed.) *Profiles and Critiques in Social Theory*. London: Macmillan.

Dawe, A. (1970) The two sociologies, *British Journal of Sociology* 21 (2): 56–75.

Dearing, Sir R. (1994) *The National Curriculum and its Assessment*. London: HMSO.

Delamont, S. (1983) Myths, monsters and misapprehensions in educational research, 1983 Presidential Address, *Research Intelligence*. Newsletter of the British Educational Research Association, London.

Dennison, W. F. (1978) Research report: the Assessment of Performance Unit – where is it heading?, *Durham and Newcastle Research Review* VII (40): 115–23.

Department for Education (1994) *The Dearing Review of the National Curriculum*. London: HMSO.

Department of Education and Science (1979) *Local Authority Arrangements for the School Curriculum. Report on Circular 14/77 Review*. London: HMSO.

Department of Education and Science (1987) *The National Curriculum 5–16: A Consultation Document*. London: HMSO.

Donald, J. (1981) Green paper: noise of crisis. In R. Dale, G. Esland, R. Fergusson and M. MacDonald (eds) *Schooling and the National Interest*. Lewes: The Falmer Press.

Dore, R. (1976) *The Diploma Disease*. London: Unwin.

Dosnon, O. (1991) Les Recherches sur l'evaluation a l'INETOP Paris: Service de Recherches de l'INETOP.

Douglas, J. W. B. (1964) *The Home and the School*. St Albans: Panther.

Douglas, J. W. B., Ross, J. M. and Simpson, H. R. (1971) *All Our Futures*. London: Peter Davies.

Duclaud-Williams, R. (1980) Teacher unions and educational policy in Britain and France. Paper presented to ECPR workshop on pressure groups and the state, Florence.

Duclaud-Williams, R. (1982) Centralisation and incremental change in France: the case of the Haby educational reform, *British Journal of Political Science* 13: 71–91.

Dundas-Grant, V. (1975) Attainment at 16+: the French perspective, *Comparative Education* 11 (1): 13–22.

Dungworth, D. (1977) Lottery may choose students, *Times Educational Supplement* 4 March.

Dunn, S. S. (1967) *Measurement and Evaluation in the Secondary School*. Melbourne: Australian Council for Educational Research.

Durkheim, E. (1947) *The Division of Labour in Society*. New York: The Free Press.

Durkheim, E. (1961) *Moral Education: A Study in the Theory and Application of the Sociology of Education*. New York: The Free Press (trans. Wilson and Schnurer).

Durkheim, E. (1977) *The Evolution of Educational Thought: Lectures on the Formation and Development of Secondary Education in France*. London: Routlege and Kegan Paul.

Ebel, R. L. (1963) The relation of testing programs to educational goals. In W. G. Findlay (ed.) *The Impact and Improvement of School Testing*

Programs – 62 Yearbook of National Society for Study of Education Part II. Chicago, IL: University of Chicago Press.

Ebel, R. L. (1965) *Measuring Educational Achievement.* New York: Prentice Hall.

Ebel, R. L. (1972) The social consequences of educational testing and some limitations of CR measurement. In G. Bracht *et al.* (eds) *Perspectives in Educational and Psychological Measurement.* New York: Prentice Hall.

Eckstein, M. and Noah, H. J. (eds) (1992) *Examinations: Comparative and International studies.* Oxford: Pergamon.

Eckstein, M. A. and Noah, H. J. (1993) *Secondary School Examinations. International Perspectives on Policies and Practice.* New Haven, CN: Yale University Press.

Eggleston, S. J. (1977) *The Sociology of the School Curriculum.* London: Routledge and Kegan Paul.

Eggleston, S. J. (1984) School Examinations – some sociological issues. In P. Broadfoot (ed.) *Selection, Certification and Control.* Lewes: The Falmer Press.

Eisner, E. W. (1969) Instructional and expressive objectives: their formulation and use in curriculum, American Educational Research Association monograph series on *Curriculum Evaluation*, vol. 3. Chicago, IL: Rand McNally.

Elley, W. B. and Livingstone, I. D. (1972) *External examinations and internal assessments.* Wellington: New Zealand Council for Educational Research.

Elwein, M. C., Glass, G. V. and Smith, M. L. (1988) Standards of competence: propositions on the nature of testing reforms, *Educational Research,* November: 4–9.

Evans, N. (1992) *Experiential Learning. Assessment and Accreditation.* London: Routledge.

Evans, B. and Waites, B. (1981) *IQ and Mental Testing: the History and the Controversy.* London: Macmillan.

Ferrara, S. F. and Thornton, S. J. (1988) Using NAEP for Interstate Comparisons: the beginnings of a 'National Achievement Test' and 'National Curriculum', *Educational Evaluation and Policy Analysis* 10 (3): 200–11.

Filer, A. (1995) Teacher Assessment: social process and social product, *Assessment in Education* 2 (1): 23–38.

Firth, R. (1969) Examinations and ritual initiation. In the *World Year Book of Education 1969.* London: Evans.

Flanders, N. (1970) *Analysing Teaching Behaviour.* London: Addison-Wesley.

Fleming, F. S. and Anttonen, R. G. (1971) Teacher expectancy or my fair lady, *American Educational Research Association Journal* 8: 151–9.

Floud, J. and Halsey, A. H. (1958) The sociology of education: a trend report and bibliography, *Current Sociology* VIII (3): 212–19.

Foucault, M. (1976) *Two Lectures*, trans. Alan Sheridan. London: Allen Lane.

Foucault, M. (1977) *Discipline and Punishment*, trans. Alan Sheridan. London: Allen Lane.

Fraser, W. R. (1963) *Education and Society in Modern France*. London: Routledge and Kegan Paul.

Fraser, W. R. (1967) Reform in France, *Comparative Education Review* 11: 300–10.

Freedman, K. (1995) Assessment as therapy. Review symposium, *Assessment in Education: Principles Policy and Practice* 2 (1): 102–7.

Frémy, D. and Frémy, M. (1978) *Quid Edictions*. Paris: Robert Laffont.

Frey, J. (1992) History and future of qualifications. *Qualifications for the 21st Century*. Wellington: New Zealand Qualifications Authority.

Further Education Unit, Institute of Education, University of London Nuffield Foundation (1994) GNVQS 1993–4: a national survey report. An interim report of a joint project. Joint publication as above.

GNVQ Assessment Review Project (GARP) (1994) *Report No. 23*, final report. London: Research and Development Services, Department of Employment.

Garrigue, P. (1980) *Etude Comparative des Systemes Éducatifs*. Paris: Ministere de l'Education.

Gentzbithel, M. (1988) Le temoinage d'un chef d'establissement. *Admistration et Education* 2: 25–30.

Gerth, H. and Wright-Mills, C. (1946) Essay in sociology. In H. Gerth and C. Wright-Mills (eds) *From Max Weber*. Oxford: Oxford University Press.

Gerth, H. and Wright-Mills, C. (1952) A Marx for the Managers. In R. K. Merton (ed.) *Bureaucracy*. New York: The Free Press.

Giddens, A. (1972) *Politics and Sociology in the Thought of Max Weber*. London: Macmillan.

Giddens, A. (1976) *New Rules of Sociological Method*. London: Hutchinson.

Giddens, A. (1981) *A Contemporary Critique of Historical Materialism*. London: Macmillan.

Giddens, A. (1982) *Profiles and Critiques in Social Theory*. Basingstoke: Macmillan.

Gifford, B. R. and O'Connor, C. (1992) *Changing Assessments: Alternative Views of Aptitude, Achievement and Instruction*. Boston and Dordrecht: Kluwer.

Gilles, M. and Associes (1990) *Bilar diagnostic des effets, chez les enseignants de l'operation evaluation-formation CE2-6eme*, consultancy report. Paris: Marc Gilles.

Gintis, H. (1980) Theory, practice and the discursive structure of education. Paper given to the International Sociology of Education Conference, Westhill College 3–5 January.

Gipps, C. (1994) *Beyond Testing*. Lewes: The Falmer Press.

Gipps, C. and Goldstein, H. (1983) *Monitoring Children: An Evaluation of the Assessment of Performance Unit*. London: Heinemann.

Gipps, C. and Murphy, P. (1994) *A Fair Test? Assessment, Achievement and Equity*. Buckingham: Open University Press.

Gipps, C., Brown, M., McCallum, B. and McAlister, S. (1995) *Intuition or Evidence? Teachers and National Assessment of Seven-Year-Olds*. Buckingham: Open University Press.

Giroux, H. (1981) *Ideology, Culture and the Process of Schooling*. Lewes: The Falmer Press.

Gleeson, D. and Mardle, G. (1980) *Further Education or Training?* London: Routledge and Kegan Paul.

Goblet, E. (1967) *La Barriere et le Niveau*. Paris: Presses Universitaires de France.

Goffman, E. (1952) On cooling the mark out: some aspects of adaptation to failure, *Psychiatry* 15 (4): 451–63.

Goldthorpe, J. H. (1980) *Social Mobility and Class Structure in Modern Britain*. Oxford: Clarendon Press.

Gonczi, A. (1994) Competency based assessment in the professions in Australia, *Assessment in Education: Principles, Policy and Practice* 1 (1): 27–44.

Good, T. L. and Brophy, J. E. (1970) Teacher–child dyadic interactions: a new method of classroom observation, *Journal of School Psychology* 8 (2): 131–8.

Gouldner, A. (1952) On Weber's analysis of bureaucratic rules. In R. K. Merton (ed.) *Bureaucracy*. New York: The Free Press.

Gray, J., McPherson, A. and Raffe, D. (1983) *Reconstructions of Secondary Education*. London: Routledge and Kegan Paul.

Habermas, J. (1970) Technology and science as ideology, for Herbert Marcuse on his seventieth birthday. In J. Habermas *Towards a Rational Society*. London: Heinemann.

Habermas, J. (1971) *Knowledge and Human Interests*. Boston, MA: Beacon Press.

Habermas, J. (1976) *Legitimation Crisis*. London: Heinemann.

Haby, R. (1975) Loi no. 75–620 de juillet 1975. Loi relative a l'education. BO no. 29 (24.7.75). Paris: Ministère de l'Education.

Hadow Committee (1926) *Report of the Consultative Committee on the Education of the Adolescent*. London: HMSO.

Halls, W. D. (1976) *Education, Culture and Politics in Modern France*. London: Pergamon.

Halsey, A. H. and Gardner, L. (1953) Selection for secondary education, *British Journal of Sociology*, IV, March: 4–7.

Halsey, A. H., Floud, J. and Anderson, C. A. (eds) (1961) *Education, Economy and Society*. New York: The Free Press.

Halsey, A. H., Heath, A. F. and Ridge, J. M. (1980) *Origins and*

Destinations: Family Class and Education in Modern Britain. Oxford: Clarendon Press.

Hamilton, D. (1981) 'On simultaneous instruction – the early evolution of class teaching', mimeo. University of Glasgow, Department of Education.

Hammersley, M. and Hargreaves, A. (eds) (1983) *Curriculum practice: some sociological case studies*. Lewes: The Falmer Press.

Hargreaves, A. (1982a) Resistance and relative autonomy theories: problems of distortion and incoherence in recent Marxist analyses of education, *British Journal of Sociology of Education* 3 (2): 107–26.

Hargreaves, A. (1982b) The politics of administrative convenience. In M. Flude, and J. Ahier (eds) *Contemporary Education Policy*. London: Croom Helm.

Hargreaves, A. (1989) *Curriculum and Assessment Reform*. Milton Keynes: Open University Press.

Hargreaves, D. H. (1979) *A Sociological Critique of Individualism in Education*. Paper presented to the annual conference of the Standing Conference for Studies in Education. London: King's College.

Hargreaves, D. H. (1982) *The Challenge for the Comprehensive School*. London: Routledge and Kegan Paul.

Harlen, W. (1994) *Enhancing Quality in Assessment*. London: Paul Chapman.

Harlen, W., Broadfoot, P., Gipps, C. and Nuttal, D. (1992) Assessment and the Improvement of Education, *The Curriculum Journal* 3 (3): 215–30.

Hartog, Sir P. and Rhodes, E. C. (1935) *An Examination of Examinations*. London: Macmillan.

Henderson, P. (1976) Class structure and the concept of intelligence. In R. Dale, G. Esland and M. MacDonald (eds) *Schooling and Capitalism*. London: Routledge and Kegan Paul.

Herzlich, G. (1980) Editorial: 'La puissance des parents', *Le Monde de l'Education* July/August: 1.

Hextall, I. (1984) Rendering accounts: a critical analysis of the APU. In P. Broadfoot (ed.) *Selection, Certification and Control*. Lewes: The Falmer Press.

Hextall, I. and Sarup, M. (1977) School knowledge, evaluation and alienation. In M. Young and G. Whitty (eds) *Society, State and Schooling*. Lewes: The Falmer Press.

Heyneman, S. (1988) Improving university selection, educational research and educational management in developing countries: the role of examinations and standardised testing. In S. Heneman and I. Fagerlind (eds) *University Examinations and Standardised Testing*, Technical Paper no. 78. Washington: World Bank.

Higginson, H. (1981) Political or educational advance through secondary reorganization. In P. Broadfoot, C. Brock and W. Tulasiewicz (eds) *The Politics of Educational Change*. London: Croom Helm.

264   *References*

Hill, L. (1981) Shades of the prison house, *Times Higher Educational Supplement*, 2 January.

HMI (1989) *Initial teacher training: the training of secondary teachers in the Academie de Toulouse*. London: HMSO.

Hoffman, B. (1964) *The Tyranny of Testing*. New York: Cromwell Collier Press.

Hogan, D. (1981) Capitalism, liberalism and schooling. In R. Dale, G. Esland, R. Fergusson and M. MacDonald (eds) *Schooling and the National Interest: Education and the State*, vol. 1. Lewes: The Falmer Press.

Holtom, V. (1988) 'A comparative study of head-teachers' conceptions of their professional role in England and France'. Unpublished MPhil thesis. University of Bristol.

Hopper, E. I. (1968) A typology for the classification of educational systems, *Sociology* 2 (1): 29–46.

Horton, T. (1990) *Assessment Debates*. London: Hodder and Stoughton.

Hoskin, K. (1979) The examination, disciplinary powers and rational schooling, *History of Education* 8 (2): 135–46.

Hoyle, E. (ed.) (1980) *World Year Book of Education 1980: Professional development of Teachers*. London: Kogan Page.

Hoyle, E. (1982) Micropolitics of educational organisations, *Educational Management and Administration* 10: 87–98.

Hurt, J. (1971) *Education in Evolution*. London: Paladin.

Ingenkamp, K. (1977) *Educational Assessment*. Slough: NFER.

Inspection Générale de l'Education Nationale (1991) *Rapport sur l'Evaluation des Acquis des Eleves a la Fin des Cycles d'Apprentissage*. Paris: Ministry of Education.

Institute of Personnel Management (IPM) (1984) *School and the World of Work: What do Employers Look for in School Leavers?* London: IPM.

Jackson, S. (1974) *A Teacher's Guide to Testing*, 3rd edn. Harlow: Longman.

Jessup, G. (1990) *Common Learning Outcomes: Core Skills in A/AS levels and NVQs*, Research and Development Report. London: National Council for Vocational Qualifications.

Johnson, R. (1976) Notes on the schooling of the English working class 1780–1850. In R. Dale, G. Esland and M. MacDonald (eds) *Schooling and Capitalism*. London: Routledge and Kegan Paul.

Jospin, L. (1991) *Propositions pour la renovation du lycee*. Conference de presse, Ministère de l'Education Nationale, 22 April, p. 5.

Judge, H. (1988) Cross-national perceptions of teachers, *Comparative Education Review* 32 (2) May: 143–59.

Judge, H., Lemosse, M., Paine, L. and Sedlak, M. (1994) The University and the Teachers. France, the United States, England, *Oxford Studies in Comparative Education*, double issue. 4 (1/2): 1–200.

Kamin, L. A. (1974) *The Science and Politics of IQ*. New York: Wiley.

Karier, C. J. (ed.) (1973) *Roots of Crisis*. Chicago, IL: Rand McNally.

Kellaghan, T. and Greaney, V. (1992) *Using Examinations to Improve Education: A Study in Fourteen African Countries.* Washington, DC: The World Bank.

King, A. (ed.) (1976) *Why is Britain Becoming Harder to Govern?* London: BBC Publications.

King, E. (1981) *Other Schools and Ours*, 6th edn. London: Holt, Rinehart and Winston.

Kirst, M. and Bass, G. (1976) 'Accountability: what is the federal role?'. Working note prepared for Department of Health, Education and Welfare, June, mimeo. Rand Corporation, Santa Monica, California.

Koretz, D. M. (1991) State comparisons using NAEP: large costs, disappointing benefit, *Educational Researcher* 20 (3): 19–24.

Larrain, J. (1979) *The Concept of Ideology.* London: Hutchinson.

Larson, M. (1981) Monopolies of competence and bourgeois ideology. In R. Dale, G. Esland, R. Fergusson and M. MacDonald (eds) *Education and the State*, vol. 2. London: Falmer Press/The Open University.

Lauglo, J. (1995) Forms of decentralization and their implications for education, *Comparative Education* 31 (1): 5–30.

Lauglo, J. and Maclean, L. (1984) *Central Versus Decentralized Control in Education: Comparative and International Perspectives.* London: School of Education, University of London.

Lawson, J. and Silver, H. (1973) *A Social History of Education in England.* London: Methuen.

Lawton, D. (1980) *The Politics of the School Curriculum.* London: Routledge and Kegan Paul.

Le Grand, L. (1980) Personal communication.

Le Guen, M. (1994) Evaluating school performance in France. In OECD *Making Education Count.* Paris: Organization for Economic Cooperation and Development/CERI.

Lee-Smith, M. (1990) *The Role of Testing in Elementary School*, SCE Technical Report 321 Arizona State University. Los Angeles, CA: University of California Los Angeles, Centre for the Study of Evaluation.

Little, A. (1987) Attributions in a cross-cultural context, *Genetic, Social and General Psychology Monographs* 113 (1): 61–79.

Little, A. (1992) *Assessment and Selection in China.* London: University of London.

Little, A. and Singh, J. S. (1992) Learning and working: elements of the Diploma Disease thesis examined in England and Malaysia, *Comparative Education* 28 (2): 181–201.

Lukes, S. (1974) *Power: A Radical View. Studies in Sociology.* London: Macmillan.

Macintosh, H. G. and Hale, D. E. (1976) *Assessment and the Secondary School Teacher.* London: Routledge and Kegan Paul.

Malan, T. (1974) L'évolution de la fonction de planification de l'éducation en France au cours des VIeme et VIeme plans (1966–1975), *Revue Francaise de Pédagogie* 26.

Marcuse, J. (1964) *One-dimensional Man.* New York: The Free Press.

Marshall, G. (1982) *In Search of the Spirit of Capitalism.* London: Hutchinson University Library.

Matthews, M. R. (1980) *The Marxist Theory of Schooling.* Sussex: Harvester Press.

Meadmore, D. (1995) Linking Goals of Governmentality with Policies of Assessment, *Assessment in Education* 2 (1): 9–22.

Mehan, H. (1973) Assessing children's school performance. In H. P. Dreitzel (ed.) *Children and Socialisation, Recent Sociology No. 5.* London: Collier-Macmillan.

Meighan, R. (1977) Towards a sociology of assessment, *Social Science Teacher* 7 (2).

Meirieu, P. (1993) Les Enjeux de la Formation des Maitres Aujord'hui en France, *European Journal of Teacher Education* 16 (1): 5–13.

Mills, I (1979) Individuality and assessment. Paper presented to the Annual Conference of the Standing Conference for Studies in Education, King's College, London, 16 December.

Ministère de l'Education Nationale (1991) *Propositions du conseil national des programmes sur l'evolution du lycée,* Second Report. Paris: Ministère de l'Education Nationale.

Montgomery, R. J. (1965) *Examinations.* London: Routledge and Kegan Paul.

Montgomery, R. J. (1978) *A New Examination of Examinations.* London: Routledge and Kegan Paul.

Morris, N. (1970) State paternalism and laissez-faire in the 1980s. In N. Morris (ed.) *Studies in the Government and Control of Education since 1860.* London: Methuen.

Mortimore J. and Mortimore, P. (1984) Secondary school examinations: helpful servants or dominating masters? *Bedford Way Papers No. 18.* London: Institute of Education, University of London.

Mortimore, P. (1983) Graded tests: a challenge or a problem? Paper given to the British Educational Research Association Annual Conference, London, 3–7 September.

Munby, S. (1989) *Assessing and Recording Achievement.* Oxford: Blackwell.

Munn, P. (ed.) (1993) *Parents and Schools: Customers, Managers and Partners.* London: Routledge.

Murphy, R. (1982) A further report of investigations into the reliability of marking of GCE examinations, *British Journal of Educational Psychology* 52(1): 58–63.

Musgrave, P. W. (1968) *Society and Education in England since 1800.* London: Methuen.

Musgrave, P. W. (1980) The limits of curricular experience: an analysis of experience and possibility. Paper presented at Society of Education Conference, Westhill College, 3–5 January.

Neave, G. (1980) Statements at 16+: a European perspective. In T. Burgess and E. Adams (eds) *Outcomes of Education*. London: Macmillan.

Neave, G. (1981) New influences on educational policies in Western Europe during the seventies. In P. Broadfoot, C. Brock and W. Tulasiewicz (eds) *The Politics of Educational Change*. London: Croom Helm.

Neave, G. (1984) On the road to Silicon Valley? The changing relationship between higher education and government in Western Europe, *European Journal of Education* 19 (2): 111–29.

Neave, G. (1989) On the cultivation of quality, efficiency and enterprise: an overview of recent trends in higher education in Western Europe, 1986–88, *European Journal of Education* 23 (1/2): 7–24.

Nias, J. (1981) The nature of trust. In J. Elliott, D. Bridges, D. Ebbutt, R. Gibson and J. Nias (eds) *School Accountability*. Bury St Edmunds: Grant McIntyre.

Nisbet, J. (ed.) (1993) *Assessment and Curriculum Reform*. Paris: Organization for Economic Co-operation and Development.

Njabili, A. F. (1987) Continuous assessment: the Tanzanian experience. Paper presented at a seminar on Examination Reform for Human Resource Development, Institute of Development Studies, University of Sussex.

Noah, H. and Eckstein, M. (eds) (1992) *Examinations in Comparative and International Studies*. Oxford: Pergamon Press.

Nowell-Smith, J. (1979) In a State, *Screen Education* 30.

Nuttall, D. L. (1984) Domesday or a New Dawn? The Prospects for a Common System of Examining at 16+. In P. Broadfoot (ed.) *Selection, Certification and Control*. Lewes: The Falmer Press.

Nuttall, D. L. (1987) The validity of assessments, *European Journal of Psychology of Education* 11 (2): 109–18.

Nuttall, D. L. (1990) The GCSE: promise vs. reality. In P. Broadfoot, R. Murphy and H. Torrance (eds) *Changing Educational Assessment*. London: Routledge.

Nuttall, D. L., Thomas, S. and Goldstein, H. (1992) *Report on Analysis of 1990 Examination Results*. Manchester: Association of Metropolitan Authorities Report.

O'Connor, J. (1980) The division of labor in society, *Insurgent Sociologist* 10 (1): 60–8.

Offe, C. (1975) The capitalist state and the problem of policy formation. In L. J., Lindberg, R. Alford, C. Crouch and C. Offe (eds) *Stress and Contradiction in Modern Capitalism*. Lexington, MA: Lexington Books.

Organization for Economic Cooperation and Development (1971) *Reviews of National Policies for Education: France*. Paris: OECD.

Organization for Economic Cooperation and Development (1989) *Education and the Economy in a Changing Society*. Paris: OECD.

Organization for Economic Cooperation and Development (1992) *The OECD International Education Indicators: A Framework for Analysis.* Paris: OECD.

Osborn, M. and Broadfoot, P. (1992) A lesson in progress? Primary classrooms observed in England and France, *Oxford Review of Education* 18(1): 3–15.

Ottobre, F. E. (ed.) (1978) Criteria for awarding school-leaving certificates. In F. E. Ottobre (ed.) *The Proceedings of the 1977 Conference of the International Association for Educational Assessment.* Oxford: Pergamon Press.

Oxtoby, R. (1973) Engineers, their jobs and training needs, *Vocational Aspects of Education* 25 (61): 3–5.

Parsons, T. (1951) *The Social System.* New York: The Free Press.

Pautler, E. (1981) Links between secondary and higher education in France, *European Journal of Education* 16 (2): 185–95.

Pennycuick, D. (1990) The introduction of continuous assessment systems at secondary level in developing countries. In P. Broadfoot, R. Murphy and H. Torrance (eds) *Changing Educational Assessment.* London: Routledge.

Pennycuick, D. and Murphy, R. (1988) *The Impact of Graded Tests.* Lewes: The Falmer Press.

Perrow, H. (1967) Hospitals, technology, structure and goals. In J. G. March (ed.) *Handbook of Organizations.* Chicago, IL: Rand-McNally.

Phillips, D. (1989) Neither a borrower nor a lender be? The problems of cross-national attraction in education, *Comparative Education* 25 (3): 267–74. – Special Number (12) *Cross-national Attraction in Education* (edited by David Phillips).

Pidgeon, D. and Yates, A. (1968) *An Introduction to Educational Measurement.* London: Routledge and Kegan Paul.

Plowden, Baroness B. (1967) *Children and their Primary Schools: A Report of the Central Advisory Council for Education.* London: HMSO.

Pluvinage, F. (1992) Evaluation au Collège: l'evaluation dans la gestion des enseignements; commentaires sur l'evaluation 1991 en sixième. Paper presented at European Comparative Education Society Conference, Dijon, 20–27 June.

Pollard, A. (1995) *The Social Construction of Pupil Identity.* London: Cassell.

Pollard, A., Broadfoot, P., Croll, P., Osborn, M. and Abbot, D. (1994) *Changing English Primary Schools? The Impact of the Education Reform Act at Key Stage One.* London: Cassell.

Poppleton, P. (1990) The survey data, *Comparative Education* 26 (2/3): 183–210.

Poulantzas, N. (1973) *Political Power and Social Classes.* London: New Left Books.

Powell, J. L. (1973) *Selection for University in Scotland*. Edinburgh: University of London Press for Scottish Council for Research in Education.

Premier Ministre, Service d'information et de diffusion (1977) *Actualitées Services: Rentrée Scolaire, 1977: ce qui change*. Paris: Ministère de l'Education.

Price, R. (1976) Community school and education in the People's Republic of China, *Comparative Education* 12 (2): 163–74.

Price, R. (1977) *Marx and Education in Russia and China*. London: Croom Helm.

Prost, A. (1968) *L'enseignement en France 1800–1967*. Paris: Armand Colin.

Pusey, M. (1980) The legitimation of state educational systems, *Australia and New Zealand Journal of Sociology* 15 (2): 45–57.

Ramirez, F. O. and Meyer, J. W. (1980) Comparative education: the social construction of the modern world system, *Annual Review of Sociology* 6: 369–99.

Ranson, S. (1983) *Centre-Local Policy Planning in Education*, Report to ESRC. University of Birmingham: INLOGOV.

Ranson, S. (1984) Towards a tertiary tripartism: new modes of control in the 17+. In P. Broadfoot (ed.) *Selection, Certification and Control*. Lewes: The Falmer Press.

Ranson, S., Hinings, B. and Greenwood, R. (1980) The structuring of organisational structures, *Administrative Science Quarterly* 25(1): 1–17.

Raven, J. (1991) *The Tragic Illusion: Educational Testing*. New York: Trillium Press.

Reimer, F. (1971) *School is Dead*. London: Penguin.

Resnick, L. B., Nolan, K. J. and Resnick, D. P. (1995) *Benchmarking Education Standards*. Pittsburgh, PA: University of Pittsburgh Press.

Rieff, P. (1973) *The Triumph of the Therapeutic: Uses of Faith after Freud*. Harmondsworth: Penguin University Books.

Rist, R. C. (1970) Student social class and teacher expectations: the self-fulfilling prophecy in ghetto education, *Harvard Educational Review* 40 (3): 411–511.

Roach, J. (1971) *Public Examinations in England 1850–1906*. Cambridge: Cambridge University Press.

Rodmell, D. (1977) The contribution of monitoring to educational policy-making. In R. Sumner (ed.) *Monitoring educational achievement*. Slough: National Foundation for Educational Research.

Rosenthal, R. and Jacobsen, L. (1968) *Pygmalion in the Classroom*. New York: Holt, Rinehart and Winston.

Rothera, H. (1968) The new Baccalaureat in its context, *Comparative Education* 4 (3):183–97.

Rubenstein, D. and Simon, B. (1969) *The Evolution of the Comprehensive School 1926–1966*. London: Routledge and Kegan Paul.

Rust, V. D. (1991) Postmodernism and its comparative education implications, *Comparative Education Review* 35 (4): 610–26.

Ryrie, A. C. and Weir, A. D. (1978) *Getting a Trade – A Study of Apprentices' Experience of Apprenticeship*. London: Hodder and Stoughton for Scottish Council for Research in Education.

Sadler, R. (1991) Rethinking certification policies for school-leavers. Australian Association for Research in Education Conference, Gold Coast.

Salaman, G. (1981) *Class and the Corporation*. London: Fontana.

Salter, B. and Tapper, T. (1981) *Education, Politics and the State*. London: Grant-McIntyre.

Sapin, C. (1980) *Deconcentration et modernisation de la gestion au ministere de l'education*. Paris: Ministere de l'Education.

Sarup, M. (1982) *Education, State and Crisis – A Marxist Perspective*. London: Routledge and Kegan Paul.

Satterley, D. (1981) *Assessment in Schools*. Oxford: Blackwell.

Satterley, D. (1994) Quality in external assessment. In W. Harlen (ed.) *Enhancing Quality in Assessment*. London: Paul Chapman.

Scarth, J. (1983) Teachers' school-based experiences of examining. In M. Hammersley and A. Hargreaves (eds) *Curriculum Practice*. Lewes: The Falmer Press.

Schofield, H. (1972) *Assessment and Testing: an Introduction*. London: Allen and Unwin.

Schools Council (1971) Question Banks: their use in School Examinations. *Examinations Bulletin 22*. London: Evans/Methuen.

Schools Council (1972) *The Predictive Value of CSE grades for FE*. London: Evans/Methuen.

Schools Council (1973) *Arguments for a Common System of Examining at 16+*. Schools Council Leaflet. London: Schools Council.

Schostak, J. F. (1983) *Maladjusted Schooling. Deviance Social Control and Individuality in Secondary Schooling*. Lewes: The Falmer Press.

Sharp, S. (1980) Godfrey Thomson and the concept of intelligence. In J. V. Smith and O. Hamilton (eds) *The Meritocratic Intellect*. Aberdeen: Aberdeen University Press.

Sharp, S. (1984) Psychologists and intelligence testing in English education, 1900–40. In P. Broadfoot (ed.) *Selection Certification and Control. Social Issues in Educational Assessment*. Lewes: The Falmer Press.

Shavelson, R. J., Baxter, G. P. and Pine, J. (1992) Performance assessments: political rhetoric and measurement reality, *Educational Researcher* May: 22–7.

Sheridan, A. (1980) *Michel Foucault: The Will to Truth*. London: Tavistock.

Shimahara, N. K. (1979) *Adaptation and Education in Japan*. New York: Praeger.

Scottish Council for Research in Education (1976) *Wastage on National Certificate Courses.* Edinburgh: SCRE.

Silver, H. (1979) Accountability in education: towards a history of some English features. Paper for Social Science Research Council Panel on Accountability in Education.

Simon, B. (1953) *Intelligence Testing and the Comprehensive School.* London: Lawrence and Wishart.

Simon, B. (1965) *Education and the Labour Movement 1920–70.* London: Routledge and Kegan Paul.

Simon, B. (1992) *What Future for Education?* London: Lawrence and Wishart.

Simons, H. and Elliott, J. (1989) *Rethinking Appraisal and Assessment.* Milton Keynes: Open University Press.

Smith, G. (1980) *Politics in Western Europe*, 3rd edn. London: Heinemann.

Smith, M. L. (1991) Meanings of test preparation, *American Education Research Journal* 28 (3): 521–42.

Spencer, M. E. (1970) Weber on legitimate norms and authority, *British Journal of Sociology* XXI (2): 123–34.

Stake, R. E. (1991) Impact of changes in assessment policy. In R. E. Stake (ed.) *Advances in Program Evaluation*, vol. 1 (Part A), *Using Assessment Policy to Reform Education.* London: Jai Press.

Stevens, A. (1980) French children are switching to technical courses, *Observer*, 28 March.

Stones, E. (1994) Assessment of a complex skill: improving teacher education, *Assessment in Education* 1 (2): 235–51.

Stubbs, M. (1976) *Language, Schools and Classrooms.* London: Methuen.

Sumner, R. (1982) *Assessment for Schools.* London: Croom Helm.

Sutherland, G. (1977) The Magic of Measurement: Mental Testing in Education 1900–1940, *Transactions of the Royal Historical Society*: 135–53.

Sutherland, M. (1977) The death of diversity. Paper presented at Third World Congress of Comparative Education Societies, London.

Sutherland, G. and Thom, M. (1983) Did the 1944 Education Act create the 11+? Paper given to the British Educational Research Association annual conference, London.

Takeuchi, Y. (1991) Myth and reality in the Japanese educational selection system, *Comparative Education* 27 (1): 101–12.

Tattersall, K. (1982) Differentiated examinations: A strategy for assessment at 16+. *Examinations Bulletin 42.* London: Methuen Educational.

Thélot, P. (1992) Mass evaluation in the French education system: problems, methods and uses. Paper given to the Fifteenth Comparative Education Society of Europe Congress, Dijon, June 20–27.

Therborn, G. (1978) *What does the Ruling Class do when it Rules?* London: New Left Books.

Thompson, P. (1974) *Assessment for Australian Capital Territory Secondary Schools*. Canberra: Australian Council for Educational Research.

Thorndike, R.L. and Hagen, E. (1969) *Measurement and Evaluation in Psychology and Education*. New York: John Wiley.

Torrance, H. (1981) The origins and development of mental testing in England and the United States, *British Journal of Sociology of Education* 2 (1): 45–59.

Torrance, H. (ed.) (1994) *Evaluating Authentic Assessment: Problems and Possibilities in New Approaches to Assessment*. Buckingham: Open University Press.

Torrance, H. (1995) Investigating Teacher Assessment at Key Stage 1 on the National Curriculum in England and Wales. Methodological problems and emerging issues, *Assessment in Education* 2 (3): 305–21.

Troman, G. (1988) Getting it right: selection and setting in a 9–13 years middle school, *British Journal of Sociology of Education* 9 (4): 403–22.

Troman, G. (1989) Testing tensions. The politics of educational assessment, *British Educational Research Journal* 15 (3): 279–95.

Turner, G. (1984) Assessment in the comprehensive school: what criteria count? In P. Broadfoot (ed.) *Selection Certification and Control. Social Issues in Educational Assessment*. Lewes: The Falmer Press.

Turner, R. (1960) Sponsored and context mobility and the school system, *American Sociological Review* 25: 855–67.

Vaughan, M. and Archer, M. S. (1971) *Social Conflict and Educational Change in England and France 1789–1848*. Cambridge: Cambridge University Press.

Vedder, P. (1992) *Measuring the quality of education*. Amsterdam: Swets and Zeitlinger.

Vernon, P. (1957) *Secondary School Selection*. London: Methuen.

Vernon, P. (1962) The contribution to education of Sir Godfrey Thomson, *British Journal for Educational Studies* 10: 123–37.

Vernon, P. (1978) *Intelligence Testing 1928–78. What Next?* Edinburgh: Scottish Council for Research in Education.

Veulard, A. (1970) Centralisation and freedom in education, *Comparative Education* 6 (1): 37–45.

Weber, M. (1923) *General Economic History*. London: Allen and Unwin.

Weber, M. (1947) *The Theory of Social and Economic Organisation*. New York: Free Press (trans. T. Parsons and A. M. Henderson).

Webster, D. (1981) Attitudes to the world of work: the relation of theory to empirical date. Paper presented to the seventh annual conference of the British Educational Research Association, Crewe and Alsager College, 4–7 September.

Weiler, H. (1981) Compensatory legitimation in educational policy: legalisation, expertise and participation in comparative perspective. Paper presented at Tenth European conference on Comparative Education, Geneva.

Weiler, H. (1988) The politics of non-reform in French education, *Comparative Education Review* 32 (3): 251–66.

Weston, P. (ed.) (1991) *Assessment of Pupil Achievement, Motivation and School Success*. Amsterdam: Swets and Zeitlinger.

White, M. (1987) *The Japanese Educational Challenge*. New York: The Free Press.

White, R. W. (1959) Motivation reconsidered: the concept of competence, *Psychological Review* 66: 297–333.

Whitty, G. (1978) School examinations and the politics of school knowledge. In L. Barton and R. Meighan (eds) *Sociological Interpretations of Schooling and Classrooms: a Reappraisal*. Driffield: Nafferton.

Whitty, G. (1980) *Block III Unit 8 E352 Society, Education and the State*. Milton Keynes: Open University.

Whitty, G. and Young, M. F. D. (eds) (1976) *Exploration in the Politics of School Knowledge*. Driffield: Nafferton.

Wilby, P. (1979) Habermas and the language of the modern state, *New Society*, 22 March.

Williams, I. C. and Boreham, W. I. (1972) *The Predictive Value of CSE Grades for Further Education*. London: Evans/Methuen.

Williams, R. (1961) *The Long Revolution*. London: Chatto and Windus.

Willis, P. (1977) *Learning to Labour*. Sussex: Falmer.

Wilson, H. T. (1977) *The American Ideology*. London: Routledge and Kegan Paul.

Wilson, J. (1975) Assessment tail wags curriculum dog. *Times Educational Supplement Scotland*, 24 October.

Wolf, A. (1993) Assessment as part of a system: incentives and control. Paper presented at International Centre for Research on Assessment Conference on Learning, Selection and Monitoring: Resolving the Roles of Assessment, London, 1–5 July.

Wolf, A. and Silver, R. (1993) The reliability of test candidates and the implications of 'one-shot' testing, *Educational Review* 45 (3): 263–78.

Wood, R. and Gipps, C. (1981) An enquiry into the use of test results for accountability purposes. In R. McCormick (ed.) *Calling Education to Account*. London: Heinemann Educational.

Wood, R. and Skirnik, L.S. (1969) *Item Banking*. Slough: NFER.

Yates, A. and Pidgeon, D. (1957) *Admission to Grammar Schools*. London: Newnes.

Young, M. F. D. (ed.) (1971) *Knowledge and Control*. London: Macmillan.

Zeldin, T. (1973) *History of France, 1848–1945*, vols I and II. Oxford: Oxford University Press.

Index

A levels, 50, 184, 189, 190, 198, 205
  GNVQs and, 197
  views of, 149
ability, innate
  concept of and belief in, 33, 34–5, 137, 178–80
  evidence against, 181
access, 160–2, 177–8
  see also equality; inequality
accountability, 37–9, 56–61, 64, 87, 155–63, 164, 199, 223–5
  centralization and, 154
  'currency' of, 200
  English system and, 199–215
  forms of, 38–9, 223
  legitimation and, 222–3
  orientation procedure and, 144
  teachers and, 211–13, 246 n20
accreditation of prior learning, 50
achievement
  records of, *see* records

responsibility for, 14, 58–60, 203–4, 206
action, ideas and, 72–3
Africa, 46
age-based groups, graded tests and, 194
Airasian, P. W., 29, 59, 88, 124, 216
Anderson, R. D., 152
anomie, 61, 78, 171
Anttonen, R. G., 12
apprenticeship, 31–2, 131, 132
APU (Assessment of Performance Unit), 60, 207, 214, 215, 219, 234
Archer, M., 102, 105, 109, 110–11, 114, 118, 129, 132, 200, 247 n1
Archibald, D. A., 154
Aron, R., 10, 152, 222
assessment
  abuse, 88

284   *Index*